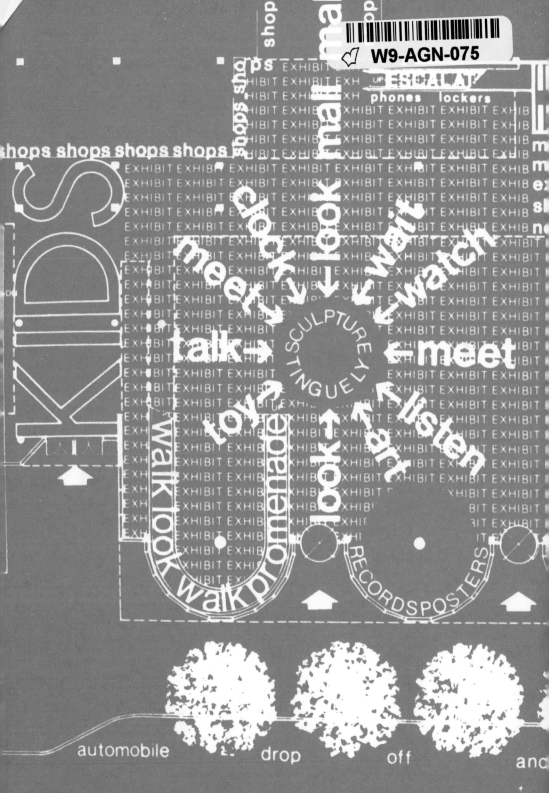

Meet Me by the Fountain

→

*The Design of Childhood: How the Material
World Shapes Independent Kids*

The Dot-Com City: Silicon Valley Urbanism

*Writing About Architecture: Mastering the Language
of Buildings and Cities*

*Design Research: The Store That Brought Modern Living
to American Homes* (with Jane Thompson)

Meet Me by the Fountain

An Inside History of the Mall

Alexandra Lange

BLOOMSBURY PUBLISHING

NEW YORK · LONDON · OXFORD · NEW DELHI · SYDNEY

BLOOMSBURY PUBLISHING
Bloomsbury Publishing Inc.
1385 Broadway, New York, NY 10018, USA

BLOOMSBURY, BLOOMSBURY PUBLISHING, and the Diana logo are trademarks
of Bloomsbury Publishing Plc

First published in the United States 2022

ISBN: HB: 978-1-63557-602-3; EBOOK: 978-1-63557-603-0

LIBRARY OF CONGRESS CATALOGING-IN-PUBLICATION DATA IS AVAILABLE

2 4 6 8 10 9 7 5 3 1

Typeset by Westchester Publishing Services
Printed and bound in the U.S.A.

To find out more about our authors and books visit www.bloomsbury.com and
sign up for our newsletters.

Bloomsbury books may be purchased for business or promotional use. For information
on bulk purchases please contact Macmillan Corporate and Premium Sales Department at
specialmarkets@macmillan.com.

They look as if they have been dropped by a helicopter flown by a blind pilot, from some giant architectural supermarket in the sky.

—ADA LOUISE HUXTABLE, "SHLOCKTON GREETS YOU,"
NEW YORK TIMES, NOVEMBER 23, 1976

Contents

Introduction
Why We Go to the Mall

From the turnpike the American Dream was a great gray blob. An earlier version of this mall, then named Meadowlands Xanadu, had worn its tacky heart on its sleeve, its vast expanse a riot of blocks and stripes of color, the patterns dramatizing the precipitous angle of the indoor ski slope as it rose from the parking lot. But now the building reposed glumly on the road-side horizon, less distinct than the green sweep of the Meadowlands or the bowl of MetLife Stadium, home of the New York Giants. Only in one spot—the outward curve of the Nickelodeon roller coaster—did American Dream's facade break its dourness, as if this ride alone could not be contained.

Inside, despite my multiyear study of the history of malls, I found myself lost. Atrium seemed to follow atrium, one with a chandelier, one with a vaulted wood ceiling, one with a plastic garden, without any sense of hier-archy or connection back to the outdoors. Long halls papered with photo-graphs suggested that one day glamorous stores might follow, but the stores that were there—Zara, Bath & Body Works, Amazon 4-star—weren't anything I needed to leave New York City to visit. Down in the lower level, near the minigolf and aquarium, signs of life: the scent of Auntie Anne's, a pastel boba storefront, masked families on their travels to the ski slope, to the indoor beach, to the candy store. After more than a year of quarantine, largely confined to my Brooklyn neighborhood, I found myself touched and thrilled by their linked hands. In May 2021, when it seemed like the summer might bring an end to the Covid-19 pandemic, seeing parents and children out and about having fun together brought me a spike of joy. I wanted to see people, I wanted to watch people, I wanted to be among people. We were all seeking that at the mall.

But as I wandered, pretzel and bubble tea acquired, this joy dropped away. There were just not enough people. Fifteen years in the making, three million square feet in area—developed by the same Canadian company that brought indoor pirate ships to Alberta and indoor amusement parks to Minnesota—American Dream felt empty. Beyond that, it felt unmoored. Sure, that was partly due to the pandemic, which closed the mall months after its 2019 opening, bankrupted department stores once slated to be anchor tenants, and made people afraid to gather. But I also felt, at a cellular and architectural level, that this was a mall that had gone too far. Too far from highway to parking lot to atrium. Too far from food to fun to frivolous purchase. While there's an amusement park at the literal heart of the Mall of America, giving visitors the collective thrill of the screamers on the roller coaster, American Dream had me venturing down a long, generic hallway to peer through the fronds of a stick-on palm-leaf decal to glimpse a Japanese-style artificial beach. At their best, malls create community through shared experience (Thrills! Tastes! Tunes!). Their architecture supports that purpose, starting with an ambitious and unmissable fountain that becomes the place to meet. If you asked me to meet you at American Dream, I would have no idea where to go.

The American dream—bootstraps, frontier, white picket fence—crossed paths with malls when they emerged in the decades after World War II, as the United States reinvented itself. In 1954, for the first time in American history, the number of children born crossed the four million mark, a level that would be sustained for each of the next ten years. The GI Bill of 1944 and federal highway acts approved in 1944 and 1956 subsidized the growth of the new residential suburbs to house these booming families, and the roads to reach them: more than a million new homes built per year, and more than forty-two thousand miles of highway. What most initial postwar development failed to incorporate, however, was the type of central—and

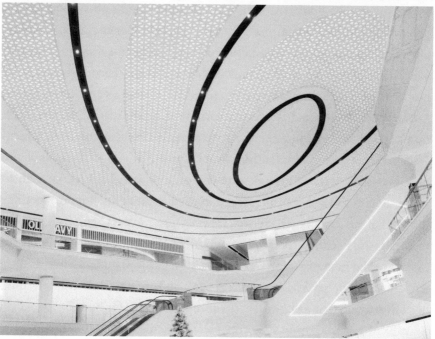

American Dream, East Rutherford, New Jersey, Gensler, December 2019.
(Photographs by Ross Mantle)

centering—space that had been part of human civilization since its earliest origins. In subsidizing the home and the road, the government failed to subsidize a place to gather. Something essential to human nature had been missed: People love to be in public with other people. That momentary joy I felt seeing happy families is the core of the mall's strength, and the essence of its ongoing utility. In postwar suburban America, the mall was the only structure designed to fill that need. People and money and controversy and larger and larger structures followed. So, in its turn, did the culture. The late twentieth-century United States doesn't make sense without the mall.

I knew going into this project that I, born in 1973, was part of the Mall Generation, raised on the smell of those pretzels, able to tune out the Muzak *and* find my car in a multilevel parking garage. As a design critic, as a child of the 1980s, and as a person devoted to the idea that architecture should serve everyone, the mall was my ideal subject. Like design for children, the subject of my last book, the mall was ubiquitous and underexamined and potentially a little bit embarrassing as the object of serious study. Shopping, like children, was a topic for after hours; and malls, like playgrounds, were places dominated by women and children. Go on Etsy and you'll find numerous unironic bumper stickers that read A WOMAN'S PLACE IS IN THE MALL. What I didn't realize was that I had been on the ground for the inception of urban inventions like the festival marketplace at Boston's Faneuil Hall, and that, even in my current Brooklyn neighborhood, I was shopping on a pedestrian street that was one of the city's responses to the flight of white dollars to the suburbs. Once I started looking at shopping not as a distraction but as a shaper of cities, I saw its traces everywhere. While architecture history tended to focus on suburban houses, and planning history looked to the highways, the shopping mall fell into the cracks between the personal and the professional, as if we as a culture didn't want to acknowledge that we needed a wardrobe, furniture, and tools for both.

When I began writing the proposal, I was still nervous, so I mentioned the idea of a book on malls to as many people as I could. Would they be excited? Would they be dismissive?

I was emboldened by the almost universal response: Oh, let me tell you about *my* mall. In contrast to many other forms of public architecture, which embody fear, power, and knowledge, the mall is personal. People told me about their first jobs, their first piercing, their first boyfriend, their first CD. I found I could sketch the plan of my first mall from memory, down to the placement of the RadioShack. When I emailed an archive for a picture of what was arguably America's first shopping center, the librarian wrote back with the needed links and added, "As a child of the 1990s, I've got many a fond memory of the mall, including the fad kiosks (pogs, especially)." The core of the mall's story was architecture, my chosen field, but the personal anecdotes pointed to all the other stories that needed to be told to paint the full picture: urbanism, practicing driving in a deserted lot; identity, collecting Pogs; maturity, going on those teenage dates. Here were hundreds of buildings, connected to everyday life and ordinary people, buildings (as I discovered) that design history had been sidelining for decades.

The less common response I got was also less satisfying. Oh, people said, you're writing about dead malls.

Whereas once the mall appeared a seat of glamour, these respondents could only call to mind the deserted atriums of recent photography, video, and social media chatter. Online communities like Reddit's r/deadmalls may allow legendary malls to live on virtually, but I was also concerned about malls' next life in the real world. I did not want to write about death for the same reason that I would be happy never to go back to American Dream. Zombie malls—physically present but stripped of animation—evoke neither the consumer pleasure that their makers intended nor the creativity and community that online message boards overlaid upon the empty halls, the quiet fountains.

That's where the predominant "malls are dead" narrative fails. Yes, technology and a pandemic boosted online shopping. And yes, we need to drive less and walk more. But in the rush to dance on the mall's grave, we risk treating the mall as only a disposable consumer object and neglecting the basic human need that it answered. We also risk throwing away the ever more valuable resources of space, material, and familiarity built into the DNA of the mall. Both a defense of and a new life for the mall are possible, but only if we open our eyes to the many roles, and many changes, the mall has undergone through the decades.

Asked by clients in Los Angeles, Detroit, and then Minneapolis to create new paradigms for the emerging postwar landscape, the Viennese émigré architect Victor Gruen developed a template: collections of stores linked by communal space and organized for strolling. Park once and spend the day. Fountains, playgrounds and carousels, and cafés accommodated women and children who might otherwise be isolated at home. That's where this book begins, in the 1950s, with the mall as a fill-in-the-blank addition to postwar suburban planning.

Subsequent chapters, each one covering roughly a decade, complicate that origin story. The 1960s bring architectural ambition, with the country's best architects and landscape architects designing a building that can change with the fashions. The 1970s bring the mall back downtown, enlivening former industrial buildings and pedestrianizing streets in an attempt to revitalize the city. The 1980s bring roller coasters; the 1990s bring pop stars; the 2000s bring dead malls and faux Main Streets. Along the journey from J. L. Hudson at one end of the concourse to Neiman Marcus at the other, there are encounters with innovators like James Rouse and Jon Jerde, with bards like Joan Didion and Ray Bradbury, with social critics like Calvin Trillin and George Romero, and with mall walkers who simply want to get on with their mornings. Some encounters are less pleasant: Mall cops have targeted teens, local law enforcement has ejected protesters, and municipalities have turned roads into moats to make it difficult for bus riders to even reach the mall.

Themes emerge: The central importance of good eats, from low-cost Woolworth's lunch counters to international food halls. The difference in experience at the mall for the Black youth and the white octogenarian, for the arcade dweller versus the middle-class mother. The ways landlords and tenants seek control through design, surveillance, and even housekeeping, and the ways skateboarders, protesters, and photographers hack the mall for their own ends. When I say "mall," you see a place in time, one shopping trip, one amazing afternoon. But even in my lifetime, the mall has changed and changed again. It's an architecture born to be malleable, and in that malleability lies its future.

$\rightarrow$

My first mall was Northgate Mall in Durham, North Carolina. Northgate was nothing special—low and tan and boxy, with an L-shaped run from Sears, at the west end, to Thalhimers (then Hecht's, then Hudson Belk, then a multiplex cinema), at the south. A dogleg, like the elongated crossbar of an *F*, jutted out from the center of the long side with a lineup of businesses best accessed from the parking lot: Kerr Drug, the dry cleaner, a beauty parlor. One of the first local lessons I learned when my family moved south was derived from weekly trips to Northgate and another shopping plaza: Kerr was pronounced "car," just as the "lion" in the supermarket chain Food Lion was pronounced "line." My northeastern mouth adapted, just as we all adapted to driving to Kroger for groceries, to Kerr Drug for medicines and toothbrushes, to Sears for clothes. In our previous life, groceries and toothpaste had been within walking distance; my parents even owned a woven-cane backpack large enough to hold several brown paper bags of food.

It was at Sears that I first began to put myself together. I drifted one back-to-school day in August from the girls' section, just inside the glass doors from the parking lot, to the boys' section beyond. Boys' was smaller and darker, with no natural light, and all the clothes blue and brown and army green and plaid. I picked out a gray canvas jacket with a soft flannel lining—a jacket like one I would wear today, sold for a hundred-plus dollars as a "chore coat" slimmed and vented for a woman's figure—and declared myself set for fall.

Past the shoe tables and the cosmetics counters lay the mall proper, a straight shot of beige quarry tile and track lighting, interrupted by a red-and-gold vintage-style carousel at the intersection of the main run and a short hallway leading outdoors. The McDonald's at the corner was too small for the in-house playgrounds that many franchises added in the 1980s, so families with Happy Meals and shakes would spill out the doors to let their kids take a turn on the carousel's leaping horses. In high school I babysat an obliging toddler, and a trip to Northgate for fries and a ride was a good way to break up a long weekend day. Ariel was tiny and blond; I was too. After a while I learned to interpret the hard looks we got in the line for a Happy Meal: People thought I was a teen mom.

Northgate was originally built in 1960 as an open-air strip serving the immediate Walltown neighborhood, a strip held down by that same Kerr Drug plus a Colonial Stores supermarket and a Roses five-and-dime. In the early 1970s, facing competition from newer enclosed malls, developers added a department store at each end, the Sears and the Thalhimers. In 1986, the year I became a teenager, it expanded again, adding another passage and a new building for Thalhimers. This was its peak moment of prosperity, with low-, middle-, and upper-middle-range department stores and passages filled out with national chains including RadioShack and Spencer Gifts. The organization known until 2021 as the International Council of Shopping Centers (ICSC) has a handy chart of shopping center classifications based on square feet, typical anchor stores, and the size of their trade areas. Northgate began as a neighborhood center, its business built around the supermarket and a sales area of three to six miles; then it ascended to regional mall status, with a sales area of five to fifteen miles, thanks to those department stores and the enclosed line of boutiques.

During my years as a middle-schooler lurching toward personal style, and as a high school student lurching toward freedom, the mall gave me somewhere to go. Northgate may have been run-of-the-mill, but it was close, and it was clean, and it offered enough variety that there was always something or someone to look at. Other places I might have gone—the strip of independent storefronts along Ninth Street, or Durham's own former-factory-to-retail conversion, Brightleaf Square—included the kinds of boutiques where young people are closely supervised, and the kinds of bakeries where you might run into a teacher from school. The mall provided the balm of anonymity.

By the time I was in my teens I stopped shopping at Sears and became more brand conscious. The first store I sought out was the Gap, then in full stacks-of-rainbow-sweaters flower. I remember the texture of its drawstring navy-blue plastic bags, soft and squishy around my purchases, and eventually collected one, two, three, four crewneck Shetland wool sweaters. Northgate wasn't a nice enough mall to have its own Gap; I had to go to South Square, located off the divided highway between Durham and Chapel Hill. South Square had a barbell plan, with a department store at each end plus a bonus one off the central atrium. J. C. Penney served the lower-end shopper, Hudson Belk the high-end one. South Square offered a squeamish sort of freedom and some of the pretension of a super-regional mall: two levels, a fountain and greenery, a food court, a department store with an arched, elegant entry off the parking lot.

Photographer and filmmaker Michael Galinsky spent the summer of 1989 chronicling malls, applying the techniques of masters like Robert Frank and William Eggleston to what he saw as the new street. As a Chapel Hill native, he made sure to stop at the local mall—South Square—and his

South Square Mall, Durham, North Carolina, Summer 1989, from *The Decline of Mall Civilization*. (Photograph by Michael Galinsky)

2019 book *The Decline of Mall Civilization* includes photographs of days I might have been there, riding the escalators in the atrium.

South Square is where I got my ears pierced at a Piercing Pagoda kiosk. South Square is where my father mortified me by breaking into a tiny boogie in response to a snatch of real jazz that broke through the Muzak. South Square is where I skim-read the adventures of Jessica and Elizabeth Wakefield, leaning against a Formica shelf, because my mother would never have let me buy books as "trashy" as the Sweet Valley High series. South Square is also where I bought my first miniskirt at the Limited when my freshman-year roommate made fun of the Sears-esque wardrobe I took to college. She thought I was hiding in those Gap sweaters, those rolled and tucked Levi's 501 jeans, those flannel shirts. When Max takes Eleven on a shopping spree in the Netflix series *Stranger Things*, whose third season is set at the Starcourt Mall, I could relate. Like Eleven, I needed a makeover.

The mall that bore the brunt of my teen angst wasn't even in Durham, but in Raleigh, the state capital, a city ringed by beltways so complex I've never untangled them. Crabtree Valley Mall was fancy, a super-regional mall that drew its customers from a twenty-five-mile radius and had brands seen nowhere else in the state. It had a Workbench, where I picked out my post-bunkbed spindle bed, elegant and timeless. It had the locally owned jewelry store, where my dad would sometimes buy my mom a gift of handmade jewelry, with hammered links and semiprecious stones. Most importantly, it had a children's boutique that sold Esprit, the it brand for the teenager who didn't want acid-washed anything.

You might think, surveying this mall ecosystem, that Northgate would have had the most precipitous decline. In the early 1990s, retail watchers began to say that the United States was "overmalled." Rather than staking out new territory, mall developers simply built structures one ring of suburbs out from existing regional hubs. Shoppers attracted by new stores, and new architecture, would abandon the older option, mimicking the cycle of planned obsolescence seen in the products those stores sold. New malls "cannibalized" the old, but their carcasses proved less easy to dispose of than used cars, toasters, and fast fashion.

But in Durham it was South Square that went down first, closed in 2002 and demolished in 2004. Its anchor department stores had abandoned it for the Streets at Southpoint, a new mall built as a "lifestyle center" a few miles away. Lifestyle centers are designed to look like pedestrianized city blocks, with shops opening outward, outdoor cafés, fountains, and trees, just like the urban interventions of the 1970s but with less pesky public-owned space. Southpoint's high-end stores and distinctive materials made it the first worthy rival to Crabtree Valley's high-end experience in decades, a sign that Durham and Chapel Hill had arrived as luxury markets and were worth the time of developers with big-city portfolios. Shoppers responded to the flattery with their feet; the new mall attracted a million visitors a year.

After South Square was demolished, and Southpoint came to dominate, Northgate shrank back but persisted. Storefronts for local entrepreneurs replaced national chains. The Friends of the Durham Library moved in near the Sears, opening a used-book emporium whose proceeds supported the library. As the department stores departed—Sears to bankruptcy, Macy's to restructuring—their giant shopping spaces were filled in with entertainment: a ten-theater cineplex and, later, a franchise of the Sky Zone trampoline park.

Facing a future in which shopping is, perhaps, the least of their functions, malls will survive by adaptation to new cultural desires: as incubators for immigrant businesses, particularly food; as containers for active entertainments; and as the Main Streets for new mixed-use neighborhoods. As big blank boxes in the middle of big empty parking lots, their structures serve as a land trust for the twenty-first century, but that land needs to be redeveloped with more care for the environment than big boxes and blacktop provide. Current plans for Northgate include total demolition of the fifty-five-acre site, with the mall to be replaced by a mixed-use development with homes, offices, and shops. Residents of Walltown, the adjacent historically Black neighborhood, have fought with the developer for the inclusion of affordable housing, fearing displacement. In response, a representative of the developer wrote to the mayor that "asking private landowners to solve the City's issues is a misdirected mission."

The late critic Michael Sorkin would have agreed with that Durham developer's conclusion, if not the logic that got him there. Sorkin earnestly wished for the death of the mall. In the introduction to *Variations on a Theme Park*, he describes how Disneyland, developer James Rouse's "festival marketplaces," and the gentrification of historic city neighborhoods all partake in the same simulation of freedom:

> The theme park presents its happy regulated vision of pleasure—all those artfully hoodwinking forms—as a substitute for the democratic public realm, and it does so appealingly by stripping public urbanity of its sting, of the presence of the poor, of crime, of dirt, of work. In the "public" spaces of the theme park or the shopping mall, speech itself is restricted: there are no demonstrations in Disneyland.

All of this is true: From their earliest days malls were built for profit on private, colonized land, with their own maintenance staffs, their own security forces, and their own trees and benches and fountains. The limits of their public nature were tested as early as 1968, in a Supreme Court case pitting unionized grocery store workers against the owners of Logan Valley Plaza. In his majority opinion, Justice Thurgood Marshall described the portico and parking lot of the Pennsylvania shopping center as "the functional equivalents of the streets and sidewalks of a normal municipal business district" and suggested that union protests today might be civil rights protests tomorrow. Malls restrict freedoms, from curfews, to codes of conduct, to standards for types of businesses, signage, and music. They are a compromised and often architecturally despised form, an ersatz version of a more ancient high street.

At American Dream I felt every bit of that compromise, from the generic marble of the floors, signifying "luxury," to the Instagram influencers' "museum" designed to give your visit an appropriately peppy backdrop (and the mall some free publicity). You can't imagine a protest at American Dream, but you also wouldn't want to protest there—it's a no-place, connected to no community that I could recognize. In 2021 the American dream is too complex and diffused to be contained in a single gray shell.

At the same time, the mall has offered freedom. Freedom from a hot day in Texas. Freedom from a boring afternoon alone in the house. Freedom from the isolation of old age or disability. In its architecture are embedded affordances often unavailable in the public realm, like air-conditioning, all-day seating, inexpensive food, and frictionless automatic doors, escalators, and elevators. Private ownership is the price we pay for a bit of city that's a little easier to take, one that can serve as an on-ramp to the real deal: the tension between the comforts of the mall and what we give up to experience them has been baked into the mall from its start. This ambiguity colors all the dialogue around it, from the way "looks like a shopping mall" is considered an architectural insult to the way "mall rats" are considered unproductive members of society. Glee over the dead mall fails to acknowledge the lack of alternatives, and the economic, demographic, and thematic transformations that the mall has already undergone. Could malls make one more shift? Could they embrace their public role without so much private resistance? The first step in answering these questions is to travel, step by step and mile by mile, the road the mall has already taken, from simple strip center to big gray box, from carousel to roller coaster, from afterthought to cultural icon.

Chapter 1
Every Day Will Be a Perfect Shopping Day

V ictor Gruen could control many things, but he could not control the weather.

He had become an American citizen. He had become a licensed architect, first in California and later in twenty-five additional states. He had built a design team in Los Angeles capable of taking on the challenges of a city expanding to fit the automotive age. He had asked his wife and former design partner, Elsie Krummeck, for a divorce. He had installed his mistress, journalist Lazette van Houten, in an apartment of their own in Greenwich Village, and met a client deep-pocketed enough to make weekly transcontinental flights possible.

When interviewers asked the short, stocky, bow-tie-wearing architect where he found the focus to develop the often-fantastic designs for the boutiques, department stores, and shopping plazas that made his name, he responded, "On planes." Several airlines had made him an "admiral" to mark his frequent-flier status. On a fall Saturday in 1948 he was doing just that—working on a plane—surrounded by his dictation machine, sketchbook, and notepad, when the flight from Los Angeles got rough. A storm accompanied by dense fog had closed all the airports along the East Coast, and his plane had to make an emergency landing in Detroit.

Gruen was not one for downtime. He had visited more American cities than most, hopping around the country with Krummeck as they plotted new stores for Grayson's, an affordable Los Angeles–based chain that grew rapidly during wartime. But Detroit was not among them. Detroit retail was dominated by Hudson's, a family-owned business, located downtown, said to be the second-largest store in the world. Gruen thought he'd make a pilgrimage.

"Before bedtime, I decided to wander through the very center of the metropolis. The walk did not take much time," Gruen reported in his posthumously published memoir, *Shopping Town*. "Everything seemed outdated, run-down, and lifeless. There was only one dramatic exception. Amid the stagnant desolation, the ten-story block-long J. L. Hudson department store, with its seemingly endless brightly lit windows, was like a bulwark . . . Every time I took a step away from the main street, I entered desolate slums, from which, smelling danger, I retreated quickly."

The next day, Gruen embarked on an eight-hour driving tour of the city, exploring everything around the center he found so desolate. His guide, the father of a colleague, told him that "real life . . . happened exclusively in the suburban areas." These, too, left Gruen cold: "palatial villas" along the lakefront, "a patchwork quilt" of boxy houses on individual plots of lawn, empty living rooms visible through picture windows.

"In passing, it seemed to me that through each of these windows I saw the same floor lamp with plastic shade, the same vase, the same flowers on the same table. This was what lay between the main roads." The margins of those main roads were also a patchwork: "a garishly advertised parade of filling stations, hot dog stands, department stores, snack bars, liquor stores, supermarkets, chain stores, used-car lots, and funeral parlors," each in its own one-story structure, most served only by limited parking parallel to the road. In short, it was a mess—of traffic, of parking, of residents, of shoppers. At one time Detroit's radial system of wide roads had been forward-thinking, but the streets had failed to keep up with the expansion of residential neighborhoods outside city limits and the movement of the automobile industry to the same. What had once been a compact city with leafy residential neighborhoods and a tight downtown core of art deco office towers, anchored by Hudson's, had become sprawl. In the space between the picture window and the filling station, Gruen saw opportunity.

Sprawl was not news to Gruen. In the decade since Viktor Gruenbaum had immigrated to the United States from Vienna, fleeing Austria after it was annexed by Nazi-led Germany, he had continued to keep an eye on the future. Upon arriving in New York in 1938 he found a job designing corporate pavilions for the New York World's Fair, opening in Queens the following year. In a run-down factory building in East Harlem, Gruen and two hundred other designers, most fellow European refugees, began to build a thirty-five-thousand-square-foot model of America in the year 1960—a vision sponsored by General Motors and intended as the centerpiece of its fair pavilion. The Futurama, as the model was called, was the brainchild of designer Norman Bel Geddes, and would eventually be housed in a streamlined structure whose exterior read HIGHWAYS AND HORIZONS. Fairgoers entered the pavilion via snaking, multilevel ramps, taking their seats in six hundred moving chairs that cycled around the model, giving them a bird's-eye (or plane's-eye) view of widely spaced skyscrapers, fourteen-lane highways, massive airports, fifty thousand cars, and—after an artificial nightfall—a lit-up amusement park. By the end of the fair's run in 1940, more than five million people had seen the exhibition. President Franklin Delano Roosevelt asked Bel Geddes to advise him on transportation policy. Futurama's imprint can be seen in the Federal-Aid Highway Act of 1944, which pledged federal money, once the war was over, for an interstate network of roads; the Federal-Aid Highway Act of 1956 would provide follow-through, funding forty-one thousand miles of roads outside and around downtowns. The imprint of the Futurama can also be seen in Gruen's first designs for Los Angeles, which included sweeping ramps, theatrical nighttime lighting, and an understanding of the social and spatial impact the highway would have on buildings and cities.

Lederer de Paris, New York City, Victor Gruen in association
with Morris Ketchum, 1939. (Gruen Associates)

While the Futurama presented a large-scale vision of modern America,
Gruen's personal work also pushed U.S. aesthetics forward, incorporating
the crisp, minimally ornamented style current in European architecture
since the 1920s into consumer culture. In partnership with Morris Ketchum,
whom he had met in architect Edward Durell Stone's office, Gruen designed
two Fifth Avenue boutiques eye-catching enough to be reviewed by influential urban critic Lewis Mumford in the *New Yorker*. Mumford wrote with
some unease that Lederer de Paris, a luxury leather-goods emporium, and
Ciro's, a jewelry store, tempted shoppers like "a pitcher plant captures flies
or an old-style mousetrap catches mice." Ciro's was particularly dramatic,
with a white, recessed front facade drawing shoppers out of the flow of sidewalk traffic and into a circular lobby with black-velvet display cases set at eye
level all around the perimeter. Before she even opened the front door the

shopper was surrounded, and hopefully seduced, by sparkle. While Mumford didn't approve of the come-on, shoppers and new clients did.

Shortly thereafter, Gruen and Ketchum parted ways; in *Shopping Town*, Gruen recounts that Ketchum's wife objected to her husband, whose family had come over on the *Mayflower*, partnering with a recent immigrant. He doesn't say whether his religion (Jewish) or his politics (socialist) were part of her consideration. In any case, Gruen decided to go into business with another designer he had met while working on the World's Fair: Elsie Krummeck, a native New Yorker born to German immigrant parents. Krummeck, a skilled artist, created the renderings that sold many of the couple's over-the-top stores to clients. Among their early successes in New York was a storefront for confectioners Altmann & Kühne that featured a twelve-by-ten-foot plate glass front and a glass staircase in pink and white like spun sugar. "We had the idea to present chocolates as jewels," Gruen wrote. "We want to influence emotional rather than rational powers."

As the authors of the encyclopedic *New York 1960* describe it, "shops were the advance messengers of the new trends of European architecture," more open to change, more fashion-forward, and more theatrical by nature than homes, offices, or schools. But Gruen had caught a glimpse of the scale that commercial development could achieve while working on the Futurama model, and soon he and Krummeck would be working not just on Fifth Avenue but on the "autopia" everywhere else.

In 1941, Gruen and Krummeck moved to Los Angeles. Their studio was flourishing, thanks to abundant work from the Grayson's chain of women's clothing stores, which found success during wartime by branding new branches "victory stores" and equating shopping with patriotism. Having taken an immediate shine to Gruen and Krummeck, the company's flamboyant co-owner dispatched them on a prop plane to Seattle, Portland, San Francisco, Omaha, and Chicago to evaluate potential store locations. When they returned, newly knowledgeable about Main Street America, he signed them up as in-house architects and strongly suggested that (*a*) they get married and (*b*) they move close to Grayson's headquarters in Indio, California. While the couple were aware of other Viennese architects who had earlier immigrated to Los Angeles, including Richard Neutra (who wrote approvingly of an exhibition of Gruen's shopping center work), their growing office was run on more corporate lines akin to that of Welton Becket, also a future mall maker.

New Grayson's locations were on wide avenues, not traditional downtowns chockablock with different stores and parallel parking. These sites often required two entrances: one from the lots located behind the stores, and the other, nominally used, from the frontage on the strip. The solution they came up with for the front was a souped-up combination of light and geometry, with the whole face of the store serving as a giant billboard. On Fifth Avenue, Ciro's jewels had provided the sparkle. For the Hollywood Grayson's, Gruen and Krummeck installed fifty-eight neon tubes, which ran from the top of a curved marquee back toward the store's recessed front entrance, like a roadway of light. The store's name was spelled out in cursive neon on top. The backside of the stores was far more modest, with small signs and inset glass show windows displaying merchandise at eye level to the shopper exiting her car.

The dramatic roadside approach used at Grayson's came in handy when the Gruen office received its largest commission to date: designing the first suburban Los Angeles store for Milliron's. The family-owned department store had decided to build a branch in the under-construction town of Westchester, where new housing was being developed for aircraft industry workers and their families. (The area is now known as the home of LAX.) The scale of new, auto-driven development required commercial architecture of a size to match. Moreover, if Gruen and Krummeck were to have their way, their structures would need to stand out both from the rush of passing cars and from the pale, windowless boxes built by suburban pioneers like Sears, Roebuck. In a 1949 article for *Women's Wear Daily*, Gruen had surveyed the postwar shopping scene and found it sadly wanting. He was dismayed by strip malls' homely rear access, where most customers entered, in contrast to their impressive storefronts facing trafficked streets, as well as by the way separate stores were strung out along those streets "like pearls on a necklace," too far apart to make walking between them pleasant. Instead, his and Krummeck's first attempt at a stand-alone department store would adapt an older pattern: the high street. This classic arrangement, which had already begun its inevitable suburban move, would inform all Gruen's subsequent forays into shopping centers, and then malls.

At the time, the most artistic pattern for shopping districts outside the urban core looked like Main Street—but a Main Street transplanted to the edge of town and built all at once. This "village center" model dated back to the 1910s and 1920s, when it had emerged alongside middle- and upper-class residential developments at the outskirts of cities, served by streetcars but also, increasingly, by motorcars. The builders and developers of these new houses had the funds to provide more than just two bedrooms and a yard. And the clientele demanded convenient shopping, close to home and with ample parking, as well as high-quality, integrated design—rather than a series of unrelated stores, the same ragged commercial strips Gruen would be dismayed to see in greater Detroit decades later.

In 1910, *House Beautiful* published a letter of complaint about just this sort of "packing-box ugliness," the "architectural patchwork, unrelated and depressing," of most shopping districts. Architect Jarvis Hunt prepared a before-and-after scenario for readers, first showing a typical Main Street with flat two-story attached storefronts, and then an improved version that resembles a series of attached Tudor- and Old English–style facades, with varied rooflines and a singular clock tower. Hunt's design proved to be inspirational for Market Square in Lake Forest, Illinois, designed in an Arts and Crafts style by local resident and architect Harold Van Doren Shaw in 1916. Stores, office suites, apartments, a gym, and a clubhouse were arrayed around a landscaped central mall with a flagpole and fountain. Shoppers could park in front of the stores on the three sides of the rectangular block, and there were service courts for delivery vehicles in back. The square was also adjacent to the city's train station, where workers would commute to and from Chicago.

Variations on this idea would pop up outside major cities around the country, often serving up Tudor pastiche in the East and Spanish Colonial Revival in the West. The Country Club District of Kansas City, Missouri, which grew into one of the largest American garden suburbs, was among the earliest and most influential. Its developer, J. C. Nichols, planner George Kessler, and landscape architect firm Hare & Hare would go on to create similar designs for cities across the United States. Nichols would become a key player in the future of shopping malls, cofounding the Urban Land Institute in 1939 to promote large-scale and long-term planning of the new suburbs.

The district was anchored by a shopping center, called Country Club Plaza, that sat between Kansas City's older streetcar suburbs and the new, auto-dependent homes Nichols was building. The plaza was designed in a pseudo-Spanish style, with a copy of Seville's Giralda tower as its center-piece, and fountains and colorful tile throughout. The plaza was edged with apartment buildings, both low-rise walk-ups and ten- and twelve-story blocks, thought to provide more support for the center's restaurants. In period photos the buildings seem to drift, slightly, in a sea of parking lot, unmoored from their original tight European urbanism.

In developing the Country Club District, Nichols set a design standard that would be imitated in many other places, choosing curving roads, cul-de-sacs, and extensive landscaping to make middle-class houses feel more like high-end estates and to differentiate the new suburb from the existing gridded center city. Nichols enforced those design values over the long term by writing form-based deed restrictions and creating a home owners' asso-ciation, a body of residents that would govern everything from how far houses needed to be set back from the road to how high hedges could be to how much new-lot buyers were required to spend on construction. The same desire for control that animated "village center" planning animated residen-tial planning too.

These deed restrictions also enforced racial segregation; only Caucasian buyers were welcome in Armour Hills, an area of the Country Club District. Sales materials emphasized the economic safety of a purchase in the Country Club District: "Have You Seen the Country Club District? 1,000 Acres Restricted for Those Who Want Protection," one advertisement read. Marketers touting stable home values in a volatile real estate market could lump racial restrictions in with appealing spatial features, like freedom from commercial neighbors, to draw in buyers. These restrictions also meant that most Country Club Plaza shoppers would be white, making it a de facto alternative to existing shopping districts open to all races. The shopping mall, from its origins in plazas such as this one in Kansas City, has to be seen as a racist form, born from speculation that a whites-only version of the city—even a city bedecked in English or Spanish garb—would prove to be a better return on investment.

For Gruen, the planning model of Lake Forest and the Country Club District—offering a one-stop shopping area identified with a specific community, and with architecture to match—held great appeal, even though he would never adopt a historicist style. In Milliron's owners he had clients interested in doing something better for the suburbs, and the opportunity to create a new store paradigm within the grid of small houses and wide roads. After Milliron's he would start to look for ways to make a modern Main Street.

In Westchester, Gruen made the striking decision to invite the car into, or rather onto, the store, embracing the techno-futurism that fueled Westchester's chief industry. Ramps for people had wrapped Bel Geddes's General Motors pavilion in 1939; ramps for cars wrapped Milliron's in 1949, a comparison not lost on critics at the time. A rooftop lot solved the problem of cars blocking and isolating the store's facade, and that lot was accessed by dramatic exposed concrete ramps that crisscrossed the building's backside. The ninety-thousand-square-foot store was originally planned as three stories, as if it were part of an established downtown, but Gruen talked the owners down to one, citing a lower cost of construction and no need for elevators. He still treated shoppers to a bright, multilevel atrium, like those in downtown department stores, by having drivers enter at the top, descending from the rooftop parking lot via escalator. On the roof, a glassed-in building held a restaurant, daycare, and community auditorium, all facilities that had once been part of historic downtown stores and would eventually make their way to malls.

Meanwhile, in theoretical projects, Gruen and Krummeck explored the limits of modern design and what a shopping center could do. The Westchester Milliron's probed structural possibilities for concrete that would turn up in the first jet-age airports of the 1950s, while its facilities gestured

Top, Milliron's Department Store, Westchester, California, 1949, street entrance, Gruen Associates in association with Elsie Krummeck. (Gruen Associates)
Bottom, rear entrance. (Photograph by Julius Shulman)

at the community amenities that would turn up in the first shopping malls of the 1950s. But it was still just one store.

In 1942, leading design magazine *Architectural Forum* asked a variety of American architects to contribute to a new master plan for Syracuse, New York, to be published in the May 1943 issue under the rubric "New Buildings for 194X." Syracuse was seen as representative of midsize American cities, with its population of seventy thousand and a central eleven-block pedestrian area bookended by city hall and a theater. By the early 1940s, downtown Syracuse merchants already feared they were losing shoppers to edge retail strips with better parking. Gruen and Krummeck, known for their Grayson's work, were asked by *Forum* editors to design a prototypical neighborhood shopping center. "I first considered the idea of a 'mall,'" Gruen recalled, "because of my daily confrontations with a problem particular to Los Angeles: though there were endless shops on both sides of the main thoroughfare, shoppers could reach them only by car."

The partners immediately started tinkering with the *Forum* editors' brief, wanting to create a space to do more than just shop. Their first sketches faced the stores inward toward a landscaped plaza, with the backs to surrounding highways, and included a "garden restaurant, milk-bars, music stand, and other recreational facilities." Architects had already begun to advocate for shopping centers as both retail and social hubs, suggesting playgrounds, schools, and theaters as add-ons to agglomerations of shops. Developers also saw such civic additions as a way to increase their profits by creating an atmosphere to encourage lingering.

Within months, Gruen and Krummeck were proposing a neighborhood shopping center serving twenty thousand to twenty-five thousand people, with a circular building as its hub. A green walkway followed the outer edge of the building, with parking lots beyond. The central building looks like an Apple store avant la lettre: Floor-to-ceiling glass faces the walk and partitions the whole pie into wedge-shaped stores. The shopper could move from store to store via the sliding-glass doors. Gruen and Krummeck had conceived a connected interior retail space that had much more in common with the glass-roofed galleries of Europe (albeit contained in a radically new form) than with the car-focused shopping plazas of America.

Architectural Forum editor George Nelson, an architect and a designer in his own right, hated their idea, writing that a circular building would eliminate the complex's most attractive feature, the courtyard, and questioning the shopping center's placement at a highway intersection. In response, Gruen and Krummeck stuffed their glass pavilion into a duller shell: a U-shaped plan with two long retail buildings facing an open-air courtyard, a covered walkway wrapping the front of the stores as all-weather protection. "For the shoppers there is a covered walk connecting the stores, a restful atmosphere and protection from automobile traffic," they wrote in *Forum.* "All necessities of day-to-day living can be found in the shopping center: post office, circulating library, doctors' and dentists' offices, and rooms for club activities in addition to the usual shopping facilities. Shopping thus becomes a pleasure, recreation instead of a chore."

Gruen and Krummeck's interest in modern materials remained in the sliding-glass doors they proposed for the courtyard-facing storefronts. In back, facing the parking, opaque facades covered in a hardwood veneer were punctuated with pop-out display windows made of the same plastic used for B-17 bomber turrets. This two-facade setup was reminiscent of the way they handled their Los Angeles commissions: bravado for the boulevard side and something smaller for the parking lot in back. They also emphasized lighting, wrapped the concrete structural columns in plastic sheathing, and specified luminescent paint for the walkway ceiling, so the whole thing would look shiny and new without the space-age styling of the circular version. As with the Milliron's ramps, the initial language of new shopping spaces was closely tied to speed, innovation, and transportation; coming out of wartime deprivation, shopping was seen as patriotic and future-oriented, if only developers and storeowners would give innovators like Gruen and Krummeck the means to experiment.

This, then, was the background for Gruen's unplanned stopover in Detroit. He knew American downtowns. He knew department stores. He knew autopia. When he visited Hudson's the day after his car tour, he could see it was an exemplary store: thirteen floors of well-chosen, well-arranged goods. The Hudson family had a close relationship with the Detroit Institute of Arts, where the store had recently underwritten an exhibition of advanced international modern design for the home. But all that good taste and all that history would be no match for the convenience of car-centric shopping outside Detroit's city limits.

When he finally reached New York, Gruen wrote a ten-page letter to James B. Webber, nephew of J. L. Hudson Company president Oscar Webber. In the months following the successful opening of Milliron's, Gruen had published a series of articles framing that store's success for different audiences. The design press praised the futuristic design and cited the civic amenities Gruen and Krummeck had embedded in a suburban structure. But Gruen wanted clients—clients rich enough to fund his experiments and forward-thinking enough to buy land at the edge of cities. He wrote for department store executives, for bankers, and for commercial developers, broadening his ideas and hoping to expand their reach outside New York and Los Angeles. He used economic language to appeal to J. L. Hudson executives, flattering their store as "superior" while dangling the threat of obsolescence. James Webber wrote back to Gruen, telling him to "drop by" if he found himself in Detroit again. Gruen made that trip happen, this time without the excuse of fog.

James Webber explained that his uncle felt Hudson's size was part of its competitive advantage: Extracted from its historic place at the center of the city, would the brand hold its mystique? Like Gruen, Oscar Webber turned up his nose at the existing shopping plazas, finding them unattractive, hard to reach, and down-market. The resplendent downtown edifice symbolized Hudson's civic importance: What form would allow it to hold that position when its customers, and its workers, seemed to prefer single-story and spread out rather than tall and dense?

The solution, in Gruen's mind, was to remake the circumstances of the downtown Hudson's somewhere other than downtown. Hudson's should, once again, be a pioneer: It should reshape the sprawl into a setting worthy of the brand and build a shopping center, with a new department store as anchor, "of exceptional size and quality . . . a cultural, social and service center for the more than five hundred thousand people who lived in its vicinity." Similar thinking had impelled General Motors, Futurama's sponsor, to transplant its executives and engineers from a tower in downtown Detroit to a spread-out campus in suburban Michigan in 1956.

Gruen always saw the next big thing—the boutique to the department store, the department store to the shopping center—and he had the publicity instincts to follow it up, articulating his ideas in blunt language for executives while he and his firm drew fresh, enticing pictures of their ideas. His shopping environments led consumers to stay longer and buy more, his architectural pitches convinced owners that building bigger would sell more. When he returned to Detroit for the third time, he presented to Oscar Webber and other store directors. At the end of the hour-long presentation, Oscar Webber asked. "How do you, Victor, imagine that we could solve all these problems by erecting a single, large-scale center? In my opinion, at least four centers are needed." Gruen, no fool, responded, "Oscar, I think you are absolutely right."

Within the week, Gruen and junior partner Karl Van Leuven were ensconced in a Hudson's boardroom, scouting suburban sites and putting together a plan. Within the month, they presented J. L. Hudson leadership with a "master decentralization plan," showing four regional shopping centers located in a broad arc at the edge of Detroit's current suburban development, approximately ten miles from the flagship store: Northland, Eastland, Westland, and Southland, setting up a mall naming tradition as well as a development pattern that would carry through the next three decades. Their site choices bet on the continuing dispersal of Detroit's population outside the established set of suburbs and encouraged speculation on what was then inexpensive Michigan farmland. They also suggested that the company buy a significant amount of land around the planned shopping centers, blocking rivals and ensuring a level of control over the surroundings that wasn't possible in the city. These centers would cure the "ugly rash on the body of our cities," Gruen said at the eventual opening of Northland. The control exerted by the architect and owner would allow for a more pleasingly ordered

landscape, with fewer signs and buildings competing for motorists' attention. The Grayson's and Milliron's stores had been among the first to
demonstrate the allure of the building as billboard, but that didn't mean that
every gas station and burger pavilion should have its name in lights; while
Gruen embraced commercialism in a way that made many of his modernist
peers uncomfortable, he still believed in design standards. (More than two
decades would pass before postmodern architects elevated the neon-lit,
uncurated roadside into the aesthetic pantheon.) The executives were
convinced, and by early 1950 they had purchased hundreds of acres in
Harper Woods and Southfield, Michigan, for development as Eastland and
Northland, respectively. Materials shortages as a result of the Korean War
put plans for Eastland on hold, while Northland went ahead in 1952.

Northland opened in March 1954 and was covered by the national press
as a state-of-the-art development in urban planning, architecture, and even
public art. *Architectural Forum* called Northland "a new yardstick." Five-
year-old Jerry Webber, the great-great-nephew of J. L. Hudson, cut the

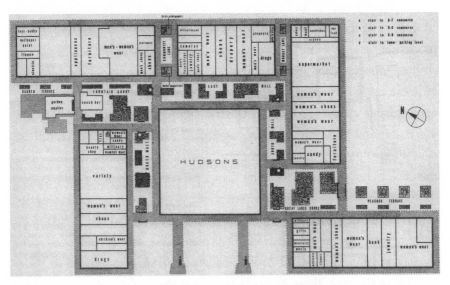

Merchandising plan for Northland Center, Southfield, Michigan, Gruen
Associates, 1954, reproduced in *Shopping Towns USA: The Planning of Shopping
Centers.* (Gruen Associates)

ribbon. An average of forty thousand to fifty thousand visitors showed up per day, far more than needed to make a regional shopping center profitable. The design itself was an attraction. The layout was simple: A large, square Hudson's department store sat at the center, dressed in simple brick with a vertical grid of white concrete columns offering some articulation and distinction from a distance. At the ground level, the edge of the building sat back from the grid, creating a fourteen-foot-deep covered passage around the edge of the whole complex. Five additional buildings with smaller stores flanked the sides and back of the anchor store in a "cluster scheme." Between each of the buildings, landscaped plazas with fountains, flowers, sculpture, and trees offered seating and shade. Each plaza had a different name and character, providing circulation and a sense of orientation for the shopper. Gruen referred to these spaces between the buildings as the shopping center's most important "town-planning element," and named them accordingly after the courts, terraces, malls, and lanes that make up European cities.

"This is a classic in shopping center planning, in the sense that Rockefeller Center is a classic in urban skyscraper group planning . . . [Northland] is the first modern pedestrian commercial center to use an urban 'market town' plan, a compact form physically and psychologically suited to pedestrian shopping," cooed *Architectural Forum*'s critic, now far better known for her defense of downtowns and urban living—in 1954 even Jane Jacobs could be a fan of the mall.

Journalists also cooed over the art. "For a really screwball fountain, the place to go is Northland Shopping Center, north of Detroit. Here is a collection of jets and sculpture that would delight Rube Goldberg, and does delight constant streams of visitors," wrote Grady Clay in *Fortune*. "People flock and stand, fascinated by the interplay of small wheels, levers, jets, spurts, and streams, a fantasy of motion and invention. Here, it seems to me, lies the promise of the future; the application of humor, inventiveness, and ingenuity to enliven display and entertainment."

Landscape architect Edward Eichstadt supervised the courtyards' arrangement and plantings. Lily Swann Saarinen (wife of famed architect Eero, whose office was in nearby Bloomfield Hills) coordinated the outdoor sculptures, contributing a work of her own, a wall-size ceramic map of the Great Lakes. A twenty-two-foot-tall totem pole in wood and steel, created by artist Gwen Lux, became the center's meeting spot. Vertical artworks of all kinds, from whimsical clocks to gilded stabiles to abstract steel figures, became a constant presence in malls thereafter. As Gruen wrote, "The average visitor to a shopping center cares less about the facade than about the character and atmosphere of the public spaces, where one might stroll or sit on benches." These totems functioned as meeting places, but on another level, they gave the shopping center identity and personality. Indoor malls' exterior facades became only more boring over time, and while stores might come and go, a single dramatic accessory could represent the place's unique character. Better to spend money on that, mall architects soon learned, than on expensive cladding and fixtures.

The shopping mall was hardly the first commercial and architectural experience to turn an errand into a treat. Many theoretical discussions of malls revolve around what has come to be called the Gruen transfer: the moment when your presence at the mall tips from being goal-oriented (must buy new underwear, must buy birthday gift) into a pleasure in itself. Gruen and his associates were not reinventing the wheel but transplanting it to new environs. As the targeting of Hudson's as a client suggests, they were building on the backs of department stores, which brought wonder, convenience, and space for women into mid- to late nineteenth-century downtowns.

The idea of the "transfer" from chore to fantasy was best described early in the department store's heyday by French novelist Émile Zola in the 1883 book *Au Bonheur des Dames* (*The Ladies' Paradise*). In that book we follow two stories of life in modernizing Paris. Denise Baudu is a country girl who moves to the city to support her family, eventually turning (as many of her kind did in reality) to work in the city's first department store, the Paradise. Her counterpart is Octave Mouret, widowed owner of the Paradise, determined to woo the city's elite from their tailors and milliners and eventually—because this is a serialized potboiler, you've got to have some romance—to win Denise's heart. Her ongoing resistance to his social, economic, and masculine power represents resistance to the transfer. She, of all the women that he has made susceptible through his sales tactics, *can* say no to shopping. Zola writes,

> Mouret's unique passion was to conquer woman. He wished her to be queen in his house, and had built this temple that he might there hold her completely at his mercy. His sole aim was to intoxicate her with gallant attentions, traffic on her desires, profit by her fever . . .
>
> But where Mouret revealed himself as an unrivalled master was in the interior arrangement of his shops. He laid it down as a law that not a corner of The Ladies' Paradise ought to remain deserted; he required a noise, a crowd, evidence of life everywhere; for life, said he, attracts life, increases and multiplies it.

Zola did his research at the Bon Marché, the Paris department store that began as a piece goods shop on the rue de Bac. By the early 1850s, entrepreneur Aristide Boucicaut had moved from peddling fabric for dressmaking to selling readymade coats and dresses, still a novelty, as well as underwear, millinery, and shoes. He extracted his store from the old world of home- and handmade goods and converted it into an emporium for everything. Innovations added over time included browsable goods, accessible without a salesperson; smaller markups and fixed prices; and a money-back guarantee. Each of these departures from the old ways of trade are explicitly called out in Zola's novel. Along with consumer innovations, however, Boucicaut also championed architectural ones. Although the store had expanded incrementally during the 1840s and 1850s, in 1869 it opened in a brand-new, purpose-built structure on the rue de Sèvres designed by architect Louis-Auguste Boileau and engineer Gustave Eiffel. Eiffel, who would go on to design the eponymous Parisian tower, applied his structural knowledge to light wells and glass-topped cupolas, bathing the store interior in light. The main selling floor of the Bon Marché was topped by a broad, flat laylight of translucent glass. Cast-iron balconies and bridges ringed the room, while a waterfall staircase drew patrons upward. All these elements would return in the skylit atriums of suburban American shopping malls.

The majority of those Parisian department store patrons were, as Zola foresaw, women. The sidewalks of nineteenth-century Paris became host to a new female pastime, window-shopping, as women of means could spend a day moving between the newly paved sidewalks and the newly built department stores. The scale and concentration of the stores—along with the labor savings that readymade goods promised—transformed the practical task of provisioning a family from a neighborhood round to a leisure pursuit. Because of the expansion of shopping districts, and their distance from homes, department stores also had to step in to provide public facilities for women, including lounges, lavatories, and casual restaurants for lunch. To keep one's skirts out of the weather, above the dirt of the streets, and to spend a whole shopping day between departments, café, and lounge—these were previously unheard-of luxuries for women of all classes.

"The ability to feed, relieve, and revive oneself outside of the home not only provided security in the urban environment, but fostered women's mobility and, hence, independence in public life," writes Chuihua Judy Chung in *The Harvard Design School Guide to Shopping*. "Feminists urged the formation of non-retail-oriented 'resting places' to hasten this public independence, both by requesting local governments to establish public lavatories and by encouraging women to provide and patronize their own facilities." The department store paved the way for downtown women's clubs that ultimately provided the same practical, educational, and social spaces—but retail did it first, and with equal design aplomb. Department stores were also major employers of women. In 1880, one out of every two women in the U.S. labor force was a saleswoman or clerk. Between 1880 and 1940, the proportion of female sales staff grew from 24 to 40 percent in department stores. Organizations for saleswomen supported women's suffrage and equal pay.

Like their French progenitors, the earliest American department stores intended to serve the growing urban middle class. Stores were often located near cities' increasingly dense business districts, which patrons could reach by trolley. Scottish entrepreneur A. T. Stewart built one of the first at the corner of Chambers Street and Broadway in lower Manhattan in 1848. His so-called Marble Palace was actually a vast structure of white-painted cast iron, a material that was strong enough to support open sales floors on thin weight-bearing columns under a central glass dome. Lewis Mumford wrote, "If the vitality of an institution may be gauged by its architecture the department store was one of the most vital institutions of the era 1880–1914." Other technical innovations followed, along with the now-expected fixed prices, set "departments" selling an array of goods, and workforces that numbered in the thousands.

Wanamaker's in Philadelphia introduced electric lighting in 1878, after a direct appeal to Thomas Edison. Wanamaker's and Macy's, on Thirty-Fourth Street in Manhattan, added elevators in the early 1880s. Later there would be escalators, air-conditioning, and pneumatic tube systems for rapid communication within the store. Department stores had the money and audience to test systems, and their attention to the fashion cycle and the competitive nature of retail forced their owners to keep up.

The material most associated with department store architecture is glass: the wide plate-glass display windows facing the street, and the intricate glass roofs above the atriums of the largest stores, which let in maximum daylight. The glass domes connected the ever-expanding department stores to the architecture of exhibition halls and train stations, also spaces of gathering, display, and the latest technology. Harry Morrison, an engineer who became a spokesman for the selling power of glass, thought it would revolutionize consumption. Morrison first built cafeterias for the Wieboldt's department stores in Chicago, adding glass cases that put the food on perpetual display for impulse purchases, just like the clothes. James Wanamaker, Philadelphia's great department store owner, hired Morrison to design his new building in 1911 after visiting Paris examples like the Bon Marché and Printemps, which already had glass floors, glass vestibules, glass elevators, and glass display cases. Wanamaker bought new fixtures with interior lights and mirrored backs, putting as much merchandise as possible on display.

The other decisive technology of the department store was the escalator. An elevator keeps customers waiting, limits the number who can ascend or descend, and underlines the division between floors. Escalators keep everyone moving. An Otis promotional brochure humanized the difference:

> The elevator is ideal for the "man with a mission." He knows what he wants. It's a specific floor; he goes to that floor, makes his purchase and leaves. If *he* wants to go upstairs because he has business there, then give him an elevator. But if *you* want him upstairs, then you must reach down and pick him up. The Escalator does this job for you.

In considering how to transfer the glamour, safety, and ease of the department store to the suburbs, Gruen and Krummeck adapted materials and technology. Their first attempts at beautiful, integrated places for shopping were heavy on the glass, from the rejected circular design for *Architectural Forum* to the accepted U-shaped plaza, which included a semicircular glassed-in restaurant, rendered by Krummeck for maximum style. Sliding glass panels allowed both the stores and the restaurant to be opened up, increasing the flow between interior and exterior.

Later, as shopping centers became enclosed malls, and added floors, escalators would again become an almost seamless way to move shoppers around, as they had in department store interiors from the Bon Marché to Milliron's. Few ambitious malls since have failed to include multilevel skylit spaces wrapped, crisscrossed, or punctuated by the moving staircases that allow customers to see and be seen. Gruen would be a pioneer of this technique too. When it came time for him to design the atrium at Southdale— what was to become America's first enclosed mall—he organized it around escalators' drama and efficiency. When *Architectural Forum* covered Southdale (alongside developer James Rouse's Mondawmin Mall) in its December 1956 issue, the headline called out the positioning of the escalators: "Break-Through for Two-Level Shopping Centers." The article noted that the "flow up and down is so easy and uninhibited, and so much gaiety is added by that second layer of moving people, lights and color, that timidity about two-level design now seems pointless." These early successes were a boon to developers, who could now confidently double their shopping area and add the final technological breakthrough that made a mall a mall: air-conditioning.

→

The success of Northland brought Gruen new clients from across the United States. The Daytons of Minneapolis—a department-store-owning family who were, like Detroit's Hudsons, important philanthropists embedded in the city's power structures—hired Gruen and Larry Smith to study the market for a suburban shopping center in the vicinity of Minneapolis. After nine months of analysis, the Dayton Company bought 463 acres of land seven miles from the downtown loop in Edina, Minnesota, paying almost three thousand dollars per acre. The land required a zoning change from residential to commercial as the company planned to turn a fifteen-thousand-person town into a true suburb of Minneapolis. Eighty-four acres were earmarked for the shopping center, but Gruen's office also prepared a master plan for the remainder. The goal Gruen had had from the start—to integrate shopping into the new suburbs ringing every major American city—was moving toward fruition.

The master plan, reprinted in Gruen and Smith's 1960 manual *Shopping Towns USA*, shows the mall set in the center of a superblock of parking lots. Adjacent blocks were separated by roads. One block contained an artificial lake wrapped in curving streets lined with single-family houses; another held a denser complex of apartment towers and offices. Elsewhere were separate buildings, with their own parking lots, set aside for a school, a medical center, and more facilities. Gruen described the development as a "blight-proof neighborhood," using the language of disease to separate his suburb from the city. He flattered his clients by claiming they supported "the first large scale planning effort made by the forces usually considered as upholders of rugged individualism." The Dayton Company agreed to develop the lot of it—but the mall came first.

For the shopping center itself, Gruen brought back an idea he had proposed unsuccessfully for a project in Houston in 1950: not just bracketing landscaped terraces between the stores but actually enclosing the whole. The rationale in Houston had been to provide cool in the Texas summers. In Minneapolis the need for weatherproofing was year-round.

"Inventions sometimes are based on coincidences. In this way, the invention of the indoor, air-conditioned shopping center took root in my observations of the weather conditions in Minneapolis, Minnesota," Gruen wrote in his memoir. During preliminary discussions for another project, he wrote, "I had occasion to visit Minneapolis repeatedly. During those visits, the city was either buried in snow and bitter cold in winter, or scorching hot in summer, or rained out in spring and autumn." The model that Southdale provided was of an exurban island with as many civic functions as possible under one roof. If downtown could not be made to hitch up to the mall, the mall would become downtown, with its own plazas and lanes, post offices and cafés, play spaces and, of course, shops. Once you had parked in the lot, you could move freely through a variety of environments and—this would be Southdale's biggest coup—you could do it 365 days a year. "Every day will be a perfect shopping day," read the ads for the country's first indoor shopping mall.

As usual in the pitch to clients, Gruen's team emphasized the economics, working together to design an indoor shopping center that could be built and operated for the same cost as an outdoor one. Gruen claimed that heating and cooling a single large space was more efficient, and that store owners could largely eliminate their storefront enclosures, making it easier for customers to flow in and out. Sales, which were known to drop on very hot, very cold, and very wet days, would even out over the course of the climate-controlled year, and the appealing interior environment would make the mall even more of a community asset. In addition, everything had to be more compact: The public space was centralized, rather than spread out as landscaped fingers (as at Northland), and the shopping was arranged on two levels.

Air-conditioning had been a selling point for department stores since 1919, when Abraham & Straus, in New York, became the first climate-controlled shopping environment, following other urban entertainment centers such as theaters. A Carrier advertisement from 1930 questioned "why one great Department Store spent $1,000,000 for Manufactured Weather" and answered, "To make 'Every day a *good* day' in their stores regardless of unpleasant outdoor weather." Improvements in climate control technology made larger, deeper indoor spaces possible; by the late 1920s, windowless stores were seen as better for sales, as they provided a controlled, clean interior with artificial lighting. Retail architects Gruen, Ketchum, Morris Lapidus, Daniel Schwartzman, and Kenneth Welch wrote in the July 1950 issue of *Architectural Forum* that "air conditioning alone can be said to have reshaped every element of the modern store beginning with the building front and ending with the display case."

Much like the debut of Northland two years before, Southdale's opening in October 1956 was a national event, with two full-size department stores

Dayton's Department Store at Southdale, Edina, Minnesota, Gruen Associates, 1956. (Gruen Associates)

(Dayton's and Donaldson's), 810,000 square feet of shops, 5,200 parking spaces, and the three-story "Garden Court of Perpetual Spring," the inspiration for all future mall atria. The parking lots were so extensive that each one of the fifteen was named for a different animal, with graphic cartoons of big-eared rabbits, sleek foxes, patterned turtles, and skinny giraffes memorably marking the locations. Publications on the new trend for malls emphasized the delights inside: "Pleasure-Domes with Parking," wrote *Time.* "A Better Outdoors Indoors," said *Architectural Record.* "The Garden Court is one of the largest indoor public areas in the United States," wrote the *Minneapolis Sunday Tribune.* Of course, it wasn't public; it was owned by the Daytons and their partners.

If people remember Southdale at the moment when it was the center of the country's attention, they remember the Garden Court. Almost a block long, it sat at the center of Southdale's cluster plan, which placed Dayton's and Donaldson's at opposite corners, with bars of shops bracketing the covered open space on either side. A supermarket faced outward, with entrances off the parking lot. Fifty-foot trees ascended toward the north-facing clerestory that let in natural light, and Gruen purposely chose species suited to warmer climates, like magnolia and eucalyptus, to emphasize the exoticism of the year-round indoor experience. The band of window, Gruen explained, "generated a visual link with the outside world: visitors could see the sky and the clouds at different times of day."

Woolworth's ran what amounted to a sidewalk café in the atrium, with wrought-iron tables and yellow umbrellas, even though there was no chance of weather. A cylindrical cage held fifty brightly colored birds. A carousel turned. The most significant works of art were by Harry Bertoia, a favorite of many modern architects: two forty-five-foot-tall sculptures made of brazed metal plates, which reflected light and drew the eye upward to the roof. Nicknamed the "golden trees," they became a marker and meeting place like the totem pole at Northland. Smaller artistic interventions included glass mosaic murals on the walls of the court—also colorful and light-catching. Crisscross escalators at one end brought shoppers to the second level, so people never had to sever contact with the delights of the court.

Outside, the mall had even less curb appeal than Northland. "For Gruen, there was no greater symbol of Southdale's reform ideals than its blank facades," biographer M. Jeffrey Hardwick writes in *Mall Maker*. "Reviewers rarely noticed the windowless walls facing the parking lots; the interior was too distracting and novel. But those blank walls were a very deliberate part of Gruen's design. No signs, no lights, no show windows, and no decoration—the exterior was supposed to be serene and uninspiring, a reaction to the bright lights of the commercial strip."

Not everyone agreed. "Who wants to sit in that desolate looking spot?" Frank Lloyd Wright sniped when the *Minneapolis Star* called him for comment. "You've got a garden court that has all the evils of the village street and none of its charm . . . You have tried to bring downtown out here. You should have left downtown downtown."

The president of Dayton's used the language of community, not commerce, when discussing the plans for what was indeed a downtown takeover of Edina: "The development will offer a pleasant place to shop, a good spot in which to work, and a fine neighborhood in which to live." As in Detroit, the traditional center of power where Minneapolis's leading businessmen worked in towers and gathered at clubs was being eroded. They wanted in on the next wave. However, it is clear from the Southdale master plan that Gruen's idea of neighborhood bore little relation to the narrow streets of European cities, where shops, offices, and housing might be neighbors or occupy the same building, and the ratio of pedestrian to car space was approximately equal. His neighborhood followed the single-use logic of American suburban development, which divided functions into discrete blocks separated by wide, car-centric roads. Even if you lived in Gruen's planned Edina high-rise, the walk from your home to the mall would be unpleasant: across a multilane boulevard and a wide parking lot.

For Gruen, the solution to the mess of the city and roadside attractions was more planning, whether by business interests or government entities.

But in his dependence on developers, he failed to acknowledge that the market, rather than community, would always be their guide. The construction of Southdale increased land prices in Edina and sparked a new wave of home construction outside the Dayton Company's 463 acres. Embroiled in the expense of building a brand-new style of mall, the company sold 208 acres to developers of single-family homes at a profit; some of the co-investors in the mall also began constructing a single-family neighborhood. No one seemed interested in the denser, mixed-use planning Gruen had imagined when, as anyone could see in a hundred other places, houses made for an easy return on investment. Again and again, Gruen's clients would buy tracts of land far larger than they needed for a mall, and again and again, they would sell those acres to the highest bidder once the mall was in progress. As Hardwick writes, "Most symbolically and practically, Gruen never found a way to create a shopping center that was not an island in a sea of parking."

Although shopping center pioneers such as J. C. Nichols in Kansas City and Hugh Prather and Edgar Flippen in Dallas, developers of Highland Park Village, one of the first outdoor shopping centers in the nation, had seen the competitive advantage of integrating mixed uses into their residential schemes, this did not become the norm. Funding streams for new construction, both federal and private, were intended for projects with a single use—either residential or commercial, not both—and most of the federal money was directed toward new homes and new roads, not what lay in between. The Federal Housing Administration (FHA) embraced more modest, drive-up retail strips with minimal landscaping, but primarily for lower-income apartment developments. The initial assumption was that middle-class families would continue to shop downtown. The so-called mess of the city that new homeowners supposedly sought refuge from in the suburbs was, in part, the mix of commercial buildings and dense homes. The dream of detached houses and generous green space didn't leave visual room for the realities of gas stations, car dealerships, and supermarkets. In one contemporary community-planning guidebook, shopping is spoken of as inimical to residential development; hedges, parking lots, and low-rise apartment buildings must screen business areas from the very people who will be shopping there. This fear of commerce as pollution sets the stage for a century of use-segregated and car-dependent suburban planning, with roads routed so that even the neighbors closest to a shopping strip have to drive around the block to access it. The beauty and convenience of integrated design and stores tuned to the neighborhood are undermined by the parking lots.

In addition, that federal money was unequally distributed, largely supporting the homeownership goals of white Americans and subsidizing the roads that made suburban commutes possible. The GI Bill, drafted in 1944, was intended to help returning World War II veterans prosper, by paying for a percentage of their education, health care, and mortgages. Many of the white families who bought in new suburban developments were able to do so thanks to low-interest mortgages backed by government guarantee. The FHA insured private lenders against losses accrued on residential mortgages, thereby changing the financial calculus most Americans performed to buy a home. Whereas in the 1920s first-time homeowners had needed at least a 30 percent down payment, FHA-secured loans required only 10 percent down. The repayment period for mortgages was extended to twenty-five or thirty years; interest rates fell by 2 to 3 percentage points to reflect the new, lower risk to the lender; and standards for home construction, set by the FHA, were improved and made uniform. This meant that more people could buy a home, and feel confident in its construction. This in turn changed Americans' expectations about their future: the single-family home with a yard and, equally important, a driveway became the dream. Between 1934 and 1972, the percentage of Americans who lived in houses they owned rose from 44 to 63 percent. Almost half of all suburban housing was financed by the FHA or the Veterans Administration, via the GI Bill, in the 1950s and 1960s. The number of new homes built during this period was also unprecedented. From 1929 to 1945, fewer than 100,000 new houses had been built per year, primarily in the suburbs, leading to a housing shortage that only became more acute as the 1940s progressed. In 1940, however, the marriage rate began to rise, and by 1943 the birth rate had also reached its highest point in two decades: twenty-two births per one thousand people. While servicemen were overseas, government, industry, and the media played up the dream of the suburban home as a reward upon return. With government-backed mortgages in play, builders responded to the unmet demand, starting 937,000 new single-family homes in 1946, 1,183,000 in 1948, and 1,692,000 in 1950. (For comparison, single-family housing starts in 2019 totaled half that, 888,200, up by 1.4 percent from those in 2018.)

In theory these benefits were available to veterans of any race, but in practice Black soldiers and their families were much less likely to benefit—or to have far fewer choices in how to benefit. Their educational options were limited to segregated colleges and universities. And the mortgages had to be issued by commercial banks, which colluded with the developers of neighborhoods with discriminatory housing covenants to keep those neighborhoods—and the shopping centers that served them—racially segregated.

The first challenge to covenants like those in place at Country Club Plaza came in the mid-1940s, beginning a wave of postwar civil rights cases that would seek to provide equal protection in housing, education, and public space. The Shelley family had moved from Mississippi to St. Louis in 1930 as part of the Great Migration of Blacks from the South. As they looked for a house to buy in the city, they found that many owners were prohibited from selling to them by racially restrictive covenants. One such owner agreed to sell them the two-story brick house at 4600 Labadie Avenue despite the covenant, thereby setting up a court challenge to the practice. Thurgood Marshall represented the Shelleys with Los Angeles lawyer Loren Miller, backed by the NAACP, when their case made its way to the Supreme Court.

In 1948 the Court ruled 6–0 in favor of the Shelleys. Chief Justice Vinson's opinion stated, "It cannot be doubted that among the civil rights intended to be protected from discriminatory state action by the Fourteenth Amendment are the rights to acquire, enjoy, own and dispose of property," thus deeming such covenants unenforceable. They were, however, honored in fact if not by law. The prevalence of such covenants is clear from the very circumstance of the court's 6–0 decision: Three members of the then all-white Supreme Court had to recuse themselves from the case because their own homes were in neighborhoods with such covenants. Afterward, Marshall wrote, "This blow to racial segregation in the field of housing opens up the pending fight against segregation in education" and "must be carried on with renewed vigor," as he and Miller teamed up for their next and more famous Supreme Court case, *Brown v. Board of Education*, decided in their favor in 1954.

Historian Andrew Wiese begins an account of the barriers to the pursuit of "African American suburban dreams" with the case study of Jim and Ann Braithewaite, middle-class Black renters in Philadelphia in 1957. "They answered newspaper ads, contacted real estate brokers, attended auctions and made an estimated 300 phone calls, but they met a 'stone wall' of resistance. 'We don't have any split-levels,' or 'That's already spoken for,' brokers told them. Others were straightforward: 'You're colored, aren't you? I can't do anything for you,' said one." In the end, the Braithewaites bought a lot from an owner willing to sell to African Americans and built their own home, checking on the contractor's progress at night. When they moved in, in October 1959, local Quakers spent the first night with them in the house, and they avoided their own picture window for "some time," fearing violent repercussions if they upset their white neighbors' vision of suburban conformity.

Rather than covenants, would-be Black homeowners faced discriminatory loan practices on the part of the FHA, which "did not insure mortgages in the neighborhoods where Black homeowners lived and chiefly targeted newly constructed homes, which almost exclusively catered to whites, and those in wealthier neighborhoods." This practice is popularly known as "redlining," so-called because of maps by the Home Owners' Loan Corporation (HOLC), issued in the 1930s, which graded neighborhoods on a four-point scale in terms of economic desirability. First-quality neighborhoods were "in demand," second-quality were "still desirable" but had "reached their peak," third were "definitely declining," and fourth, coded red, were already in decline and labeled "hazardous" on the basis of the age of the housing stock as well as the race and income of the inhabitants. Recent scholarship has shown that the HOLC, rather than being guided by the maps, actually did offer loans to Black homeowners, while the FHA engaged in discriminatory lending practices. The FHA did not insure mortgages in majority-Black neighborhoods and offered preferential treatment to buyers of newly constructed houses, who were likely to be white. Descriptions of Black neighborhoods in planning literature of the period often referred to them as "blighted," adopting an agricultural metaphor for a socioeconomic configuration. Eventually, "hazardous" neighborhoods were more likely to be walled off by or demolished for highways, following disinvestment after white flight to the suburbs. As Andrew Herscher writes in "Black and Blight,"

> Definitions of blight have consistently applied to property owned and occupied by people of color, while, on the other hand, the remediation of blight has consistently served to transfer property from people of color, through the state, to predominantly white investors, developers, or owners. Property has thereby served as both an instrument and reward of racism.

Many banks would not loan to renters seeking to buy in redlined neighborhoods, while suburbs would not accept Black buyers, locking generations of Black Americans out of the opportunity to own a home and accumulate generational wealth. In New York and northern New Jersey, writes historian Ira Katznelson, "fewer than 100 of the 67,000 mortgages insured by the GI bill supported home purchases by non-whites" in the newly constructed suburbs. The practice of "blockbusting" also played on white homeowners' economic fears: Predatory realtors and developers would suggest that Black families were planning to move into a neighborhood, thereby "contaminating" its real estate values. White families would sell at a loss, while the realtors would flip the houses to Black families with fewer options at a higher cost. Even when such families successfully settled in the suburbs, they often returned to the city, or to more established Black communities for church, personal services, and shopping.

The success of FHA programs that subsidized the purchase of new construction leached money from downtown cores. It was more expensive to develop multi-unit housing, as in denser urban areas, and renovation loans to fix up existing or historic homes were smaller and had to be repaid over a shorter term. The Interstate Highway Act of 1956 also subsidized the suburbs to the detriment of downtown. When the act became law, Congress agreed to fund 90 percent of a forty-one-thousand-mile interstate highway system, the direct result of lobbying by trucking, car, bus, and roadway operators led by General Motors, which had proposed a car-centric vision of the future way back in Norman Bel Geddes's (and Victor Gruen's) Futurama of 1939. Money was set aside for roads rather than public transportation, privileging those with cars, and for roads that went anywhere but downtown. Ring roads to take drivers around the downtown core, beltways to take you swiftly from downtown to suburb, and multilane highways to speed the way from city to city were all funded by taxes, while railroads went begging and 1 percent of postwar transportation money went to public transit.

Shopping centers and malls piggybacked on the exploding population and new homebuilding. In devising the catchment districts for their new neighborhood and regional centers, developers, planners, and architects were aware of whom their new shoppers would be. Through seemingly innocuous decisions such as whether, and where, to include a stop for public buses, they created additional barriers for Black shoppers less likely to own a car and more likely to live—not necessarily by choice—in older neighborhoods closer to the center city. In proposing a downtown outside downtown, protected from the elements, ringed by parking lots, designed for a single use and rigidly planned, Victor Gruen had also created a mechanism to protect white, upwardly mobile homeowners from those unlike themselves.

Seen in this context, Southdale's tagline, "Every day will be a perfect shopping day," means more than just protection from Minnesota's chill or humidity. The indoor shopping mall offered a promise of control extending from the weather onward, including art curation, landscape design, store selection, security, and transportation—everything from the maps in the mall to how shoppers got to the mall to the income level and appearance of those shoppers. As malls began to spread countrywide in Southdale's wake, the next decades would demonstrate how that control made shopping easier and more seductive for some and compounded the segregation of others— often at the same time.

Chapter 2
The Garden

In the 1960s the mall grew up. Nancy Nasher grew up with it. NorthPark Center was conceived in her family's living room. It was her parents' dream for the future of Dallas, conjured from undeveloped farmland, a brand-new cloverleaf interchange, and a successful modern apartment building. It was never meant to be just a mall. As the fact sheet for NorthPark's August 21, 1965, opening grandly explained:

> In the dream stage of planning, NorthPark was projected as a Taj Mahal of great stores and shops surrounded by theatres, restaurants and cafes, skyscraper office buildings, medical buildings and clinics, high- and low-rise apartment living residences, and recreational areas with tennis courts, swimming pools, spas—all bordered by a green belt of grass and ground coverings and engulfed by the warmth of a forest of trees and the sparkle and brilliance of ever-blooming seasonal flowers.

Nancy's parents, Raymond and Patsy Nasher, like so many other designers and builders of the time, were dismayed by the motley, piecemeal nature of development at the edge of cities. Echoing Victor Gruen, the critic Peter Blake called the roadways "God's Own Junkyard" and "the mess that is man-made America" in a book published in 1964. By controlling the planning and design of their new shopping center, inside and out, the Nashers believed they could improve on a model then in its toddler stage, wobbly and unformed.

During the 1960s the mall went from being a curiosity to a ubiquity, expanding its geographic and stylistic range. With that expansion came more variety in shape, size, amenities, and ambition, with accompanying heroic profiles of mall makers—both developers and architects. Then and now NorthPark serves as an example of the perfection of the mall, and provides a rare opportunity to trace how a family, their architects, and their employees make and manage that perfection over decades. This era is also when the mall starts to fall through the cracks of mainstream architectural criticism; there are simply too many to look at, and while the nation's top-ranked architects would continue to design malls throughout the 1960s, by the end of the decade that connection began to slip as familiarity bred contempt.

Sixteen department store branches opened in shopping centers between 1946 and 1950. Between 1950 and 1955, sixty were built, a nearly fourfold increase. Southdale opened in 1956, which is, not incidentally, the same year the International Council of Shopping Centers was founded. From 1961 to the end of 1970, right when the Nashers were plotting in their living room, 240 regional malls, with multiple anchors and up to one hundred stores, were built in the United States. The majority of them were the work of specialized developers, including Edward J. DeBartolo Sr., the Rouse Company, the Simon brothers, and A. Alfred Taubman. Architecture firms including John Graham & Company of Seattle (Northgate), Welton Becket & Associates (Stonestown) and Albert C. Martin & Associates (Lakewood) of Los Angeles, Morris Ketchum of New York (Shoppers' World), and, of course, Gruen of Los Angeles contributed to the shaping of this new American form.

The Simon brothers—Melvin, Herbert, and Fred—started in strip malls, developing relationships with the low-cost national chains like Woolworth's and Sears to anchor roadside shopping centers in their native Indiana. Their first indoor malls, one in Bloomington and the other in Fort Collins, Colorado, opened in 1964. Both were located near university campuses and incorporated the flagship department store of their respective closest cities. DeBartolo—based in Youngstown, Ohio, and by 1973 the country's largest developer of malls—started the same way, financing his first enclosed buildings by selling off approximately one hundred neighborhood shopping centers. DeBartolo was notorious in his day for taking a literally high-flying approach to locating new malls, hopping around the country to check on construction in his Learjet. "Across this landscape zigzags trelliswork of straight, strong, skinny lines, the highways and expressways," a 1973 profile of DeBartolo described, "and wherever these straight lines meet, at each convergence of asphalt, the face of Edward J. DeBartolo, master builder of shopping malls, takes on [a kind of] bliss." The Nashers followed the same practice, locating their mall near that cloverleaf intersection where US-75 and Northwest Highway intertwined.

DeBartolo, like the Simons, was all business in terms of style. Live plants were a must, as were flattering lighting and plashing fountains. But above all else, cleanliness. "DeBartolo Modern," as defined by one of his employees, "is clean lines, functional, efficient, well landscaped, with colors and textures that look pleasant and suit the region—warm brown brick in Chautauqua, N.Y., textured concrete in Palm Beach. Our whole idea is easy maintenance, prevention of decay, keeping the place from looking seedy . . . Disorder is costly." Here DeBartolo and the Nashers would part ways: The Nashers' priorities went beyond low-maintenance efficiency toward art.

In 1960, when the Nashers were negotiating NorthPark's ninety-nine-year lease with the Hillcrest Foundation, which then owned the property, the nearest built-up areas were the historic Caruth homestead to the south and the Sparkman-Hillcrest Memorial Park to the west and the Preston Hollow neighborhood beyond. Highland Park Village sat within a three-mile radius of NorthPark's location. (They remain rivals to this day.) "The thing is we have sufficient room to create more than a conventional shopping center," a "soft-spoken" Ray Nasher told the *Dallas Morning News* in 1961, responding to critics blocking his requested residential-to-commercial zoning change. "Our goal is to produce something that will be aesthetically pleasing—a new urban complex impossible to realize in a smaller area." What makes NorthPark compelling today is how well he succeeded. Even mall skeptics—downtown denizens who turn up their noses at the suburbs,

Aerial view of NorthPark Center, Dallas, Texas, under construction, 1964. (NorthPark Center)

aesthetes who pretend they never shop at chain stores, socialists who think there are better reasons to gather than shopping—have been charmed by NorthPark's combination of architecture, art, and something very like community. And NorthPark's success has kept it intact: Most malls of the 1960s are hardly recognizable as such, thanks to additions and subtractions and demolitions. In certain spots at NorthPark it can still feel like 1965, and the twenty-first-century visitor, even a skeptical one, can catch a glimpse of the mall as an ambitious urbanist's dream.

Architecture was an intrinsic part of the NorthPark equation. Back to the fact sheet:

> The chaotic confusion of climate-controlled shopping buildings— which normally are a mass of diverse forms, elements, materials, and colors—would become in NorthPark's mind's-eye a single building composed of a single material, a white brick—the whitest available

natural clay with a soft finish—with white flush joints, and a natural cast stone. The retail homes for one hundred merchants would be transformed into a dignified, unified, strong structure; a piece of architectural sculpture.

At that point, Ray Nasher's major development achievement was 2300 Riverside, a twenty-one-story luxury apartment building in Tulsa, Oklahoma, designed by the young architect E. G. Hamilton in partnership with George F. Harrell. Hamilton had studied architecture at Washington University in St. Louis, then after the war worked in the Detroit office of Minoru Yamasaki, later the architect of the World Trade Center towers. There Hamilton fell in with an active and experimental group of architects and designers including Kevin Roche and neighbor John Dinkeloo, both of whom worked for Eero Saarinen, then at the height of his fame among U.S.-based architects.

Hamilton met the Nashers socially through the Seldins, a young couple for whom he had designed a never-built modern house. "Donald [Seldin, a Brooklyn-born nephrologist who transformed the University of Texas Southwestern Medical Center into a national leader] took me aside and he said, 'Now you keep your eye on this man, he's going to be a millionaire.' Ray was thirty years of age at the time, Patsy was 23, I was 32," Hamilton told an audience in 2010. He was already aware that the Nashers had modern taste—a small Ben Shahn painting of a tennis player caught his eye the first time he visited their house—and that came through on the Tulsa project. "Patsy and Ray wanted good architecture. They wanted to be involved in the process . . . Patsy had to look at every cabinet, every fixture, every fitting in our plans. So I learned that they wanted something good and they were willing to work at it."

Raymond Nasher had grown up in Boston, the only son of Jewish immigrants from Russia and Germany who worked in the garment industry. He attended the Boston Latin school and visited the nearby Isabella Stewart Gardner Museum on the weekends with his parents, along with the city's other public collections. He went to Duke, where he focused on economics and athletics, becoming president of the class of 1943 and captain of the varsity tennis team. (Later he would give the founding gift for the university's new art museum.) After serving as a lieutenant in the navy for four years, he returned to Boston and studied for a master's degree in economics at Boston University. There he met Patsy Rabinowitz, a Smith graduate, at an election night party in November 1948; she was the only one to predict a Truman victory. Married a year later, the two soon returned to Rabinowitz's native city, Dallas, which seemed primed for postwar growth.

While histories of NorthPark tend to focus on Ray Nasher, their daughter insists her mother deserves equal credit. "She was the more decisive of the two," Nancy Nasher told me. "She had the eye. The art collection is her work, the design of NorthPark, the selection of materials, the selection of stores, the marketing, the advertising. Everything you see, she was intimately involved with." Early meetings about the project were held at the Nashers' then-modest home, with their daughters passing refreshments. Ray Nasher used to drive Nancy, his youngest daughter, by the mall on her way to school, checking on its construction as a gardener might check for new buds.

When Nasher decided a shopping mall should follow the Tulsa apartment building, he partnered with Sidney Greenberg of Strouse Greenberg, a Philadelphia developer with retail expertise. They turned to Hamilton for the same kind of light, geometric masonry architecture as 2300 Riverside, an elegant slab tower open to the play of sunlight and punctuated by landscaped spaces. Their mall was to be more than DeBartolo Modern: It was to embody the most advanced architecture of the time, while still accommodating the ebb and flow of commerce. Hamilton told the same 2010 audience,

> In the beginning of the process, we got together—the architects, the landscape architects, the graphic designers—two or three times to discuss the basic design philosophy for the project . . . We very quickly were able to agree on some of the ground rules. One of the most important points with people was the fact that we should have

a single palette of materials. Up until that time, if you had a [shopping] center, and you had three department stores, you had four palettes of materials and you had four types of graphics.

In design meetings, landscape architect Lawrence Halprin pushed for red brick, Hamilton for sand silver, a pale gray. But Patsy Nasher preferred white. Hamilton found a Texas source of white clay and commissioned Henderson Brick Company to make a new brick with a smooth, sanded finish custom for the project. The bricks were installed with a flush mortar joint, with mortar to match the white clay, so that the overall effect was of a lightly textured but monolithic wall. Outside, with the sharp shadows cast by the architecture under the Texas sun, light and dark create a brilliant contrast.

At first, the multiple department store owners Nasher and Greenberg courted insisted on their own architects. But in the end, only the owners of Neiman Marcus chose another set of designers. Stanley Marcus hired Eero Saarinen as his architect; after Saarinen's death in 1961, successors Roche and Dinkeloo took over the design, seamlessly working with their friend Hamilton.

By the mid-1960s Stanley Marcus was a legendary retailer. His father, Herbert, cofounded Neiman Marcus in downtown Dallas with his sister Carrie and her husband, Al Neiman, in 1907. Stanley worked at the family store from an early age, leaving to attend first Harvard College and then Harvard Business School. In 1932 he married Billie Cantrell, who worked in the Neiman Marcus Sports Shop until she had their first child in 1936. He also began to expand the role of Neiman Marcus in the city, adding weekly couture fashion shows, the over-the-top Christmas catalog, and, once he was elected president and CEO in 1950, the "International Fortnights": two-week fairs, focused on a single foreign country, that brought art, music, food, and fashion to downtown Dallas. The Marcuses, the Titches, the Nashers, and a handful of other professionals were members of a Jewish elite in what was still a Christian and conservative city, a dynamic repeated in many other Southern cities, by many other Jewish merchants.

In 1951 Marcus had opened his first suburban store at Preston Center, an open-air shopping center in the Preston Hollow neighborhood, so he

Top, Neiman Marcus Department Store at NorthPark Center, Kevin Roche for Eero Saarinen Associates, 1965. *Bottom*, Titche-Goettinger Department Store, E. G. Hamilton for Omniplan, 1965. (NorthPark Center)

understood his customer as someone requiring easy access from a car. He chose the site at NorthPark closest to Preston Hollow, facing west onto Boedeker Street, and asked his architects to create a building for the store with exterior presence: a roof and thick cornice like a strong brow, and, on two sides, a series of half-cylinders popping from the smooth surface of the white brick wall. Even in construction photos those curves stand out, thanks to their crisp shadows. For the shopper pulling up to the store's outside entrance, they would have been a tease. I imagine her journey from wondering what those bumps on the outside of the building are, to wandering among the jewelry cases, riding the escalator down to lunch at the café, purchasing a few makeup items, and then heading to the heart of the store: the designer floor. Only after a sales associate has gathered an armful of goods would she have been ushered, with ceremony, into her curved cubicle and realized— aha! The half-cylinders are fitting rooms. Not merely a decorative flourish but a minimalist expression of the department store's most intimate purpose: dressing you. They even offered the most flattering illumination—daylight— thanks to skylights made possible by their exterior location.

From outside, the NorthPark Neiman Marcus was all Corbusian forms in space. Inside, it was a haze of sensual pleasures—sparkling jewelry, bright purses, perfume samples, and the crafty, clunky goodness of Bjorn Wiinblad's blue-and-white tiles for the café, which served Danish open-faced sandwiches and was originally known as "The Little Mermaid," after the Copenhagen sculpture. The interior design was by Eleanor Le Maire, a longtime collabo-rator on the interiors of Neiman Marcus stores. Marcus didn't have to explain to her, as he did to Roche, that the interior of a store known for cutting-edge fashion had to be designed with future refurbishments in mind. "We found ourselves educating most of the architects as to what the philosophy of a store was," Marcus told an interviewer. "One of the things we had to teach them was that we were positive of only one thing with any store—that we would want to change it within 10 years . . . [Roche] was very convincing that a building had to have some discipline even if you did have to change it a little."

Even after agreeing to be an anchor for NorthPark, Stanley Marcus was dubious that his high-end clientele would want to enter through the mall proper, rather than from the Boedeker side. Within weeks he turned out to be wrong: Traffic via the mall was greater than from any other entrance, leading to a rapid expansion of the cosmetics area. There was nothing to be done with the relatively small, single-story opening between the mall and Neiman's—even in 2020 it was still simply marked NEIMAN MARCUS in the standard NorthPark lettering.

Outside Neiman Marcus, a series of square mountains rise from the floor, faced in the same taupe glazed tile that runs around the edge of NorthPark's long halls. A shallow pond, lined with blue tile, sinks below the concrete surface of the floor, with tiny flat bridges crisscrossing the water. Daylight filters down through a clerestory, with direct sunlight blocked by a series of thin wooden slats, painted to match the concrete. Wide benches of wooden slats frame the fountain. It is a pocket park, a sculpture garden, and a resting place all in one, and almost never without a parent or caregiver sitting on a bench watching a child climb up and slip down, climb up and slip down one of the hard-sided mountains. As critic Virginia Postrel writes, "Long before malls were installing play areas, NorthPark created one accidentally. Instead of worrying about wear and tear or lawsuits, or taking a hint to install traditional play equipment, NorthPark embraced children's spontaneous use of its space." Other malls have a circular fountain, a few benches and plants; NorthPark has playable sculpture by a designer on par with Saarinen.

The fountain was designed by landscape architects Lawrence Halprin and Richard Vignolo, called "Viggy" by the NorthPark team. Halprin himself was a bearded Northern California type who created dramatic and pedestrian-friendly parks for downtown Portland, Oregon, and wild, light-on-the-land plans for the coastal development Sea Ranch, about a hundred miles north of San Francisco. In collaboration with his wife, dancer Anna Halprin, Lawrence led urban workshops for architects, dancers, and students that were intended to tune them in to city patterns, the way people move through space, and intuitive design, and tune out professional boundaries and straight lines. He's easy to pick out in photographs of the NorthPark design team since he's the only one without a suit and a clean shave. What he brought to the table at NorthPark and the other shopping mall landscapes his firm designed was a sense of play. While NorthPark is now known for its superlative collection of art, particularly large-scale sculpture—the square mountains were plinths for works of art that had yet to appear—Halprin and Vignolo's atrium set the mall's standard for art that was also physically engaging, conversation pieces that could be admired and also explored. Halprin's firm would go on to design a number of urban pedestrian malls in the 1970s.

Graphic design was the final element in NorthPark's coordinated concept. The architects designed steel-framed, glass-topped porte cocheres to mark the major entrances and cover the walk from curbside to glass doors. Lighting in the parking lot was uniform, the lamps set higher than usual to create a clear line of sight from car to entrance. Herb Rosenthal, whose firm was based in Los Angeles, created a series of design specifications for the center. All the exterior signs were to be of the same type, height, and material, and all the interior signs had to fit within the frame proscribed by the architecture: a projecting course of white brick running up the sides and over the top of the storefront. Rosenthal's most indelible contribution was the treelike mark, nicknamed "the bug," which appears as a cast-stone relief at the two upper corners of each storefront's white brick frame. A 1965 ad introduced the mark, along with the center, to Dallas. "This is the symbol," it reads. "In it you see a tree form combined with a north arrow symbolically expressing the name—NorthPark," and it quotes Rosenthal: "In both form and color it represents the park-like quality of the center." Early printed materials featured the mark in dark green with a lighter green background; later versions played with coloring the petals green.

On opening day, all three Nasher daughters were outfitted in matching blue sleeveless A-line dresses with green trim, matching pendant necklaces with the NorthPark bug symbol in white on green looped around their necks. They cut the ribbon, arranged in a row with their parents, and then the three girls, along with Hamilton's three daughters, handed out guides and showed people around. The family pressed handprints into the concrete in the corner of the SouthCourt; Nancy's handprint is in the middle, marked with an N.N. Some families squish their palms into the sidewalk outside their houses; the Nasher girls had a whole mall to play in. After NorthPark opened, Nancy remembers walking the mall with her father analyzing which stores were busiest, and with her mother, watching her dust every leaf in the landscaped medians. For the holidays, Patsy Nasher created a series of reindeer and other holiday decorations, covered in pecans, sour cherries, marshmallows, and raisins, most of which still make an annual appearance.

As Hamilton noted in 2010, "At the opening of NorthPark, there was no art." The architecture and design were intended to stand on their own. In 1970, NorthPark won the American Institute of Architects' Design of the Decade Award, which came with funds to commission a piece of public art. Patsy Nasher chose sculptor Beverly Pepper, who moved to the city to work on *Dallas Land Canal: Canal and Hillside*, unveiled in 1972. The piece, made of triangles of Cor-Ten steel and mounded earth, draws a dramatic line down the parking lot approach to the mall from the south, culminating in a miniature, fragmented pyramidal form. The unveiling of Pepper's artwork was announced via a type-only ad in the *Dallas Morning News*, couched in NorthPark's signature understated idiom: "A sculpture to see through a car window," it read. "Beverly Pepper designed it. Then she left her home in Rome for four months to participate in its construction. It's in our South parking area. And it's actually designed to be admired from a car in motion. Drive by and see it. Then park and come in."

Patsy had already begun to build a sculpture collection, owned by the couple but displayed at NorthPark. She bought the couple's first work of sculpture, a bronze by Jean Arp, as a birthday present for Ray in 1967, thinking that, as a builder, he could better relate to its materials. Sculpture was also, at that time, undervalued on the art market. Today, the mall's two largest and most iconic pieces are *Ad Astra*, a forty-eight-foot-tall orange steel sculpture by Mark di Suvero, the soaring centerpiece of the addition's NorthCourt; and Jonathan Borofsky's *Five Hammering Men*, whose motorized labor long held down the SouthCourt—right at the end of Luxury Row, the prime real estate just outside the Neiman Marcus store. In the years leading up to Patsy's death—at age fifty-nine of cancer, in 1988—the elder Nashers' collection eventually grew well beyond their home, and the mall; in 1997 Ray Nasher purchased a plot of land in downtown Dallas and spent seventy million dollars to found, and build, the Nasher Sculpture Center. Its design by Italian architect Renzo Piano includes a pale materials palette, a single story, and an elaborate ceiling to safely channel daylight down to artworks and patrons. It shares these elements, of course, with NorthPark, whose slogan today is "The Art of Shopping."

$$\rightarrow$$

The Community Builders Handbook, published by the Urban Land Institute (ULI) in 1947 and updated annually thereafter, was an early attempt to establish best practices for the postwar shopping center and that new concept, the enclosed mall. Too little thought had been given to building neighborhoods of enduring value, wrote the members of the Community Builders' Council, following the lead of ULI founding member J. C. Nichols, developer of the pioneering Country Club Plaza. Shopping centers had been built hastily, without proper analysis of community needs and adequate parking. The council was, nevertheless, conservative. It stressed that central business districts remained important, but satellite shopping areas were necessary as suburban development, underwritten by the federal government, turned toward automobility. That conservatism went double for architecture: "The ultra-modernist and the seeker for radical, unorthodox, or socialized departures in this field will not find them here."

As the pace of first shopping center, then mall construction picked up in the 1950s and 1960s, some leaders of the development community wanted to get a handle on it. The Nashers intended NorthPark to serve as a physical model of good design and good business—a combination of traits associated at that time with leading corporations like IBM. The handbook was a separate attempt to tame "God's Own Junkyard" by compiling what were thought to be best practices. For the reader today it provides insight into the underlying structure of the shopping center and mall—why these stores, in this arrangement, in this size parking lot?—and also into overarching planning patterns that were ultimately destructive: Why do malls turn their backs on the neighborhood, and on downtown?

The handbook laid out the basics of planning, listing thirty store types and the order in which they should be added to a center. A small strip of up to twenty stores, serving approximately one thousand families, should include a grocery store, a drugstore with a lunch counter, a dry cleaner, a beauty parlor, a filling station, and other such everyday needs. This is a "neighborhood center." A larger version, a "community center," should have a florist, a milliner, a gift shop, and a liquor store, as well as a junior department store, among its twenty to forty businesses. The next tranche of need included a dress shop, a theater, a café or drive-in restaurant, and a toy store, plus doctors' and dentists' offices. Like stores ought to be grouped with like, so that a woman shopping for an outfit could move from dresses to hats to alterations at the dry cleaner without passing the mechanic or car showrooms. The "100 per cent locations," the best in a center, should be reserved for bakeries, bookstores, clothing shops, and candy emporiums, the guide authoritatively states. "Regional centers," with forty to one hundred stores, needed to be destinations unto themselves for 100,000 to 250,000 people, with a full-size department store as anchor.

Although the early editions of the book discuss outdoor shopping centers, single-loaded corridors of stores with entrances off the parking lot, the same principles of organization and emphasis on uniform appearance carried over into indoor malls. Control, indeed, was a large part of the appeal for shoppers and a way that suburban retail could initially distinguish itself from town. "One of the things which disgraces the business districts of American cities both central and outlying, along with poor architecture, is the indiscriminate use of signs," the authors write. "In many centers the original purpose of directing attention to a particular shop has been lost in the effort of shops to outdo each other. The result is chaotic, confusing, and self-defeating." Nichols had set a limit of eight- to twelve-inch letters, and only white lighting, on the signs at his centers, and many that followed added sign-approval provisions to their lease agreements. That total control would, in turn, allow the retailers' ideal customer—a white, suburban mother—to relax. "He, or usually she, wishes to feel free to bring the baby, to come on a bicycle, or in shorts, house dress or other informal attire. She wishes to be able to visit with friends on the street or in the shop, take more time for lunch, park her car as she wishes."

The handbook discusses four different layouts: the simple strip, the open-air mall with facing rows of shops, the U or court type, and the cluster, with multiple anchors around a central court, mentioning Gruen's as-yet-unbuilt plans for Southdale. Malls, they say, are the most attractive because there is "no best side of the street." The maximum desirable distance from storefront to storefront across the promenade is sixty-five feet, but Northgate (1950), the large Seattle shopping center planned by architect John Graham and conceived by Bon Marché president Rex Allison, has a mall forty-eight feet wide, creating a pleasant "closed-in" feeling and making it easy to cross from one side to the other. Outdoor shopping centers should be enlivened by landscaping, the handbook says, but by 1968 it recommends that indoor malls include "active features such as statuary, bird cages, kiosks, small animal cages (but be careful to avoid having monkeys), aquariums, and the like, provid[ing] most enclosed mall and court areas with an active and attractive environment which creates an appeal not possible on a conventional pedestrian sidewalk."

Inexperienced designers try to innovate at the mall, the authors write, adding complex layouts, frequent jogs and corners, and poor sight lines. But it is best to keep it simple: straight runs of forty to fifty feet in width between the anchor stores, with sixteen- to twenty-foot ceilings in the shopping areas and up to fifty feet in a court or atrium. Daylighting, variations in ceiling height, and the aforementioned enlivening elements should be deployed to keep shoppers from getting bored along the way. "Good architecture is functional as well as beautiful," the builders write. "A shopping center can be so appealing that it brings customers repeatedly simply to browse and enjoy its beauty. It can make itself a public attraction, a focus of civic pride and interest. Southdale in Memphis, North Park [sic] in Dallas, Lloyd Center in Portland, Cherry Hill near Camden, and Oakbrook near Chicago are new examples of such customer-appealing centers." The architecture to which the builders refer, however, is largely internal: the plants, the fountains, the artworks inside what became blander and blander exterior shells. To reach the beautiful, appealing parts of the mall shoppers must first cross the moat of the parking lot and the battlements of blank walls, searching for elements (signs, porticoes, canopies) that say ENTER HERE. Design was valued as a method of increasing dwell time and tying a mall conceptually, if not physically, to its community.

People often tell me that they get lost in malls. Malls are a habitat. Some of us are natives. If you grew up hiking, you know to look for blazes. If you grew up with malls, you know to look for the anchor stores, the fountain, the food court. Orient yourself to those cardinal points before you set out.

When you look at the plan of the mall, the first thing you see is stores. On some mall plans, the stores are color-coded by type: clothing, media, food. On others, they are identified by number—high, nonsensical numbers like 903 and 227. On some the department stores get logo callouts; on others a brand has paid to be the brightest color on the map. What concerns you is not the size or shape or number of the stores, or the exterior shape of the mall, or the pillowy layer of parking lot around it. What concerns you is just the shape of the corridor between the stores.

Indoor shopping malls of the 1950s and 1960s took their cues from the origin of the word "mall." Pall Mall is a London street, long home to gentlemen's clubs at which the aristocracy drank, ate, and played together. One of the games they played was *pallamaglio*, or pall-mall, an early version of croquet that employed *palla* (ball) and *maglio* (mallet). Players used their mallets to move balls down a long, linear course, really an alley, at the heart of the city. While the game fell out of fashion, that name for spaces that suited the requirements of the game persisted. A linear, landscaped promenade came to be known as a mall, in England as well as the United States. The court for an aristocrat's game gave its name to that symbol of democracy, the National Mall in Washington, D.C., and the shopping mall too. That is the simplest form of shopping center, an I shape: two department stores, two lines of stores between them, with an enclosed hallway running straight up and down. The malls of the late 1950s and early 1960s were Main Street under glass, their dimensions taken from the street fronts of prewar downtowns but without the clamor. The "regional center" was clean and neatly maintained; it was new, sporting a cool, nonreferential modernist vocabulary; it lacked vehicular congestion, jostling crowds, street noise, the "wrong" social elements, and crime—all departures from qualities associated with downtown. Urban historian Richard W. Longstreth writes: "The regional center was a bastion of middle-class ingenuity, respectability, and order; it was touted as a cure for the purportedly ailing condition and antiquated arrangement of the core."

One level up in complexity from the Main Street–like two-anchor mall is the L: three anchor stores, one at the elbow. As long as you remember which department store your destination is closest to, and park next to that one, you're golden. Other three-store options include the T, with a store at each endpoint and an atrium connecting the runs, and the X, with four stores spidering out from a central court. When you get to plans that look like an E or its uncompleted cousin, the F, you see malls starting to sprawl, showing their many phases in new legs, protuberances, and satellites. It is difficult today to find a mall from the 1970s or before whose original plan is recognizable. Longstreth: "Like the department store interior of earlier decades, the regional mall is in more or less a continual state of flux."

The best mall maps make the relationship of private stores to public passageways clear, differentiating them by color rather than lumping them together under one cartographic roof. What you see of a mall from the sky never syncs with one's experience of the mall. The outside is purposefully bland—architecture, except to indicate entrances, doesn't pay—while the inside bursts, to whatever extent mall management will allow, with color, water, and brands. Much was made, early on, of the environmental impact of having to condition only one giant airspace in an enclosed mall, but shoppers don't feel the mall as a giant bubble. The scents of Bath & Body Works, the music spilling out of the teen boutique, the smoky undertone of cookie and pretzel—these make the mall feel like a real street.

Despite its primacy, Southdale had very little influence on the anatomy of the malls that followed. Its influence was conceptual, in the way Gruen ruthlessly exploited its firstness to become the most famous name in malls. Gruen structured Southdale around an atrium—the triple-height Garden Court, top-lit by clerestories, animated by escalators, and given sparkle by a fountain and the golden Bertoia sculpture—and this is what people remember. Southdale has a cluster plan, with legs of stores pinwheeling off the corners of the court, and its department stores—Dayton's and Donaldson's—

NorthPark Shopper's Guide, 1965. (NorthPark Center)

on opposite sides. The advantage of the cluster plan is less hallway: Visitors would pass quickly down the corridors from the parking lot into the Garden Court and then spin out from there in the direction of their choice. But this type of plan works only when the number of stores is small and set. Southdale opened with fifty-eight shops, pocket-size compared with the regional and super-regional malls of a decade later. The cluster offers little room for organic growth, since the whole point of the plan is to keep things tight and centralized. The proper way to expand would be replication, adding a second court and a second set of pinwheeling volumes to one side. But when its owners added on to Southdale in the 1970s, they instead built an arm off to a new J. C. Penney, turning it into a lopsided T. Further additions in the 1990s and 2000s obliterated any sense of structure and Gruen's original simplicity. That's why letterform malls, rather than baby Southdales, litter the American landscape.

NorthPark, in contrast, provides a textbook example of the community builders' formula. When it opened in 1965 as a regional center, sprawling over twenty-five acres, with three department stores and eighty shops, it was reverse L-shaped, with two straight runs of shops facing each other along thirty-eight-foot-wide daylit hallways. The twelve feet in front of each store were left clear, with a fourteen-foot center strip for benches, plants, and artwork. Unlike most malls, this strip has never been used to make money: no Sunglass Huts, no Piercing Pagodas, no kiosks selling airbrushed T-shirts, phone cases, greeting cards. Hamilton credits leasing agent Sidney Greenberg with insisting that the mall be a single path. "We debated about having H's and different kinds of paths, but he said the merchants would not survive off of a main street," he told an audience in 2007. "Stanley got first choice of where Neiman's was, then Titche's got their choice and Penney's was last. But the idea of width was discussed and there weren't a lot of precedents. Most of them that came later were a little less wide." While working on schemes for the center, Hamilton happened to visit the Metropolitan Museum of Art in New York City. "Centers up until that time, inside, were just a continuous row of shopfronts. There was no sense of architecture; there was no sense of belonging to the building's exterior," he said in 2010. "It occurred to me that the sequence of spaces [at the museum] was a lot more interesting than a long corridor, so we arranged it so we had malls and courts and a variety of connected spaces." Courts with higher ceilings, clerestory lighting, and fountains beckoned visitors from Neiman Marcus to the mid-price Titche-Goettinger, and from Titche-Goettinger to affordable J. C. Penney. "Not a 'street of stores' but a flowing series of natu-rally lighted plazas, each with direct access to parking," wrote *Architectural Record*, praising the development and design team, which "recognized from the beginning that this center had to be the logical and disciplined culmi-nation of shopping center evolution from the chaos of unbridled competition to the superior drawing power of order and delight." That sense of flow is underlined in NorthPark's appearance in David Byrne's 1986 cult film *True Stories*, where the narrator (Byrne) smoothly strolls the center's wide halls, past tasteful garbage cans and tasteful modernist sculpture, noting, "Shopping itself has become the activity that brings people together."

Grouped near Neiman Marcus at the luxury end of the mall were Linz Brothers, which sold jewelry, china, and silver; Seeburg Piano and Organ, self-explanatory; women's boutiques the Carriage Shop, kitted out to look like a converted carriage house, and Margo's la Mode, which sported chandeliers from Spain; and I. Miller Shoes, the first branch of the Fifth Avenue shoe store west of the Mississippi. More practical matters could be taken care of in the run of stores close to J. C. Penney, where a Singer Sewing Center, a SupeRx drugstore, and an Olan Mills portrait studio were located, alongside a generously sized Woolworth's and the Marriott Cafeteria. A separate outdoor plaza on the north side of the parking lot included a Kroger supermarket, the NorthPark National Bank, and a liquor store. Smaller storefronts arranged along the hallways connecting the main thoroughfares to the parking lots held services like a barbershop, shoe repair, and, on an outside corner for quick pickups, the Black Forest Bakery. Looking at a map from NorthPark's opening year, with the community builders in mind, I found that the organizing commercial logic behind NorthPark became clear in the same way mall plans reveal the hidden simplicity of their layout. Middle-class shoppers could park to the west, avoiding Neiman's and its high-end neighbors. A mother pressed for time could pull up to the bank or the Kroger. Picking up dry cleaning or a cake could be accomplished without entering the belly of the mall, while a lunchtime meeting would come with a view outside. We don't have to be confused by the mall once we read the handbook.

Like gardens, malls require constant tending: weeding out underperforming stores, rotating successful ones to better locations, policing wayward signage, replacing a chain that's become too commonplace, adding food courts, movie theaters, VR boutiques. There are cleaners, gardeners, window dressers, and window washers, maintainers of perfectly folded displays and maintainers of acres of concrete. There are more ephemeral types of upkeep too: scheduling the story time at the children's branch of the Dallas Public Library just off the central garden, scheduling the mall's annual Lunar New Year celebration or the holiday chorus. Some programming populates the mall at off-hours—when I arrived at NorthPark at ten A.M. on a temperate

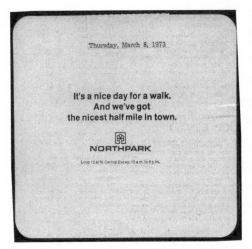

Thursday, March 8, 1973

**It's a nice day for a walk.
And we've got
the nicest half mile in town.**

NORTHPARK

Loop 12 at N. Central Expwy, 10 a.m. to 9 p.m.

"It's a nice day for a walk." *Dallas Morning News*, March 8, 1973. (NorthPark Center)

Monday in February to meet Nancy Nasher, seniors were already walking circuits of the mall. The center has over two million square feet of retail, more than 200 stores, with more than 26 million visitors per year and annual pre-pandemic sales of over one billion dollars. It won the Texas Society of Architects 25-Year Design Award in 2007. Today it is owned by Nasher and her husband, David J. Haemisegger. That lifetime of family ownership makes NorthPark one of few places in the country where you can see, hear, and even smell the history of the mall in America, from its distinctive museum-like white brick walls to the Muzak-free plash of fountains to the scent of Mrs. Fields. My guided tour of NorthPark offered me the opportunity to see how a mall built in 1965 stays fresh in 2020, from the inside out.

When Stanley Marcus told Kevin Roche that department stores required change every ten years, he understated the case. At NorthPark, tenants are required to renovate every four to six years. Hamilton designed the mall once, but Nasher, Haemisegger, and their management office, which employs 150 people, have to redesign it every day. In 2019, the only store that remained from NorthPark's 1965 opening was Neiman Marcus. But even as the mall, this most fashion-driven of architectures, can be a case study in creative destruction, the ongoingness and dailiness of the work required to sustain a mall reveal that capitalist churn is not the whole story. Malls are also spaces of maintenance, spaces of care.

Nasher, a Duke Law School graduate, began working with her father and husband on NorthPark in 1985, with her mother's encouragement. Haemisegger, who has an MBA from Wharton, had worked for Ray Nasher since business school, rising to president and CEO of the Raymond D.

Nasher Company before the couple created the NorthPark Management Company and purchased the mall from Raymond Nasher in 1995. NorthPark is one of only a handful of malls in the United States under family ownership, and part of a slightly larger group that are not owned by real estate investment trusts, or REITs, publicly traded companies that own hundreds of commercial properties. Also among this small cohort is the Forbes Company, based in Southfield, Michigan (just like Gruen's pathbreaking Northland), which owns four high-end malls, including Mall at Millenia in Orlando, Florida, and Somerset Collection outside Detroit. Founder Sidney Forbes, who began his company in the 1970s building average malls in small Michigan cities, changed his strategy to focus on a few luxury properties in the early 1990s—going the opposite way of rivals who went public and began a chain of mergers and acquisitions.

South Coast Plaza in Orange County, California, has a story with even greater parallels to NorthPark's. The mall began as a real estate play by Harry Segerstrom, the son of Swedish immigrant farmers who owned extensive acreage. In the early 1960s, postwar Orange County was moving from agriculture to industry. The construction of the 405, a limited-access highway running south from the west side of Los Angeles, opened up the possibility of commuting from the county to the city; Orange County could draw hundreds of thousands of new residents, which is to say, new customers. Representatives of Sears and the May Company approached the Segerstrom family about building on some of their land and became the project's first anchor tenants. The first phase of the mall opened in 1967 and was designed by Victor Gruen and his associate Rudi Baumfeld. Over the decades since, South Coast Plaza, like NorthPark, built up its portfolio of art, architecture, and luxury brands. Marion Sampler, head of graphic design for Gruen, created the Jewel Court Dome for the plaza's first expansion in 1972. Frank Gehry designed the interiors of the J. Magnin branch, a boutique California department store, with a restaurant by Gere Kavanaugh and graphics inspired by Corita Kent. Isamu Noguchi and Shoji Sadao designed California Scenario (1980–1982), an outdoor public plaza anchored by a thirty-foot-high pyramidal mountain. Nordstrom, which opened its first California

Top, NorthPark Expansion with Anthony Caro, *River Song* (2011–2012) in foreground. *Bottom*, NorthPark Cafes, NorthPark Expansion, Omniplan, 2006. (NorthPark Center)

store there in 1978, helped South Coast Plaza to attract international luxury brands, starting with Courrèges, whose minis were all the rage in the mid-1970s, and then adding Yves Saint Laurent, Halston, and others. Meanwhile, the Segerstroms began to surround the mall with cultural institutions, now known as the Segerstrom Center for the Arts. Today the mall encompasses 2.8 million square feet on three H-shaped levels and a 1980s annex, South Coast Plaza West. Harry's son Anton Segerstrom is the general manager of South Coast Plaza and one of its three primary stakeholders.

In 2006, NorthPark doubled in size, adding a second L of retail space that included a Nordstrom on the opposite corner from the original Titche-Goettinger site, and creating a 1.4-acre garden within the center of what became a square donut-shaped plan. The $225 million expansion (a far cry from the center's 1965 $18 million cost) was designed by Omniplan, E. G. Hamilton's firm, and overseen by principal Mark Dilworth, who had worked at Omniplan since the late 1970s. The expansion, which includes a two-story row of shops crisscrossed by long-span bridges, manages to refer to all of NorthPark's original details—white brick, polished concrete floors, framed storefronts, daylight everywhere—while also looking as crisp and tasteful as an art museum.

A series of moves, both planned and unplanned, paved the way for the expansion. The center's original movie theater, General Cinema, which had a freestanding building in the northwest corner of the site, closed in 1998, freeing up that area. J. C. Penney left the mall in 1999, allowing for a revamping of that store (now a Macy's). Then Lord & Taylor, which had always been awkwardly placed along the side of the 1973 expansion, declared it would close in 2003. Suddenly, the mall's owners had two empty anchors as well as a newly freed-up parking lot that would allow them to complete the square.

"We had all the greats come through here, Rem Koolhaas, Renzo Piano, Richard Rogers," said Nancy Nasher, dressed for our mall walk in a compli-cated tweed jacket, sensible black-on-black designer sneakers, and impressive emerald-cut diamond earrings. Those architects were all in town to discuss the sculpture center commission that eventually went to Piano. "They all said, 'It's impossible—you'll never succeed in adding on to 1962.' In the retail world they all said, 'You need to tear it down and start over.'"

"I didn't know it was impossible," Dilworth, the gentlemanly local architect she eventually chose, commented dryly. "It was three of the happiest years I ever spent. I hadn't been doing that much designing, but you said, 'I want you to come to every meeting.'"

This ambitious renovation included three elements NorthPark had never had before: an embedded multistory multiplex movie theater, a branch of Nordstrom, and a food court. Previously, individual restaurants had provided seating for customers, both within their spaces and in discrete areas inside the mall. For the first time NorthPark would build an open-seating area adjacent to a set of smaller food windows. Of course, this being NorthPark, the fitting out of the food court became an aesthetic project in itself: no neon, no Orange Julius, no orange. The NorthPark food court features white contemporary chairs by Ron Arad often seen at museum cafés, as well as a glassed-in open-air garden, planted with trees and flowers, that looks like a high-end terrarium. The influence of the café at the Nasher Sculpture Center is clear, even if you and your family are getting Popeyes.

The care expended on the food court extended to the design of the entire addition, whose materials mimicked those of the original as closely as possible while offering some twenty-first-century upgrades. The most obvious difference to the trained eye is in the sharpness of the edges and lightness of materials—the difference between the 1960s technological modernism of Dieter Rams and his collaborators' Braun appliances and their 2000s update at the hands of Jonathan Ive and Apple. The new L is two stories, rather than one, and is crossed by narrow bridges every five or six shops so that no shopper suffers the thwarted desire to cross to the other side for long. The bridges are made of the same off-white brick as the interior and exterior walls, with glass railings from the bed of the bridge up, so that the solid crosspiece is only a few feet thick. This choice means that the views down the long corridor, from Macy's to Nordstrom, remain largely clear, and it is easy to see the shop signs on the second floor from down below.

The two-story leg running across the north side of the extension was devoted to youth brands—a previous weakness of the center—including Hanna Andersson, Janie and Jack, Build-A-Bear Workshop, Lego, and Swatch. In 2010, Texas's first H&M opened along that corridor. In 2020, the same stretch was under the process of strenuous refreshment. "There are very few children's concepts left," Nasher said. When I ask about that mall staple, Mrs. Fields, whose vanilla odor I can smell a level away, Nasher wrinkled her nose. "We have one, one cookie store."

Design historians' interest in maintenance, caretaking, and repair developed in the mid-2010s, spurred by Steven J. Jackson's essay "Rethinking Repair." In that essay Jackson asked of his colleagues, "What happens when we take erosion, breakdown, and decay, rather than novelty, growth, and progress, as our starting points in thinking through the nature, use, and effects of information technology and new media?" As historians of technology Andrew Russell and Lee Vinsel, founders of the research network called the Maintainers, have written, "Focusing on infrastructure or on old, existing things rather than novel ones reminds us of the absolute centrality of the work that goes into keeping the entire world going."

Media anthropologist Shannon Mattern, writing for *Places Journal* in 2018, broke down the types of decay into four categories: "Rust" for infrastructure, "Dust" for architecture, "Cracks" for objects, and "Corruption" for data. Dusting, both literally and figuratively, is essential to the maintenance of the mall. Literally, in the sense that floors must be mopped, windows squeegeed, and leaves wiped on a regular schedule. This is part of how the mall differentiates itself from the disorder of the public street—a necessity that mall makers acknowledged from the start. But there's also a figurative form of dusting, a constant vigilance about visual standards and upkeep, required to keep the mall forever young. All these tasks are historically constructed as women's work and, in fact, the employees responsible for managing the upkeep of the mall are mostly women. Historian Vicki

Howard writes that salesclerking at department stores had long been a path to advancement for white women. "While top executives were largely male, with a few standouts like Dorothy Shaver [Lord & Taylor] and Beatrice Fox [G. Fox & Co.], women could work their way up the ranks to become buyers, middle managers or department heads, and fashion advisors." Malls' irregular hours, including opening on nights and weekends, made them an appealing option for mothers to pick up part-time work close to their homes and children's schools in the 1950s. As a skill, caretaking for customers overlaps with the caretaking women are acculturated to do in the home.

During World War II female consumers were encouraged to plant victory gardens, cook with less meat, collect their scraps, and save their pennies. In the postwar era, they were the target of a very different message: The patriotic thing to do was to spend. "In the context of World War II, good citizenship and good consumer-ship were promoted as inseparable, and women gained special stewardship over both," writes historian Lizabeth Cohen in *A Consumers' Republic*, citing a November 25, 1946, issue of *Life* that proposed the "Family Utopia" was a ranch-style home and the new goods to fill it. Between 1940 and 1950, the percentage of American homes with refrigerators jumped from 44 to 80. Consumer credit and buying on installment became part of the commercial landscape, along with universal credit cards. Previously, department stores and gas stations had issued their own cards. Such credit was, however, available only to married women through their husbands.

Feminist theorists have long argued that obsession with labor-saving technology obscures all the work, including housework, that women do to keep family life on track. In her classic 1983 book, *More Work for Mother*, Ruth Schwartz Cowan examined home technologies—such as washing machines and vacuum cleaners—and how they fit into women's ceaseless labor of domestic upkeep. One of her more famous findings was that new housekeeping technologies, which promised to save time, literally created more work for mother as cleanliness standards rose in response to these "improvements."

Yet while the maintenance of the home, shopping at the mall, and, indeed, many retail jobs were considered women's work—Jack Follett, a designer for

Seattle mall architect John Graham said, "I wouldn't know how to design a center for a man"—the development, financing, and construction of malls were dominated by men. The mall reproduces the same structure of labor as the suburban home: women working, men benefiting the most financially. And, like good housekeeping, good mall-keeping is left out of the narrative of design. The mall was designed as a delivery system for planned obsolescence, but the best malls, by keeping up with the Joneses as capably as their consumer base, managed to keep themselves from becoming obsolete. The percentage of retail trade in suburbs doubled in the postwar era, from 31 percent in 1948 to almost 60 percent in 1960. The malls' rigorous maintenance programs create spaces that are simultaneously being repaired and being replaced, being cleaned and being novel. What sets the mall apart from the goods it sells is that it does, in fact, have systems in place to keep itself working.

Brenda Buhr-Hancock is the director of design and special projects for the NorthPark Management Company. That makes her de facto design director for every brand that wants to lease a store in the center, and an enforcer of NorthPark's detailed handbook of tenant dos and don'ts. Talking to her provides a window into the machine that keeps NorthPark looking mint, and how mall management keeps all the brands in line.

Some of these are macro-level regulations. Every storefront is set four inches back from the lease line—the threshold to the mall—to preserve the effect of Hamilton's white brick frame; every bathroom must be accessible to the public, and not require a detour through a stockroom. Others are micro-: Floors must be wood, stone, terrazzo, or through-body porcelain tile, so that chips are less noticeable; no plastic laminates or shingles on storefronts. No recessed lights are allowed, because they make for a dark store, and signage and screens are kept to a minimum. "The longest letter I have ever sent [a tenant] was twelve pages of 'Here are things that need to change,'" said Buhr-Hancock. "We have rejected a whole set of CDs [construction documents] because they didn't follow our handbook."

Taking long-term maintenance into consideration, the handbook also tries to save brands from themselves by excluding materials that are hard to clean, show wear, or are, like twelve-by-twelve-inch tile, simply too ordinary. Johnny Was, a "boho chic" store that opened at NorthPark in 2018, originally proposed a vinyl sticker representing grillwork for its front window; Buhr-Hancock suggested it get the grillwork made in metal. But the residents of Luxury Row also have to bow to NorthPark's edicts. "The lease will ask for their best flagship store," which, for fashion companies, will often be a proto-type ready for rollout in major international cities. "If it's not the quality of store that we want at NorthPark, we have asked for an older design," she said.

Brands born on the web often struggle with their first brick-and-mortar stores. "If they aren't used to merchandising, it can look rather sparse," Buhr-Hancock said, with too little in the store, or too little variety from rack to rack. Take Outdoor Voices, which opened one of its first brick-and-mortar outlets at NorthPark in 2018. The interior is designed to look like a citrus-hued gym, with speckled rubber floors, a curved set of risers, and dressing rooms styled like a locker room. "They took too much space," Nasher said, looking at the storefront. "They don't have enough product." It was dismissive but it was true, and a botched store rollout was one of the factors that led to the ouster of Outdoor Voices founder Tyler Haney right around the time of my Dallas visit. Racks of sports bras and stretch pants are pretty dull to look at, and the Outdoor Voices product line doesn't have enough color or pattern to create the kinds of fashion stories that draw a shopper deeper into the store. More than a third of the store's footprint is dressing room, invisible from the front windows. When we duck in there, a young woman is getting her leggings hemmed, a nicety that had never occurred to me. Isn't the best thing about leggings their accommodating stretch?

Nasher seems equally at home with the sporting goods stores, the teen outposts, and the posh boutiques along Luxury Row. Professional, sensible, luxurious. She insisted that I see the bathroom in the new Dolce & Gabbana boutique, towing me past upholstered walls and flower-bedecked heels (as the salespeople greet her by name) to a hidden door. The bathroom is a wonder, a box of book-matched marble behind a mirrored door that is, as she says, like a Rudolf Stingel painting.

While Outdoor Voices disappoints, another recent addition, Golden Goose, is much more to their taste. The Golden Goose product line is, essentially, old-school low-rise sneakers that cost three hundred dollars. I'm reminded that shoe stores were the mainstays of the earliest shopping malls, while thinking that the mother shopping for Buster Browns never imagined that her kids, much less the owner of the mall, would pay that much for tennis shoes. Nonetheless, the Golden Goose store feels much more replete than Outdoor Voices, with oversize fluorescent parkas, stacks of art books, and a small table set up at the entrance that's offering while-you-wait customization of your new sneakers via paint markers and heat-sealed patches. (In 2020, personalization was big.) Youthful saleswomen and shoppers, almost indistinguishable, chat around the table like instant friends. The room feels like a club, thanks to its crumpled-silver walls. I ask how it was done, and it turns out that the wallpaper is a giant sticker, like an artfully fucked-up application of the contact paper your mother used to line her kitchen drawers.

While Buhr-Hancock was initially skeptical of Golden Goose's metallic walls, she ultimately signed off on it after going over how to clean and maintain a giant tinfoil sticker with the same intensity as a museum conservation specialist: the store interior as a fragile work of art. And while she praised Yves Saint Laurent's marble-on-marble shop, premanufactured in Italy to within one sixteenth of an inch, she also raved about Isabel Marant's totally Brooklyn terrazzo floors and Instagram-bait fuzzy sofa. "That's an interesting piece, but it is as hard as a rock," she warned, eye on the bottom line. "You don't want them sitting too long."

Chapter 3
The Mall and the Public

It was a muggy August day in downtown Boston, the dog days of summer, not good for an opening. The college students were not back, the vacationers were at the Cape, and the office workers were clinging to their air-conditioned cubicles. But the market was done, banners flying, just in time for the country's bicentennial, and if there was a place that had more to celebrate in 1976, Bostonians did not want to know about it. Their city was the birthplace of the revolution. On August 26, 1976, it was also the birthplace of the festival marketplace.

Mayor Kevin White stood between two of the fat columns in front of Quincy Market, a Greek Revival stone building constructed to house the overflow of merchants from neighboring Faneuil Hall. Boston branding was out in full force: The brass band played "The Star-Spangled Banner," a man in a tricorn hat rang a cowbell, White unveiled a statue of a predecessor, Mayor Josiah Quincy, who presided over the market's opening in 1826. On the porch with him: developer James Rouse and designers Benjamin and Jane Thompson, who soon followed the kilt-clad Scottish bagpipers inside to sip champagne under the building's glorious dome.

Articles leading up to the opening emphasized the proximity of the dome to the city's real center of power. From his office in city hall, a brutalist behemoth completed in 1968, Mayor White overlooked the sad state of Faneuil Hall. "Every morning this scene of ruin and litter reminded White to do

Faneuil Hall Marketplace, Boston, Massachusetts, Benjamin Thompson and Associates, 1976–1978. (Photograph by Steve Rosenthal © Historic New England, from the Steve Rosenthal Collection of Commissioned Work at Historic New England)

something to make it into a more fitting symbol of the new Boston he hoped to build," write Bernard J. Frieden and Lynne B. Sagalyn in their lively history of this period of American urban development, *Downtown, Inc.*

The hall's copper dome was corroding, adjacent market stalls were empty, rats were making homes, and the basement of one of the market buildings was flooded with seepage from the harbor. Meanwhile, several hundred thousand people walked by the site each year, between those with business at city hall, the tangle of downtown T stations, and tourists on the 2.5-mile-long Freedom Trail, a popular walking route linking sixteen historic sites.

White described the new market in the old buildings as a "truly a historical event, a rebirth," and ended with a simple call to any citizens listening: "This market is yours, the public's. Use it, enjoy it."

For more than twenty years, the narrative of American downtowns had been blight and destruction. Stores closed, buildings demolished, highways built. An evacuation of social and cultural life, and of spaces that had once been pedestrian, urbane, and central to business, in favor of infrastructure for cars. The only way to save downtown, the narrative went, was to make it more like the suburbs. This even though when downtown was at its peak, it beckoned with the glamour of department stores, the treat of lunch counters, the convenience of streetcars. Victor Gruen, flush with the success of building a new downtown—as he saw it—in Edina, had also started selling his planning services to urban leaders. He argued that downtown—with parking, with pedestrian promenades, with design guidelines as rigid as a shopping mall's—could compete with the mall.

Some of the solutions he and others proposed were radical. In Rochester, New York, that took the form of Midtown Plaza, which opened in 1962: the nation's first enclosed urban shopping mall, with an interior "town square" and skyways and tunnels linking it to existing towers, parking garages, and the new Midtown Tower, which held a hotel, a restaurant, and offices. The suburban shoppers it attracted back to the city did not actually have to touch the city; they could simply drive in and drive out, meeting friends at the signature Clock of the Nations. Angelo Chiarella, the Gruen & Associates architect who supervised the project, later returned to run the mall for its owners, Rochester department store magnates Gilbert McCurdy Sr. and Maurice Forman.

Gere Kavanaugh, *Clock of the Nations*; Midtown Plaza, Rochester, New York, Gruen Associates, 1962. (Gere Kavanaugh)

In Montreal, the first tunnels in what would become the twenty-plus-mile Underground City were completed in 1962, connecting the aboveground Place Ville Marie Tower to an underground shopping mall, planned by Vincent Ponte and designed by Henry N. Cobb of I. M. Pei & Associates. In Calgary, architect Harold Hanen developed the Plus 15 Skyway network, connecting dozens of downtown office buildings to shopping centers and the city's flagship department stores via transparent walkways fifteen feet above the city streets.

Some were literally more down to earth: "Urban society's growing frustration with the automobile, and the congestion it causes, is a major factor behind the Pedestrian Revolution," wrote the authors of a book of the same name, published in 1974. "Pedestrianism enhances our physical well-being both by reducing air and noise pollution and by encouraging, through the creation of urban strollways and urban bikeways, the greater use of footpower." Their revolution consisted not of enclosing sidewalks but of removing cars from streets, making connected, walkable zones downtown that would knit existing storefronts and department stores together with decorative pavements, designer seating and lighting, and public art.

As they solved the problem of the city—too much weather, too much dirt, too little parking, too many signs—by pedestrianizing it, heating and cooling it, and imposing graphic standards on it, these new structures also created new barriers. Who could afford the higher rents fifteen feet above, or below, the sidewalks? Whose appetites were being served at the cafés in Rochester's new "town square"? As Frieden and Sagalyn write of a famous urbanist conference, convened in suburban Hartford in 1957, "A reader searches the conference report in vain for some recognition that whatever else the city is, it is also a place where ordinary people live, work and play."

> With so little understanding of popular taste and even less interest in it, how would [downtown specialists] ever figure out what would bring people to visit or live in the new buildings? And how could they rebuild the inner city so thoroughly without pushing out the very people and businesses that had not yet left for the suburbs?

The Faneuil Hall model was a little bit different. Rather than new boxes, the frame would be old buildings. Rather than chain stores, the businesses would be quirky and local. Rather than fast food, the cafés would sell fresh pastries and the delis fresh fish. The developer was a mall owner—a booster of suburbs, a believer in design control—but his vision of the mall, the suburbs, and the city diverged from the norm. What thirty years of public policy had set apart, James Rouse believed he could put back together—with a little help from his friends.

→

The first time James Rouse heard about Faneuil Hall he was at Disney World. Rouse had been a longtime fan of the parks, noting,

> Some may reject the whole thing as a stage set: false, flimsy. But it seemed to me an authentic fairyland that made joy, caprice—yes, and beauty, real beauty, out of such widely diverse subjects as fairy tales, aerospace, submarine rides, haunted houses, monorails, the tropics, and early America.

He told an audience at Harvard in 1963 that Disneyland in California was "the outstanding piece of urban design in the United States." He advised Walt Disney himself on the design of EPCOT, which Disney originally envisioned as a model future city with monorails and a greenbelt centered on a glowing collection of skyscrapers rather than a giant geodesic sphere. (Disney had also consulted Ray Nasher, developer of NorthPark.) Into this space of futurist thinking and family entertainment came a letter from Robert E. Simon, visionary developer of the planned community of Reston, Virginia. Simon's friend, the Cambridge architect Benjamin Thompson, had a "glamorous project looking for an enlightened and imaginative developer." Simon, ousted from Reston for poor economic performance, didn't have the means to help, but he thought Rouse might.

Rouse's early career ran parallel to Gruen's. His first major project as head of James W. Rouse & Company (later simplified to the Rouse Company) was Harundale, an enclosed suburban shopping mall south of Baltimore that opened in 1958, two years after Southdale. In speeches of the 1950s, Rouse spoke of shopping malls as "convenient, gay and human," fostering better community and familial relationships and filling out the needs of suburban residential patterns. Rouse Company malls built over the next decade included churches, public libraries, and post offices, as well as fountains and atriums in which to gather. Cities seemed to him at the time "grim, impersonal," and as a member of the Greater Baltimore Committee, Rouse pushed for the transformation of that city's downtown through so-called slum clearance—large-scale, hard-nosed urban renewal, paid for by the federal government on the premise that historic cities were obsolete and needed to be remade with new buildings and separate zones for living, working, and shopping.

The 1954 Federal Housing Act set aside 10 percent of federal capital grant funding for renewal of nonhousing areas, which meant demolishing old buildings and old businesses and replacing them with new, larger structures. By the mid-1960s, 1,300 downtown redevelopment projects were underway, with 129,000 demolished buildings. As urban historian Alison Isenberg writes in *Downtown America*, retail analysts framed the problems of downtown as a "housekeeping" crisis. Downtown was disorder, ugly, outdated, while shopping malls were fresh and new. "Urban renewal—the era's most drastic and influential solution for cities—sought to make America's downtowns appealing to white, suburban, middle-class women." Planners assumed a white woman would judge the city on the same standards of appearance and cleanliness as she would her own home. Other consumers, including African Americans and ethnic minorities, lived closer to the core. African Americans had been loyal downtown shoppers, partly because of their more limited choices for transportation, housing, and retail. But instead of capitalizing on or catering to this population, the new downtown developers by and large decided to chase the white middle class.

Rouse soon saw that individual malls, however economically and socially successful, wouldn't be enough to change the "nonsense" patterns of city growth. They were too disconnected from the fabric of residential patterns, and while many included community spaces, they failed to link the anchors of public town life—city hall, schools, and parks—to retail patterns in the way that classic Main Streets or town squares had. Unless a single central authority was developing homes, stores, and public facilities as one, there was no way to control the result in terms of land use, commuting patterns, and community building. The only solution was to build his own town.

In a speech titled "How to Build a Whole New City from Scratch," given to members of the National Association of Mutual Savings Banks in 1966, Rouse spoke decisively about the challenge ahead. To meet estimated population growth, developers would need to build a new branch department store, three new supermarkets, and dozens of neighborhood stores every week for the next twenty years—a quantity of new construction that, to date, he saw emerging haphazardly and with serious environmental consequences.

> Let's look at how our cities grow. A farm is sold and begins raising houses instead of potatoes. Then another farm. Forests are cut. Valleys are filled. Streams are buried in storm sewers. Kids overflow the schools. A new school is built. Churches come out of the basement. Then more schools, more churches, traffic grows, roads are widened, front yards cut back to make room for the automobiles. Service stations are built; Tasty Freeze, MacDonald Hamburgers [sic] pockmark the old highway . . . Thus, the bits and pieces of cities are splattered across the landscape.
>
> . . . And what nonsense this is. What reckless, irresponsible dissipation of nature's endowment and of man's hope for dignity, beauty, and growth. By this totally irrational process, non-communities are born.

He describes postwar construction—the highways, the suburbs, the gas stations, the signs, the malls—with all the same vocabulary of distaste as the architecture critics and urban planners upset by the mess: formless, monstrous, graceless, tasteless, natural landscapes reduced by man-made clutter that "stretches out the distance people must travel to work, to shop, to worship, to play."

Rouse had the means and desire to do something about it. The result was Columbia, Maryland, a new town he developed in the late 1960s on fourteen thousand acres of farmland outside Baltimore. Columbia was organized around nine small "villages," each with its own shopping area, town green, and elementary school, ringed by a few hundred houses. Apartments and subsidized housing were part of the plan, so that residents of Columbia could be drawn from across the income spectrum. Columbia would also be an integrated community, at a time when most suburbs were implicitly or explicitly segregated. Employment zones—areas that could be built out for offices or light industry—were designed into the plans, as were public transportation routes. At the same time, existing streams, forests, and open space were preserved, and the artificial Wilde Lake was added. Rouse himself lived in a house overlooking its shores.

"The [county was] willing to accept shopping centers, high-rise apartments, garden apartments, townhouses—the very land uses that they had been fighting for years—when they were gathered together in a rational, well-planned new city," Rouse told the bankers. The objections to the lack of segregation, and the mix of uses, of incomes, of work and leisure were overcome by money and design. Rouse made it clear that his goals were not just high-minded but profit-making, ending his pitch with the suggestion that better city building was his generation's moon shot. A decade later, after building a better burb, Rouse wanted to try again with the city.

Rouse flew up to Boston with his resident "art guru" Ned Daniels to meet with Ben Thompson and his partner in work and life, planner Jane Thompson. The group met on the upper floor of one of the three Faneuil Hall market buildings, so Rouse would get the full flavor of decay. To contrast with the buildings' decrepit state, the Thompsons put on a show: bouquets of fresh flowers, tempting market foods, architectural models and renderings of what the nineteenth-century buildings could be, culminating in a mood-setting slideshow that included Venetian gondoliers selling melons from boats. As Daniels later said, "It was so romantic, it was so human, it was so colorful. And it involved people. It was people to people."

A Boston-owned firm had already bid on the project, planning to fit out the buildings with more office space. The Thompsons proposed no department store, no national chains, shoe stores, or underwear stores—just small, locally owned businesses selling jewelry, seafood, ethnic goods. It reminded Rouse of the open-air farmers market on Olvera Street in Los Angeles, while Ben Thompson brought up Ghirardelli Square in San Francisco, brick warehouses refitted as a complex of shops and offices around a courtyard in the mid-1960s. Thompson argued that the fresh concept of the marketplace would prove enough of a magnet on its own, especially given the city beyond. Those two elements would be the new anchors.

While Rouse's community-building vision and financial acumen would prove to be important in launching the festival marketplace, it was Ben Thompson who gave them an instantly recognizable look and the "authentic" atmosphere that contemporary food halls still ape. Scenic slideshows had been part of Ben Thompson's arsenal for years, as had his attention, unusual in an architect, to the textures and tastes of domestic life. He had spent twenty years as one of former Bauhaus leader Walter Gropius's partners at the Architects Collaborative (TAC). In the late 1940s TAC was one of the first firms to design a modernist subdivision. First at Five Fields and then at Six Moon Hill, both in Lexington, Massachusetts, Thompson and his partners tried to bring modernism to the masses, with modestly sized, light-filled houses with flowing floor plans, all opening onto communal greens. As TAC clients furnished their new homes, they realized that traditional American furniture didn't work in these spaces. They needed lighter, leaner pieces, without historical details—furniture more like that being designed by Europeans including Alvar Aalto and being sold to the trade through the American showrooms of Knoll and Herman Miller.

Ben Thompson saw an opportunity to combine design and commerce and, in 1953, opened the store Design Research in a clapboard row house on Brattle Street in Harvard Square. That store was his first marketplace, and his first encounter with remaking historic architecture to new purpose— what would come to be called "adaptive reuse." He cut holes for plate glass windows in the solid wooden front and hollowed out skylights to bring light from floor to floor. He designed squashy down sofas and practical butcher block tables, hung Noguchi Akari lamps, and sourced pottery, knitwear, and silks on trips to Central America, southeast Asia, and southern Europe. Most famously, he spotted Marimekko, the Finnish fabric company known for large-scale designs and freeing silhouettes, on hostesses at the 1958 Brussels World's Fair and brought their dresses and tablecloths to a grateful American female public.

When the *New Yorker* covered D/R's Manhattan opening in 1963, Thompson gave a good accounting of why an Ivy League–educated architect, head of the architecture department at the Harvard Graduate School of Design, would want to open a store.

> I think that for art to be part of our life we must live with it, not just go to museums. In a way, things like museums and Lincoln Center kill art and music. Art is *not* for particular people but should be in everything you do—in cooking and, God knows, in the bread on the table, in the way everything is *done*. In Cambridge, I think we've served a little as a museum and a little as a store, and we hope to do the same here.

Jane McCullough Thompson had an equally diverse career before 1976. As a recent Vassar graduate, she started working for Philip Johnson, then director of the Department of Architecture and Design, at the Museum of Modern Art. In 1954 she cofounded *Industrial Design*, a pioneering publication that covered product design but also the latest developments in architecture, graphic design, and interiors. She met Ben Thompson in the early 1960s, when TAC was hired to design a new high school in Bennington, Vermont, where her family was then living. She joined his firm as a planning associate in 1967, the year they married, and from then on focused her work on the urban scale. Together they founded the restaurant Harvest, located on the ground floor of the concrete-and-glass building that Ben Thompson designed to house the expanded Design Research headquarters as well as the offices of TAC. Food, travel, shopping, home—all the elements in the Thompsons' presentation to Rouse ran as threads through their previous work.

Thompson began trying to interest the city in his ideas for the market buildings in 1967, seeing them as the three-dimensional application of his 1968 lecture "Visual Squalor, Social Disorder or A New Vision of the 'City of Man.'" In Ben Thompson's view, the built environment had become increasingly impoverished not, as many of his colleagues would argue, by "slums," the physical manifestation of "blight," but by "the hollow world of supermarkets, canned music and deodorant on everyone in their path," "the vast middle-class slum created by business and bureaucratic indifference," and single-use, single-purpose "developments that segregate the elderly and unprosperous, of cultural centers in pretentious heaps in the centers of cities."

> Today's environment displays our deeper social values as if on giant billboards: "BOREDOM, DRABNESS, SQUALOR, CONFUSION, OVERSCALE . . . LIFE IS NO FUN . . . PLEASURE IS FORBIDDEN . . . NO LEFT TURN, NO RIGHT TURN . . . KEEP OUT . . . KEEP OFF THE GRASS (if you can find any)."

Thompson's solution to the alienation of the environment at large is affective architecture: the creation of buildings and places that offer variation, choice, and personality. "Everything we build must inject the affirmative values human beings need as much as food—the pleasure of tactile and visual things, assurance of physical security and freedom, variety of stimulating impressions and experience." His vision for cities (as well as for schools and homes) was the opposite of the kind of totalizing design that brought about Midtown Plaza in Rochester or John D. Rockefeller III's Lincoln Center in New York.

Rouse took the Thompsons' Faneuil Hall renovation idea home to his mall-development team in Columbia, Maryland, but stopped them before they did the kind of market study they would typically perform for a new location. He knew it wouldn't look like a profitable project—and back-of-the-envelope calculations said the same—but his eyes and his feet told him differently.

Rouse's competitors, even Rouse's longtime financial backers, thought he was crazy. Rival mall developer Edward DeBartolo said in 1973, "I wouldn't put a penny downtown. It's bad. Face it, why should people come in? They don't want the hassle, they don't want the danger . . . So what do you do? Exactly what I'm doing, stay out in the country, that is the new downtown." TIAA, the teachers' insurance company that had funded many Rouse projects through the 1960s, agreed to a permanent loan only after the first phase of the project was built. The Rouse Company eventually got half of the cost of construction from David Rockefeller, who had made investments in other downtowns, and decided to do it in three phases, with the $7.5 million restoration of the central Quincy Market building to start. After the 1976 opening, Rouse raised the second half of the construction money from eleven different Boston banks, which allowed him to open phases two and three in 1977 and 1978.

Despite the humidity, one hundred thousand people visited Faneuil Hall and Quincy Market on opening day. More came the first year than visited Disneyland in 1977. Half of the visitors lived in Boston, but a quarter came from the suburbs, and a quarter were tourists. Foot traffic quickly doubled the per-square-foot sales Rouse expected from his *suburban* properties even though, at eighty thousand square feet, the Boston markets were a tenth the size of a regional center. Rouse's doubters were proved wrong: Downtown still had life in it yet.

The easiest way to think of Faneuil Hall is as a shopping mall whose anchor stores are Boston City Hall and the waterfront. Those two draws attract politicians, government workers, document seekers, and tourists daily. Between them the long, narrow market buildings flank a pedestrian street, with benches, plantings, and lighting creating a corridor for walking and people-watching. The open space in front of the hall's 1805 Greek Revival porch, as well as the rotunda within, offer indoor and outdoor versions of a mall's central atrium. The analogy is not perfect—the six-lane Central Artery formed a barrier between the end of the market and the waterfront—but the concept holds. While Faneuil Hall upended many commonly held ideas about how commercial real estate worked, its underlying structure built on twenty years of successful mall-making. Critic Roberta Brandes Gratz, writing about downtown malls in 1981, emphasized the importance of "layering" for robust urban places. "The successful cities" such as Ithaca and Saratoga, New York, and Burlington, Vermont, "have competed on their own urban terms, respecting the street, restoring what's left of the fabric built over time, wearing the new to fit in with the old, and continuing the layering process through which cities evolved in the first place."

The architecture of Faneuil Hall distinguished itself from that of the mall through materials: worn brick, granite pavers, exposed structural beams, carved shop signs, and copper accents. The new crept in through shiny additions: transparent canopies that expanded the covered shopping space, single large panes of glass inserted into the old openings, and stainless-steel bins to display cheese and pastries. Inside Charles Bulfinch's 1805 Faneuil Hall building, the ceiling of the first floor was cut out so that visitors could look up two stories to the great dome.

The difference between Faneuil Hall and suburban malls was spelled out in myriad ways in tenant leases. No plastic wrapping. No shopping carts. No Muzak.

As Jane Davison wrote in the *New York Times* in 1976, "Thompson's approach has for over a decade been as much dramaturgy as city planning or architecture." Quincy Market was "a conspicuously empty stage" waiting for a director to set the scene, attract an audience, and put on a show. The original architecture was stripped back to its bones, so that the market buildings' rows of pillars, painted gleaming white, were free of signs, and the colonnade was uncluttered by merchandise. Signs identifying individual stalls between the pillars were hung from above like heraldic banners. Meanwhile, at ground level, merchants were encouraged to show items in profusion: overflowing baskets, stocked tables, merchandising in the same way as Thompson had in his own store, with everything out to touch. All these scene-setting details were laid out in a handbook for tenants, spelling out the philosophy of the market like a corporation's in-house design guide, even as the details spelled out "authenticity."

$\rightarrow$

The opening of Faneuil Hall and Quincy Market was treated as a game changer for cities. Finally, a solution to what ailed downtown! Surely every city had a brick warehouse, even more than one, that, with added globe lights and exposed beams, cheese counters and café tables and wooden toys, could become a hub of activity after offices closed and parking garages emptied out. The banners and jugglers and carts gave the pedestrian walk between the old buildings the aspect of a fair, and thus a new name was spawned: the festival marketplace. New uses, old buildings, shopping as entertainment. Rouse and the Thompsons teamed up twice more, first to build Harborplace on the Baltimore waterfront, and next South Street Seaport in Manhattan. Rouse made the cover of *Time* magazine in 1981 with the headline "Cities Are Fun!"

One hundred new downtown retail centers opened between 1970 and 1988, with cities as co-investors in three-quarters of those projects. Festival marketplaces accounted for fewer than three in ten of those projects, but they got the most press and required the most artistic hand, both in the selection of buildings for adaptive reuse and in the curation of stores. Before Faneuil Hall, most observers agreed with DeBartolo: Downtown was dead. After Faneuil Hall, cities wanted in on the action but also looked for ways to reimagine the mall downtown at less expense than the full festival marketplace treatment.

On the cover of the 1974 book *The Pedestrian Revolution*, men in bell-bottoms and women in vests stroll between planters of lush blooms, dine under a purple umbrella, take a tram—all surrounded by blocky towers. *Streets Without Cars*, the subtitle, offers the promise of leisure, sunshine, family time on some not-so-mean streets. The pedestrian mall was an urban phenomenon broader than that of the marketplaces, and one with a clear boom-and-bust cycle. From 1959 through the early 1980s, more than two hundred American cities closed blocks of their downtowns to car traffic. By 2000, fewer than twenty-four of those original malls remained. The design intervention that was supposed to bring people back from the suburban mall had, instead, exacerbated the very problem it was trying to solve, turning downtowns into car-centric, retail-first monocultures rather than pedestrian-first, mixed-use places. And the man who popularized the downtown pedestrian mall was the same man who popularized the suburban shopping center: Victor Gruen.

In 1955, Gruen spoke at the influential Aspen Design Conference, unveiling his revitalization plan for "City X" (actually Fort Worth, Texas). His animating idea was to bring the level of design and management control of the shopping center or mall back to the city—and potentially double his client base. *Business Week* covered the plans in an article titled "Downtown Needs a Lesson from the Suburbs": "One of the troubles with technical progress, Gruen feels, is that it has showered us with all manners of machines and gadgets to make it possible to go where we want. But it has also reduced the number of places to which it is really worthwhile to go."

Today many elements of his City X plan read like a "what not to do" list for urban renewal. To save downtown, according to Gruen, cities needed ring roads (paid for with federal highway funds), satellite parking decks for tens of thousands of cars, and an underground network of tunnels for trucks. In return, citizens would get a fully pedestrianized set of downtown streets, with planters, benches, fountains, and public art. The *Business Week* article draws parallels between the planning of Northland—Gruen's original suburban breakthrough—and City X, which makes the resemblance clear: The ring road is the highway, the parking decks are the parking lot, and the pedestrian streets are the terraces and lanes between the stores. To deal with the larger scale of a city site, he proposed limited public transit.

"Gone also would be traffic lights and curbs to stumble over," wrote the *Fort Worth Star-Telegram* in 1956, when the city was revealed as the plan's sponsor. "For bad weather, disabled persons and shoppers burdened with packages Gruen envisioned noiseless, battery-powered shuttle cars similar to those at world's fairs." Futurama had struck again.

Asked by the *New Yorker* in 1956 what he would do for Manhattan, Gruen offered a vision of the island girdled by superhighways, with "ribbons of multiple-decked parking lots covered over with gardens and broad walks" adjacent to apartment buildings up to 150 stories high. "Down the spine of the island will be grassy malls, skating rinks, outdoor theatres, playgrounds, and more gardens," the authors write. " 'The chief means of travel will be walking,' said Mr. G. 'Nothing like walking for peace of mind. And, for when our feet get tired, there will be thousands of comfortable benches and scores of charming sidewalk cafés.' "

Gruen wasn't the only leading architect who wanted to impose a hierarchical, designed order on the evolving city. Louis Kahn's 1952 Traffic Study project for Philadelphia suggested a similar ring of high parking garages "protecting" downtown from the onslaught of cars, as defensive towers had once protected the medieval city. Even when they were putting pedestrians first, the car, physically and psychologically, dominated.

Despite the scale of these proposals, the first pedestrian malls were, relatively speaking, small. In 1959, Gruen's first downtown project opened on Burdick Street in Kalamazoo, Michigan. It was two blocks long, later expanded to four, and cost only sixty thousand dollars, paid for by the city and local business owners whose stores fronted the street. Gruen biographer M. Jeffrey Hardwick writes, "Cities saw Gruen's concept as a cheap and quick fix that would lure suburbanites and their dollars back downtown."

Cities also embraced the opportunity for greater control. The new pedestrian malls included signage programs, privately funded trash collection and security measures, and the same kinds of national brands as the out-of-town malls. In Gruen's pitch to Fort Worth boosters, he included three stories of hypothetical citizens satisfied by what City X had to offer: a businessman pleased with the orderly downtown, a merchant whose sales were enhanced, and a housewife who took the bus in from the suburbs for a day of errands. Not represented: workers, downtown residents, children, or people of color. Hardwick again: "The salvation of downtown, Gruen argued, rested on convincing white, middle-class females to return to the city center for shopping."

As Lizabeth Cohen writes, suburban shopping centers, like suburban housing developments, were planned to exclude.

> When developers and store owners set out to make the shopping center a more perfect downtown, they aimed to exclude from this public space unwanted urban groups such as vagrants, prostitutes, racial minorities, and poor people. Market segmentation became the guiding principle of this mix of commercial and civic activity, as the shopping center sought perhaps contradictorily to legitimize itself as a true community center and to define that community in exclusionary socioeconomic and racial terms.

The space of the mall looks like public space, but with their private cops and rules about loitering and unaccompanied minors, most shopping centers were never truly open. As the same designers moved from the suburbs back into the center, selling downtown's salvation as a series of design and regulatory moves, what was once publicly policed and publicly maintained public space became something else. This counterproductive focus outward and upward is nowhere more apparent than in the long history of Fulton Mall in downtown Brooklyn.

Fulton Street first became a shopping destination in 1883, upon completion of the Brooklyn Bridge. Abraham Abraham, one of the founders of department store Abraham & Straus, invested in the bridge and purchased Wheeler's Folly, a broad, cast-iron building on Fulton that had struggled to find a use for its generous floors. Upon completion of the bridge, what had been a thriving center of commerce at the ferry landing was suddenly obsolete, and the high ground along Fulton Street became easily accessible by carriage from the bridge. In 1888, an elevated railway opened, extending from Fulton Ferry to Nostrand Avenue and including a stop on Fulton Street. Over the next half century, Fulton Street became the crown jewel of Brooklyn shopping, as more local merchants joined A&S's grand emporium and more transportation systems made downtown Brooklyn a hub. When the el was torn down in 1940, shoppers had a variety of transit options to choose from, including the Jay Street station on the Independent Subway System, or the Atlantic Avenue subway station served by both the Brooklyn Rapid Transit and the Interborough Rapid Transit lines.

But by 1960, the high-end retailers were being undercut by discount stores. By the 1970s, even lower-end department stores like Korvettes were finding it hard to compete. Retail was bad all over, thanks to the recession. "The owners of Fulton Street's largest stores perceived the root of the problem differently . . . white people were making up a smaller and smaller percentage of the street's shoppers," writes Rosten Woo in a recent history of Fulton Mall. Business wasn't bad—in fact, business on Fulton Street has never been bad—but it didn't follow the City X template.

The solution for the owners, even in dense, popular, transit-rich Brooklyn, was pedestrianization. In 1979, architect Lee Harris Pomeroy was hired to rationalize the street, designing a project initially called the Fulton Arcade. For eight blocks, cars would be banned, though buses would still run. Orange cylindrical kiosks and bubbly Plexiglas bus shelters, a sans serif signage system, and semicircular benches would turn a city street into a facsimile of a suburban mall. Pomeroy's first proposal even included low-tech climate control: a tensile structure of red fabric to offer shade, like a perpetual version of Christo and Jeanne-Claude's *The Umbrellas*.

Pomeroy's design articulates the festive elements of the Thompsons' work at Faneuil Hall into an existing streetscape, echoing the rounded forms, warm colors, and fabric structures that proved so popular there. But just as important as the coordinated look was the coordinated governance over the street. Malls had both a central aesthetic command and a central selector for stores. Fulton Mall, which took the word "mall" back to its origin as an urban strip, would be run the same way despite its city environs. The written summary included with Pomeroy's plans noted, "When a shop window gets dull—they change it or go out of business. The same selective process applies to the mall. It will never be complete—creative changes and improvements and additions must prevail."

One of the most powerful tools for bringing mall values back downtown was an entity called the "business improvement district," or BID. The first BID was established in Toronto in 1970 on Bloor Street West, an urban

Fulton Mall

New York City Department of Highways
The Plaza, 2 W 45 St, New York, N.Y. 10019

Bodyn, Electronics, Feiner & Smith, Inc.
Office of Downtown Brooklyn Development
48 Park Avenue, New York, N.Y. 10016
Consulting Engineers

Pomeroy, Lebduska Associates
Architects Partners

Freelund and Associates
Landscape Consultants

Roland Brandese Lighting Design, Inc.
Lighting Consultants

Page, Arbitrio & Resen, Ltd.
Graphics Consultants

View at Fulton Street   **8**

Top, Fulton Street Pedestrian Mall rendering, Lee Harris Pomeroy Architects, 1976. *Bottom*, Fulton Street Pedestrian Mall and Transitway, Brooklyn, New York, Lee Harris Pomeroy Architects, 1980. (LHPA)

shopping strip populated by such core everyday businesses as a bakery, jewelry store, and greengrocer. Local merchants feared their strip was doomed, unable to compete with newer suburban malls. What if, the owners wondered, they marketed and styled themselves as a group, rather than individual shops? What if, they argued as they agreed to tax themselves, they added lights and flower boxes to the street, coordinated holiday shopping days, and acted as a team rather than as competitors? From this beginning the BID (or the business improvement area, as it is known in Canada) was born. After receiving approval from local government, businesses pay into a central fund run by a board of directors drawn from business and property owners and local officials. The fund in turn pays for streetscape improvements and group advertising, as well as trash collection and maintenance and, in some cases, private security guards. Such arrangements now cover major Manhattan commercial districts such as Bryant Park and Thirty-Fourth Street, as well as smaller strips in all five boroughs. The first New York BID was one of the earliest in the United States, a special assessment district, ratified in June 1976, to cover Fulton Street in downtown Brooklyn as it transformed from a traditional shopping strip to a pedestrian mall. The largest contributor was Abraham & Straus, which had anchored the area since its earliest days.

Yet along with the improvements—fewer cars, cohesive urban design, cleaner streets—there was a trade-off. Malls were clearly private property, and when you went in the door it was apparent that you were standing on private land. The boundaries are much less clear for a BID, where one sidewalk can be policed and maintained by the city, but if you cross the street, you are suddenly under the jurisdiction of private security and private rules. BIDs drive up rents, since property owners have to pay into the fund as well as paying rents. And despite the presence of public officials on BID boards, property and store owners hold the majority of seats. Which means that certain slices of the city are governed not by citizens—walkers, shoppers, small-business owners, lunchers—but only by those with the means to buy in. As Max Rivlin-Nadler wrote in the *New Republic* in 2016, "What was once an emergency measure by business owners in cities with a diminished tax base has become a power play for the future of urban space. By removing the interests of small business owners as well as community members from the equation, property owners can remake a neighborhood as they see fit. Already these actors wield enormous power, but have had to deal with democratic mechanisms that would temper their vision." *Who is the district being improved for?* became the critical question as more cities turned their streets over to be run by consortiums of business owners.

Ultimately, only a fraction of Pomeroy's streetscape elements were built; the tentlike arcade was eliminated early on. In addition, the suburban shoppers never came. And yet Fulton Mall was a success. Smaller, nimbler retailers kept up with the times as national department stores could not. The twelve nearby subway lines brought shoppers from all over the city. Storefronts were subdivided, so merchants could start small and grow as needed. By the late 1980s Fulton Mall was considered an epicenter of hip-hop style, reflected in the Biz Markie song "Albee Square Mall" released 1988. He raps about his experience roaming the mall: "You wouldn't think it's a store / You'd think it's my home." Junior's, a restaurant at one end of the mall, had been operating as a Jewish diner since its founding by the Rosen family in 1950; in the 1980s, it started selling soul food, crossing over to become a Black cultural hub (and a popular photo op for Brooklyn politicians). Major retailers, Woo writes, "believed that [Fulton Mall] was too tacky or poor to attract a Gap or Banana Republic, when in fact the opposite was true." As of 2022, Fulton Mall includes both—but their factory stores only.

"Fulton Street has maintained its place over the years as an important place for shopping in Brooklyn even as trends in shopping have changed. Landlords have stayed in front of the curve," said Regina Myer, president of the Downtown Brooklyn Partnership—the successor organization to the street's original BID—when I interviewed her in 2019. "I had teenagers that were highly aware [that] when new sneakers came out, they came out on Fulton Street."

$\rightarrow$

As Faneuil Hall got built out through the end of the 1970s, it became clear that the Thompsons were right to set specific guidelines for store design and selection. They wrote memos to Rouse executives outlining the atmosphere the market should strive for and the tenant mix needed to keep it feeling special. By 1978, those memos were becoming increasingly agitated. "The success of fast food and singles drinking operations tends to drive out serious shoppers for groceries, fashion and durable goods. The present local image of the Marketplace is something like 'pizza, piano bars, no-park, push and shove,'" the couple wrote in a missive titled "Guiding the Future of Faneuil Hall Marketplace," underlining the fact that homogenization was the project's biggest enemy. They were less concerned with copycats than with the encroachment of fast-food chains and tourist trinkets, with the fresh food market becoming, increasingly, a show for out-of-towners.

The truth was, however, that the Thompsons' vision limited the audience, and the sales, for the marketplace. Not every shopper is interested in local gourmet cheese, and once you've seen one copper-bottomed pot, you've seen them all. While the festival marketplace disrupted the status quo of retailing, it also quickly hardened into a parody of bourgeois consumerism. In addition, its status quo came in at a significantly higher price point than those fast-food chains, mass-market clothing stores, and souvenir shops. By making downtown a destination for middle-class shoppers searching for an authentic Boston experience, the festival marketplace put downtown out of reach for those who might want a more everyday shopping experience.

In 1977, less than a year after Faneuil Hall's triumphant opening, Calvin Trillin skewered it in the *New Yorker*—a magazine read by precisely its target audience of Julia Child–loving, imported-coffee-sipping, suburban-ennui-having adults. His piece, published under the rubric "U.S. Journal: New England," was subtitled "Thoughts Brought on by Prolonged Exposure to Exposed Brick." In the piece, Trillin travels south from Portland to Portsmouth to Boston, cobblestones beneath his feet, "never far from succor" should he need a copper bowl or wire whisk, the better to froth egg whites. He writes,

> The brick exposed in Ghirardelli Square in San Francisco tended to look like the brick exposed in Pioneer Square in Seattle, which

has some similarity to the brick exposed in Old Town, Chicago, or Underground Atlanta or the River Quay in Kansas City or Larimer Square in Denver or Gas Light Square in St. Louis.

Trillin quotes political journalist Andrew Kopkind, who published a February 1977 essay in the *Real Paper* titled "Kitsch for the Rich." Boston "will remake an area of warehouses, wharves, working-class markets and ethnic enclaves into a high-life playground, a theme park of nostalgia and a theater of consumption," Kopkind writes. Barring collapse and revolt, eventually the city from Government Center to Copp's Hill may become "one vast stack of exposed bricks, a forest of butcher block, a jungle of asparagus ferns." The highway that interrupts the flow of people from Government Center to the waterfront, in Kopkind's view, is a protective moat, saving the traditionally Italian, working-class North End from the predations of middle-class taste.

That middle-class taste reflected a change in the economics of building and development. In a major shift since the 1950s, as a result of rising urban and suburban land prices, redevelopment and renovation were now more affordable than new construction. Changes in urban politics also factored in; the protests of 1968 had slowed inner-city highway construction and wholesale neighborhood demolition, and the advocacy of thinkers like Jane Jacobs for old buildings, small-scale neighborhoods, and mixed uses had had time to filter out to a wider public. "'Preservation,'" Kopkind writes, "became the favorite rationale for the middle-class takeover of urban territory" from Boston's South End to Washington, D.C.'s Capitol Hill, Manhattan's SoHo to San Francisco's Mission. He quotes MIT urbanist Lisa Peattie calling the process "reverse blight." The same areas of cities that Gruen saw as dangerous and that lenders saw as hazardous were now— cleaned up and dressed differently—an opportunity. Those new development opportunities, however, suffered from the same narrow-audience focus as the marketplaces. "A city of classy playgrounds and retail amusement parks, of tourist-shoppers and rootless workers, eventually will decay of its own irrelevance," Kopkind concludes.

Trillin's critique is largely aesthetic, based on the sameness and precious-ness of these developments, their upscale–Holiday Inn nature. He recognizes Kopkind's critique as deeper: "There are some, like Andrew Kopkind, who look on it as a group of middle-class sophisticates taking territory away from working people—a phenomenon he describes with a marvelous word that is apparently used by British planners, 'gentrification.'" What may well be the first use of "gentrification" in the *New Yorker* arrived in relation to shopping, not housing.

While critiques of the festival marketplace continued to turn on the question of audience, by 1980 the phenomenon had become a known quan-tity and a recognizable brand. Rouse had struggled to get financing in the early 1970s; now his company was synonymous with urban adaptive reuse. Before settling on Baltimore and, subsequently, Manhattan's South Street Seaport, the Rouse Company evaluated downtown projects including the Ferry Building in San Francisco, Horton Plaza in San Diego, and Navy Pier in Chicago—all of which would be developed by others.

Instead, Rouse went to Baltimore. Harborplace opened there in 1980 with a fifty-seven-boat flotilla and fireworks. The model was the same: an underutilized but picturesque urban site, a partnership between the Rouse Company and Benjamin Thompson Associates, and a significant amount of public support. One hundred and fifty million dollars in federal funds had already been spent on a waterfront promenade, a Harry Cobb–designed office building, a science center, and plans for the proposed National Aquarium. When Baltimore's mayor, William Donald Schaefer, had toured Faneuil Hall with Patty Rouse, he said, "Baltimore has got to have one of these."

Baltimore's Inner Harbor boasted dramatic abandoned industrial archi-tecture, in the form of a disused power plant with distinctive smokestacks, but Rouse thought its location was all wrong. The site he picked out was at the northwest corner on the Inner Harbor, closest to downtown. Thompson's firm was asked to design two new buildings, taking their cues from the idea of a fair. They shaped broad, tentlike green metal roofs, balconies projecting

Harborplace, Baltimore, Maryland, Benjamin Thompson and Associates, 1979–1980. (Photograph by Steve Rosenthal © Historic New England, from the Steve Rosenthal Collection of Commissioned Work at Historic New England)

into multilevel interior spaces, and windows pointed toward downtown and toward the water, emphasizing the buildings' role as a link between the two. One was to be a fresh food market, like the ground floor of Faneuil Hall; the other to be enclosed shops, restaurants, and cafés. As in Boston, the city was one anchor store, the harbor the other, and office workers would fill up the weekdays while tourists took over on weekends.

Though the mayor was on board in Baltimore, concerned citizens had questions about whether new construction and private development were the best use of their now recreational waterfront. Baltimore was not without existing marketplaces: Rouse's son Jimmy remembers visiting Lexington Avenue Market and North Avenue Market, part of the city's historic network, with his father in his youth. "When he started Harborplace, part of the

vision was to recreate that, have an independent meat and cheese dealer ...
produce, flowers, all these individual merchants in there, along with retail
that was impulse buying," the younger Rouse said in 2020. Would the new
offerings include minority-owned businesses and serve the Black community that still lived close to downtown? Or would the market orient itself to
white suburban workers and tourists?

Two ballot referendums in 1978 took these questions to voters. One was a
yes or no vote on any future development in the Inner Harbor; the other a
vote on whether construction could proceed on just the 3.2 acres set aside for
the project. Baltimore's majority Black voters were swayed toward votes in
favor of development by two factors. First, Rouse had long-standing relationships with Black community leaders, established in the 1950s—and
Columbia's track record as an integrated garden suburb was well known.
And second, Rouse promised jobs at the marketplace to Black candidates
early in the approvals process and had said he would recruit minority tenants
for the stalls and stores. For once it seemed as if the Black community would
have a chance to profit, not just consume, in the rebuilt inner city. When
Harborplace opened, its offerings included twenty-two minority business
owners, including Sandra Dotsun, a seller of local relishes and sauces, who
made her pitch to Rouse at Union Baptist Church. When *New York Times*
food writer Marian Burros visited the Inner Harbor in 1983, she tried to
wave readers away from everywhere food like pizza and fried chicken and
toward unique local offerings such as the city's cheese bread, kielbasa with
sauerkraut, and the Baltimore lemon stick, a peppermint stick inserted into
a whole lemon. The food gave the place specificity, even if the architecture
was a postmodern take on a refreshed factory building.

Faneuil Hall, Harborplace, and Fulton Mall all opened within a few years of
one another, now four decades ago. The Rouse developments—with their
political support, elaborate curation, and Ben and Jane Thompson designs—
might have seemed like the odds-on favorites for long-term survival. But of

all urban malls—including festival marketplaces, pedestrian malls, and indoor shopping centers—the ones that have fared the best have been those that best served their workday and weekend audiences and catered to the transit-oriented community, rather than chasing tourists and purchasers of copper pans.

"Faneuil Hall's Promised Retail Revolution? We're Still Waiting," read the headline on a *Boston Globe* article in 2019. The article wasn't referring to Rouse and the Thompsons' original vision for the marketplace, but to what it had become by the early twenty-first century: chain stores, everywhere food, representing "Boston" only to tourists. All the fears the Thompsons laid out in their memo in 1978 had come true. Ashkenazy Acquisition Corporation, which bought the site in 2011, promised more local tenants and refreshment of the physical premises, but these improvements had yet to come to fruition.

In some ways, Faneuil Hall was a victim of its own success: Pedestrianization came for downtown Boston in a major way with the completion of the Big Dig, which sunk the Central Artery in a tunnel and swept away the barrier between Government Center, the marketplace, and the waterfront. Who needs the sometimes-crowded brick streets of the market when you have the broad, planted, parklike Rose F. Kennedy Memorial Greenway? In addition, the idea of a food hall with local vendors and communal tables had spread to other locations in the immediate area and across the city. The Thompsons were right about what would draw people, but they also spawned a thousand imitators.

The story is similar in Baltimore, where the two Harborplace pavilions are in receivership and planners say it is time to demolish one if not both. In a 2020 essay, "What Happened to Baltimore's Harborplace?," Ethan McLeod writes, "It's hard to overstate how transformative Harborplace was for Baltimore's sense of itself in the 1980s and '90s. Even locals who shunned the twin pavilions as cartoony tourist traps often found themselves drawn to the waterside, especially when hosting out-of-town visitors. Baltimore held plenty of more 'authentic' haunts, but it was Harborplace, and the circuit of

Inner Harbor attractions it anchored, that dominated every television ad or visitor's center brochure." But what happened at Harborplace happened in Boston, in New York, in San Francisco. "What was once a one-of-kind attraction became just one of a network of glitzy waterfront shopping emporia. The homogenization was internal, as well, as national brands began to replace the local merchants."

To save Harborplace, observers agree, would require going back to basics. "It needs an owner that cares. It's had two really bad owners in a row, both from out of town," Jimmy Rouse told McLeod. It would need small, local merchants you can't buy from anywhere else; a focus on the new residents living downtown, often in conversions of former office buildings; and an appeal—through refreshed spaces and Baltimore-centric marketing—to the tourists who continue to visit the superlative National Aquarium and Maryland Science Center. Recent design competitions have suggested radical updates to the dated postmodern architecture, from stripping it back to its concrete structure to opening more sides to the street. Some have even suggested replacing one or both pavilions with green open space—a return to the original criticism that private development shouldn't dominate the harbor.

As malls moved back into cities in the form of festival marketplaces and pedestrianized streets, questions of race, ownership, and audience moved from the background to the foreground. And even as some suburbs diversified in their second or third decades, the change in shopper demographics was not part of the developers' plans. As comedian Chris Rock noted in a November 1996 *Saturday Night Live* monologue:

> And every town's got two malls! They've got the white mall, and the mall white people *used* to go to. 'Cause there ain't nothing in the Black mall! Nothing but sneakers and baby clothes!

The Black mall became Black not with intention but by default. Investment capital fled to chase white shoppers, and malls built for their use ended up

Top, The Gallery at Market East, Philadelphia, Pennsylvania, with Harold Kimmelman, *Burst of Joy* (1977), Bower Fradley Lewis Thrower/Architects, 1977. *Bottom*, interior. (Special Collections Research Center, Temple University Libraries, Philadelphia, PA)

serving the Black consumer because of changes in residential ownership patterns or, in urban malls, transportation patterns. In recent years, when the forces of real estate and revitalization have come back for "the mall white people *used* to go to," there's typically little care for what the mall has become; private equity wants to make it back into a white mall.

One of the best-known examples of this phenomenon is the Gallery at Market East in downtown Philadelphia—another Rouse Company project, but without the flotilla and flourishes. The Gallery opened in 1977, part of the wave of downtown investment intended to bring middle-class shoppers back from the suburbs by offering them the same amenities downtown. Gallery I was developed under the leadership of Philadelphia's visionary planning commissioner Ed Bacon as a public-private partnership, with the city Redevelopment Authority paying two thirds of the construction cost through funds earmarked for urban renewal, and the Rouse Company the final third. As happened in Boston, national merchants were initially wary, and leasing took 30 percent longer than expected, though Philadelphia stalwart Strawbridge's signed on as one of two anchor department stores. Also as in Boston, those wary tenants were wrong.

Dan McQuade wrote in a *Philadelphia Magazine* tribute to the Gallery in 2015, "Get this: *It was successful from the start.*" "In a shopping mall, to gross $100 per square foot is average, $150 is considered a hot property, but we have three that gross over $250, and one is The Gallery," Rouse's Scott Toombs told *Progressive Architecture* magazine in 1978. By 1983 the Gallery was the Rouse Company's third most valuable commercial property, grossing approximately $300 per square foot. In the second phase, which opened in 1984 with ninety more shops, minority leaders pressed for inclusion. A quarter of the new stores were minority owned and operated.

But by the late 1980s, the Gallery's demographics began to change. The ends became a revolving door of department stores, as Strawbridge's unsuccessfully tried to hold on to its local clout. The mall's remaining stores and restaurants increasingly catered to the lower-middle-class population that worked in the area and found a mall with excellent public transportation access both convenient and necessary.

In *The Cosmopolitan Canopy*, ethnographer Elijah Anderson observes the Gallery during this era:

> Here, in the gap between the well-to-do areas of Center City west of Broad Street and the emerging chic of Old City on the edge of the Delaware, black people from the neighborhoods ringing Center City and readily accessible by public transport found a comfortable place to shop and congregate . . . At some point in the last decade, the transition became complete, and the Gallery acquired a clear and lasting reputation as a "black place," catering to black patrons from lower economic classes.

As Anderson and McQuade discover, the organic change in retailers and customers hasn't actually signaled financial trouble. As with the stores along Fulton Mall, a "black place" doesn't mean financial failure, even though retailing stereotypes may perceive it as such. When the real estate investment trust that owned the Gallery was pressured to sell low-performing malls in 2014, the Philadelphia property was considered an asset, still making $327 per square foot—less than Cherry Hill, always among the country's top malls, but still well above average.

Nonetheless, revitalization came for the Gallery too: It reopened in 2019 as the Fashion District, with an increased emphasis on entertainment, food, and fitness in its store selection, and a third floor with coworking and maker spaces. The new owners did make an effort to include Black store owners, and as *Philadelphia Inquirer* architecture critic Inga Saffron noted, "Based on the opening day crowd, the Fashion District appears likely to serve the same customers it served before, but with better decor and brighter lighting. [They are] hoping more Center City residents, millennials, and tourists will join them." The latest iteration of the Gallery suggests the possibility of a happy ending: a mall that draws a new, multiracial generation of residents, workers, and visitors to central Philadelphia while remaining a "black place" and fostering Black entrepreneurship.

→

The 1968 documentary *Fresno: A City Reborn* describes the Central California city, and cities in general, as in a state of crisis—a disaster movie looking for a hero. "They have become unsafe, unhealthy, and often ugly," says the narrator, over grainy images of New York and Chicago, downtown streets and commercial signs. "One product of our technology in particular has encouraged urban sprawl and the exploding metropolis . . . the private automobile." The camera zooms back to show cloverleaf highway interchanges and curving cul-de-sacs. "Entering the city center . . . he joins a grim battle for space and time . . . Without decisive action our cities may become dreary ghost towns."

The documentary then celebrates the people responsible for that "decisive action": the producers of the film, Victor Gruen Associates. The film was meant as a victory lap for the firm's six years of work in Fresno on what would become the Fulton Street Pedestrian Mall. Planned by Gruen Associates, with a landscape by leading California design firm Eckbo, Dean, Austin and Williams, Fulton Mall was dedicated in September 1964: six blocks of automobile-free city adjacent to the courthouse, new and remodeled department stores, and a new high-rise office and hotel building, paid for through a combination of federal urban renewal funds and an assessment on downtown property owners—a precursor to the BIDs of the 1970s.

The willingness of business owners to tax themselves was precipitated by the departure, in 1956, of a large Sears store that had been a downtown anchor. What would replace the solid, respectable store was an explosion of downtown amenities. Decorative pavement featured a stylized wave pattern in sandblasted concrete, striped with bands of red pebbles; new water features included round pools with cascades and jets, some of them setting off sculptures. Shade trees and canopies sprouted, with seating areas under the trees and next to the moving water. There was even the occasional playground, with a Jim Miller-Melberg concrete turtle for the weary small shopper. Art and design would lure people back to the city, just as they had

"Nothing happens unless first a dream"
—Carl Sandburg

Forward looking Fresnans dreamed their dream then pursued its fulfillment and the Mall was born — a grand design in convenience and beauty united to serve practical needs. The 9 blocks of walkways and promenades encompass a great variety of sculpture and art interspersed with waterways, fountains and grassy oases. Amid these pleasant surroundings thrives a broad and diverse collection of stores and businesses serving Fresnans and valley citizens.

FULTON MALL, TULARE TOWARD KERN STREET

Top, Fulton Mall rendering, Fresno, California, Gruen Associates in association with Eckbo, Dean, Austin and Williams, landscape architects, 1965. *Bottom*, Fulton Mall promotional brochure featuring Eckbo fountains and the pedestrian mall's sixty-foot-tall wood clock tower by Jan de Swart. (Gruen Associates) enticed patrons to the outdoor pedestrian spaces at Northland ten years earlier. The Fresno art program was particularly striking, including a sixty-foot-tall wood "clock tower"—because every mall needs a statement clock—designed by Jan de Swart, plus urban-scale sculpture by California modernists Peter Voulkos, Stan Bitters, Claire Falkenstein, and George Tsutakawa. It was a museum-quality sculpture park, thoughtfully designed for Fresno's hot climate, embedded in the center of the city rather than at its car-dependent periphery.

In a story for *Reader's Digest*, Bernard Taper described the scene in "A City Remade for People": "I am sitting contentedly, a cool drink at my elbow, right in the middle of Fulton Street—the main street of Fresno, California . . . What I am doing now is simply a part of a new pattern of life this bustling city of more than 150,000 has adopted: one starting from the premise that downtown is for people."

The Fresno documentary picks up this theme of rebirth: "Where wires disfigured the sky, tree branches filter the sunlight; where there were parking meters, now there are flowers; gas stations have given way to drinking fountains. Debris-filled gutters are gone, and the sight and sound of cooling water have taken their place." The mall received a U.S. Department of Housing and Urban Development Award, following a 1965 *Progressive Architecture* Design Award for the city agencies and design team. Delegations from as far away as Rotterdam, home of the oft-cited Lijnbaan pedestrian shopping street, visited with praise.

Despite its pedigree, however, Fulton Mall had limited success. While sales along the mall initially increased, within a decade additional suburban shopping centers had siphoned off even more business. In addition, as Gruen historian Alex Wall points out, the images used to sell Fulton Mall to Fresno residents show sidewalk cafés, landscaped medians, and shady streets populated by people who are entirely "white and middle class, precisely the people who chose in the mid-1960s, rather than remaking and reinhabiting the city, to leave it." By the early 2000s, the lack of business for the stores, long-deferred maintenance on the mall, and the city's rising population of the unhoused caused city officials to turn back the clock and allow cars back on to the mall—demolishing Eckbo's landscape and saving the sculptures as individual art pieces rather than as an ensemble. The pedestrianization had been paid for with urban renewal funds; now the return of automobility was backed by a federal Transportation Investment Generating Economic Recovery (TIGER) grant, demonstrating the long-term automotive focus of U.S. government transportation priorities.

As part of the run-up to the demolition of Fulton Mall, the Downtown Fresno Partnership sponsored a study, "The Experiment of American Pedestrian Malls: Trends Analysis, Necessary Indicators for Success and Recommendations for Fresno's Fulton Mall." The study provides useful assessment tools for the entire pedestrian mall phenomenon. In its present condition, the authors found, Fulton Mall would fail as 89 percent of America's pedestrian malls had failed. The 11 percent that continued to succeed into the twenty-first century had three things in common: 80 percent were in areas with populations under one hundred thousand people, all were short in length, and all were anchored by a university (as in Burlington, Vermont, and Charlottesville, Virginia), a beach (as in Santa Monica), or a major tourist location (as in Las Vegas or New Orleans).

Americans walk when they are in college or on vacation; the rest of the time, automobility rules. Pedestrian malls in places with existing foot traffic succeed. Americans also walk in cities where there is enough population density to support retail, restaurants, and entertainment downtown as well as public transportation to get there. Teaching people to drive downtown to shop didn't work. But capitalizing on and improving resources for existing-consumer desire lines did.

Many pedestrian malls stumbled because they disrupted car routes in and around downtown, and patrons felt cut off within the pedestrianized areas. By the same token, a subset of those that succeeded incorporated public transit. Buses, light rail, or trolley routes up and down a largely pedestrian area counterintuitively improve foot traffic, adding liveliness and providing more connections to the rest of the city.

The ongoing success of Brooklyn's Fulton Mall offers clues to how pedestrian malls—and festival marketplaces too—might meet twenty-first-century needs. The future of these spaces should not involve chasing this century's "ideal" consumer, but instead improving the experience for the shoppers who are already there. The process begins by not disdaining the people spending money downtown, especially when center-city stores have historically served a far broader racial and economic spectrum than those in enclosed shopping malls. The nomenclature used to refer to car-free streets has changed too. "Pedestrian mall" is dated, freighted with negative connotations of blight, and it limits the interpretation of such streets to their commercial role. "Shared streets," by contrast, doesn't privilege one form of transportation over another except by implication: When have cars and their drivers ever shared?

Avoiding the word "mall" offers more flexibility, opening the possibility of a pedestrian-first space that isn't constrained by consumerism. A shared street can be a built-out play street—a concept pioneered by I. M. Pei and M. Paul Friedberg in the mid-1960s—or the "home zones" proposed for residential neighborhoods in Seattle, which eliminated sidewalks in order to slow everyone down and limit streets to local traffic. In Long Island City, Queens, a nascent Street Seats program turned a de facto employee parking lot into a pedestrian plaza, inspired by the unusual glacial rock formation popping out of the asphalt. Imagine such a slow zone centered on a school, or overlaid, as it could be in my Brooklyn neighborhood, to encompass a park, an elementary school, two ice-cream shops, and a public library. Such plans would recognize there's more to life than shopping, and that people's homes, work, schools, and play zones are far more mixed than any mall of the 1950s, or the 1970s, ever managed.

James Rouse, in his speech on constructing new cities from scratch, and Ben Thompson, in his speech about visual squalor, both made it clear that building housing, shopping, government, and cultural buildings separately led only to boredom, traffic, and urban vacuums. Their festival marketplaces, like the pedestrian malls, attempted to put the pieces of mixed-use neighborhoods back together again, embedding shopping within existing nexuses of offices, theaters, and public facilities. And yet, those shopping spaces devolved quickly into monocultures—stores you could find

Fulton Mall, Downtown Brooklyn Public Realm Plan, BIG Architects and WXY, 2021. (Downtown Brooklyn Partnership)

elsewhere, tourist traps good for only one visit—because they failed to maintain the balance of vendors and the connections to their specific community necessary for long-term stability.

New ideas for Fulton Mall reflect the shifting paradigm and include elements that are clearly the offspring of Eckbo's Fresno designs. In January 2020, Bjarke Ingels Group and WXY Architecture + Urban Design unveiled concepts for the 240-acre public realm, sponsored by the Downtown Brooklyn Partnership. The plans were prompted by the tremendous residential growth in the area after a 2004 rezoning, which was originally intended to spur office development. Many of the ideas in the plan were reminiscent of the first round of pedestrianization, from curving fountains and bright public sculpture, as with Fresno's Fulton Mall, to orange, treelike shade structures, like Pomeroy's original bright canopy. Going forward, streets will not be repaved but repainted, with zones for bikes and pedestrians, and wavy benches added, leaving lanes that are wide enough to let cars through but make it clear they aren't wanted. Smaller streets branching off Fulton proper may be de-mapped entirely and made over into playgrounds, with surrounding buildings' hard edges softened with murals and neon.

In 2019, as an interim measure, the Department of Transportation turned several blocks of Willoughby Street into shared streets, with five-mile-per-hour traffic, café seating, and planters to accommodate the area's lunchtime crowds. That was the first time the agency had installed a shared street outside Manhattan. It was immediately adopted—a small, relatively inexpensive gesture, without architectural distinction, that allowed the public to make the neighborhood their own.

"I've been amazed how quickly the public responds to new open space in downtown Brooklyn," Regina Myer of the Downtown Brooklyn Partnership said. "No one has been like, Oh, maybe we didn't need that."

Chapter 4
Make Shopping Beside the Point

T he major commercial strip in Waukegan, Illinois, is called Genesee
Street. As an industrial hub halfway between Chicago and Milwaukee
on Lake Michigan, Waukegan grew prosperous in the early twentieth century,
with a handsome row of masonry buildings lining the street, including
Waukegan National Bank, the Genesee Theatre, and the S. S. Kresge five-
and-dime with a soda fountain. When Ray Bradbury, born in Waukegan in
1920, wrote nostalgically of small-town America in the 1953 short story
"Dandelion Wine," it was his hometown that he fictionalized as "Green
Town," the place where he discovered L. Frank Baum and Edgar Allan Poe,
cinema and comic books and circuses.

Even after a family move to Los Angeles in the late 1930s, Bradbury still had
a sweet shop, soda fountain, and movie theater within easy reach, roller-
skating his way around Hollywood to meet movie stars. The commercial strip
in his neighborhood, he wrote, felt like Main Street. But then, lunch counters
began to be replaced by fast-food restaurants, street-front cinemas by multi-
plexes, strolling teens by honking (or cruising) drivers. Teens were told to
move on, but really, an entire culture was told to move on. "How can we bring
it back?" Bradbury asked, thinking of Genesee Street. What would give teens
what he would eventually label "Somewhere To Go"?

In Mexico, in any small-town plaza every Thursday and Sunday night
with the band playing and the weather mild, the boys walk this way,

the girls walk that, around and around, and the mothers and fathers sit on iron-scrolled benches and watch. In Paris, with miserable weather, in thousands of outdoor drinking and eating places, the generations gather to talk and stare. Even this late in the century in many crossroads-country-junction American towns, Saturday night finds pumpkin boys rolling in from the farms to hold up cigar store-fronts with their shoulders and paw the sidewalk with their hooves as the girls go laughing by. Which is what life is all about.

By 1970, few such places existed in Los Angeles, at least outside the pages of Bradbury's fiction. As the city expanded and its residents came to rely on private rather than public transportation, the tissue connecting residential communities to retail streets was cut. Shopping meant driving to a free-standing store with a moatlike parking lot, or to a strip shopping center with angled parking, its access roads interrupting sidewalks where pedestrians might once have strolled. Science fiction starts with world building: an accumulation of new sights and sounds, channeled through a narrative, that allows the reader to get oriented in the environment invented by the author. Bradbury, a writer perhaps best known for the classic sci-fi collection *The Martian Chronicles*, was well positioned to use his skills, in an essay eventually published in *West: The Los Angeles Times Magazine*, to sketch an alternative Los Angeles.

> A vast, dramatically planned city block. One to start with. Later on, one or more for each of the 80 towns in LA . . . A place where, by the irresistible design and purpose of such a block, people would be tempted to linger, loiter, stay, rather than fly off in their chairs to already overcrowded places.

Bradbury imagines the center of this place as a bandstand or stage, with other functions arrayed around it like the layers of an onion. A conversation pit. A mosaic-floored plaza. A ring of food purveyors including a malt shop, a pizza parlor, a delicatessen, a candy store. Shops selling the things "most delicious in our lives": books ("why not three" bookstores?), a record store, an art gallery, hardware, stationery, toys, magic. At the four corners of the block, his anchor stores would be not vast emporia but entertainment: one cinema for new releases and another for classics, a theater, a coffeehouse for music.

What Bradbury proposed as an urban fiction would, over the next decade-plus, become reality, thanks to a new mall-maker named Jon Jerde. Like Bradbury, Jerde was born in Illinois but grew up roaming remote areas of the United States, following his father's career in the oil business. In his later personal mythmaking, he dramatized these years as lonely ones, contrasting his childhood with that in the typical American family. When he was twelve, he said, he experienced community for the first time at an amusement park on the ocean cliffs near San Diego. Theme parks, California, the lure of public conviviality—all these would get translated into the places he and his partnership made. A scholarship to Italy added another influence, the architecture and choreography of picturesque hill towns such as San Gimignano. "On his return to Los Angeles," Ann Bergren writes, "he formed the founding conviction that the only place left in the city for creating communality is the shopping mall."

Malls would become more urban. Malls would become more entertaining. If the designers and developers would get their way, malls would replicate what draws people together in plazas, squares, and Main Streets—food, people-watching, reasons to laugh and cry and kiss. This was the second generation of shopping malls, building on the more straightlaced and contained precedent Gruen had sketched at Southdale, and cemented into I-, T-, V-, and O-shaped plans by Urban Land Institute manuals and developers including DeBartolo, Rouse, the Simons, and Ernest Hahn. Malls sought innovation because they sold innovation; unlike other architecture that was built to last, malls were built to sell fashion and newness and they, too, had to turn over every decade or so, just as the Nashers predicted. By 1980, the first generation of mallgoers was old enough to have children. These families expected more: more to do, more reasons to go to the mall, and a more urban approach to suburban life in general. In 1980, the media also raised the specter of the death of the mall for the first time. It would be far from the last.

→

As Ray Bradbury later told an interviewer, Los Angeles in the 1970s "was falling apart at the seams." By the start of the decade, Bradbury had already made the leap from speculative fiction into real-world forecasting through collaborations first with designers working on the United States Pavilion for the 1964 World's Fair in Queens and then for Walt Disney's EPCOT. In both cases, architects asked him to write the script for the places they were building, offering a bridge from the 1960s to a future envisioned (in EPCOT's branding) as Spaceship Earth.

In 1976, Jon Jerde visited Bradbury and asked him, " 'Have you seen the Glendale Galleria?' " " 'I said, 'Yes, I have,' " Bradbury later told the *Paris Review*.

> "Did you like it?" he asked. I said, "Yes." He said, "That's your Galleria. It's based on the plans that you put in your article in the essay in the *Los Angeles Times*." I was stunned. I said, "Are you telling me the truth? I created the Glendale Galleria?" "Yes, you did," he said. "Thank you for that article that you wrote about rebuilding L.A. We based our building of the Glendale Galleria completely on what you wrote in that article."

In the early 1970s Glendale, a bedroom community east of Los Angeles, feared its commercial downtown was on the edge of collapse. A newly formed redevelopment agency sponsored street beautification and mandated design upgrades for existing storefronts, but also supported a new 1.6-million-square-foot shopping center. From the outside, the Glendale Galleria was your average brown box, closed off from the neighborhood around it in ways Bradbury certainly never scripted. But inside, Jerde disrupted the straight shot from department store to department store with a bend. On the second floor, the mezzanine is a maze. Above visitors' heads, a curved glass skylight embraces the whole with a three-level garden court at the center.

Top, Buffums Department Store at the Glendale Galleria, Glendale, California, Jon Jerde for Charles Kober Associates, 1976. *Bottom*, holiday display. (Glendale History Room, Library, Arts & Culture Dept., Glendale, CA)

When he designed the Glendale Galleria, Jerde was working in-house as design director for Charles Kober Associates, one of the West Coast's largest retail architecture firms. Charles Kober, who had an undergraduate degree in economics and a master's degree in architecture, ran his firm like a businessman, paying as close attention to the financial prospects for the projects he took on as to the design. Kober malls of the era typically had sober, brutalist exteriors, in solid brick or tan concrete, and multilevel earth-tone interiors, their atriums laden with plants like then-trendy ferns. They were elegant but not exciting. Jerde kept trying to interest clients in the mall as more than a literal shopping center. It should be "a vessel for heightened human experience to occur," he told *Los Angeles Magazine* writer Ed Leibowitz. "Make shopping beside the point, [Jerde] argued, and paradoxically more shopping would be done. So many patrons would come, and they would stay so much longer that sooner or later they would end up buying something," Leibowitz added in a revealing 2002 profile of Jerde.

Kober Associates clients didn't listen, happy with their return on investment with standardized malls. Jerde quit the office and spent a few unhappy moments renovating historic buildings in Seattle, before returning on his own to Los Angeles and the problem of the city, the mall, and Somewhere To Go.

In 1977 Jerde came back to Bradbury with a request for a custom scenario for San Diego, where developer Ernest Hahn, once Kober's biggest client, had hired Jerde to prepare a scheme for a downtown redevelopment site. Jerde later reminisced that Hahn had been having trouble selling the city on a standard mall and called him up saying, "Jerde, that crap you used to talk about? Its time has come. Come out of retirement and save me and San Diego." Jerde looked to Bradbury in turn for help. Bradbury produced "The Aesthetics of Lostness," a manifesto for the mall that imagined not the legible, bilaterally symmetrical, top-lit spaces that Kober, Hahn, and others had been producing at a rapid rate, but something a little more writerly, drifty, lost.

Why lost?

To be lost. How frightening.
To be *safely* lost. How wonderful

To not know where we are, as children, is a nightmare.

To not know where we are, as adults, traveling, is a perfect dream.

Bradbury's ideal shopping mall would offer that feeling without the cost of travel. It would build in twists and turns—literally—and with the right amount of confusion, profusion, and curiosity. Bradbury even imagines a use for the third levels of malls, the narrow hallways under the eaves where good businesses fear to tread. That's where the teens should hang out, giving them options apart from the grotty arcade or the corner of the food court, away from the disapproving adults.

Hell, why not, at the very top level of some future mall rear an entire floor labeled: THE ATTIC? Up there stash all your antique shops, antiquarian booksellers, Victorian toy merchants, magic shops, Halloween card and decoration facilities and little cinemas running "Dracula" fourteen hours a day, or name another half-dozen specialty stores that wouldn't mind being half-lit and fully exciting.

It was up to Jerde and his team to translate that idiosyncratic vision into a three-dimensional project. Margaret Crawford, a keen historian and critic of the shopping mall, writes that only Gruen and then Jerde have been able to shape the form: Gruen by enclosing the mall at Southdale and making it possible for shopping centers to weatherproof themselves and re-create the city in compressed form; and Jerde by taking Gruen's vision of (sub)urban sociability and theming it, so that each "city center" had its own look. The Bertoia sculpture and carousel, the "sidewalk café" and aviary at Southdale look far too sedate in contrast to the roller coasters and waterways Jerde and his partners would place at the center of their expanding portfolio of malls.

Hahn's plea was for Jerde to redevelop San Diego's Horton Plaza Park and environs, a historic area that had turned into a political battle: Once used for concerts and rallies, it had grown into a skid row adjacent to the local adult-entertainment district by the early 1970s. The city council began to think along much the same lines that would impel Boston, Rochester, and numerous other cities to build urban malls over the course of the decade:

Malls had drawn city dwellers to the suburbs; now perhaps a mall could draw them back. In 1972, San Diego approved a general plan for the fifteen-block area around Horton Plaza; at its center would be a hotel, offices, and a new shopping center, though many observers were dubious that San Diegans would ever shop downtown again. Mayor Pete Wilson (who would subsequently become first a California senator and then the governor) was elected in 1971 on a platform to prevent the "Los Angelizing" of San Diego by bringing people back.

Jerde's first design presentation for Horton Plaza was made of cardstock pasted with patterns, theatrically lit and displayed to the San Diego powers that be by a team dressed in the black turtlenecks of stagehands. Downtown San Diego had very little historic architecture to work with: no brick factories or cobblestones like Faneuil Hall, no earlier urban renewal scars to fill in like Baltimore. Jerde's references weren't local but global, a postcard pastiche of sunny plazas and dramatic hill towns and landmark towers of Europe, a little bit Spanish, a little bit Moorish, a little bit Italian. Earlier California architects including Julia Morgan and Irving Gill had looked to other places with similar climates for inspiration, and so would he. The 1920s-themed shopping districts in English Tudor and Spanish colonial styles paved the way too, but Jerde's strongest precedent came from the same environments for which Bradbury had already written scenarios: world's fairs and theme parks, which shamelessly mashed up countries, decades, architectural styles, and artificial topography in the interest of creating the most exciting visual narrative in the minimum quantity of space.

The finished product, which opened in 1985, retained that sense of theater: The edges of the 11.5-acre development followed the right angles of the existing city blocks, notched in at the corners to preserve some existing buildings and create a parking lot. The spine of the mall cuts diagonally across the street grid, creating the longest possible internal passage. Bracketed by three department stores and 150 shops, this pedestrian street is subdivided into six sections, each assigned to a different design team to simulate a real city's diverse architecture. Curved walkways and glass-topped coves cut in and out of this passageway, with stairs and escalators and bridges crisscrossing the route and suggesting alternate paths up, down, and across.

Aerial view of Horton Plaza, San Diego, California, Jerde Partnership, 1985. Partially demolished 2020–2021. (Photograph by Charles Lenoir; JERDE)

Although Horton Plaza was originally proposed as a covered mall, Jerde and Hahn convinced their clients that the local climate was balmy enough for year-round outdoor shopping, and saved millions of dollars on the roof to use elsewhere. Bradbury's notion of attics actually seems appealing when the fourth story of the mall can be reached by, for example, an undulating teal-green bridge. In *Downtown, Inc.*, Bernard J. Frieden and Lynne B. Sagalyn write, "The story of Horton Plaza is one of steady change in the character of the project, from an early plan dismissed as 'a suburban shopping center set on four levels of parking' to one of the most unconventional retail centers in the country—a blend of theme park, theaters and department stores in a compact, multilevel, open-air plan that left very few industry standards unbroken."

John Simones, the design director at Jerde Partnership and an employee since 1984, disagrees with that assessment. "Horton Plaza follows the rules of Retail 101—anchor on each end, one in the middle," he told me in a 2020 interview. "But it twisted it and created an adventure as you walked through. The idea of creating a journey and moving through a project became the idea of moving from a typical mall, a place of consumption, to a place of experience."

The most photographed section of Horton Plaza resembles a Sienese palazzo, with square sides and thick black, white, and terra-cotta banding like the cathedral in that Tuscan town. Jerde's version reads as more toylike because the materials are more cardboard than marble: stucco tinted a variety of colors and scored to look like the stone panels or stacked masonry of the Italian originals. The overscaled elements make the fakeness of the results clear—there's no attempt to make it appear authentic—so instead it resembles a collage blown up to city scale. When Walt Disney reproduced his Missouri childhood Main Street at Disneyland, he was trying to make the simulation feel real. Jerde set that ambition aside. Fake was fine; what he wanted to generate was the feeling of festival, of community, sharing the goals of Gruen, and then Rouse, but with a very different aesthetic.

The architect with the largest influence on Jerde's design for Horton Plaza was Charles W. Moore, who praised Disneyland in his 1965 essay "You Have to Pay for the Public Life" for its simulacrum of the Main Streets that so many sprawling California cities lacked, identifying the same problem as Bradbury did. Moore, who taught at UCLA from 1975 to 1985, was a popular and populist architect and theorist, whose work had an unusual undercurrent of joy. "Singlehanded," Moore wrote, Disneyland "is engaged in replacing many of those elements of the public realm which have vanished in the featureless private floating world of southern California."

Moore's own designs incorporated a variety of historicist and graphic elements, ranging from Corinthian colonnades to hand-painted signs, and he continuously played with level changes, interior windows, and big circular and arched cutouts in projects that ranged in scale from his own home in New Haven, Connecticut (where he was dean of the Yale School of Architecture for five years), to the Piazza d'Italia in New Orleans. The first project introduced disorienting views and theatrical displays into a historic house. The

Piazza d'Italia, completed in 1978, is a city-funded plaza centered on a large, shallow fountain shaped like that country, intended to knit together new retail, residential, and entertainment development in central New Orleans, like a mall atrium waiting for its bars of shops. It is easy to see how Moore's ideas might translate into retail environments, whether cut into the historic fabric of a city or introduced like a stage set into a place without landmarks of its own.

Moore was one of the foremost theorists and practitioners of the style known as postmodernism. As a response to the modernist white walls, grids, and glass that had dominated postwar American architecture, postmodernism was, for its partisans, an opportunity to explore the older visual language of classic and classical buildings for a new audience. Moore and contemporaries including Robert Venturi and Denise Scott Brown thought deeply about how to make architecture communicate. Venturi and Scott Brown had a special appreciation for the very roadside architecture that Gruen et al. described as a blight. They shrugged off judgment about the commercial, accepting it as a fact of American life, just as Moore had shrugged off judgment about Disney being too "theme park." Jerde and Moore knew each other in Los Angeles and shared a distaste for drawing lines between the commercial realm and so-called serious architecture.

Horton Plaza was a hit, with twenty-five million visitors in its first year. It launched Jerde Partnership as a designer of dreamscapes for consumers. Over the next decades, those dreamscapes would become larger and larger, incorporating first fragments of historic buildings, then whole neighborhoods, then the world. Horton Plaza, like the malls of old, was anchored by department stores. But as Jerde's spatial ideas caught on, more mall developers were willing to take a chance on a mall maker who promised chaos rather than certainty. He created retail projects with different types of anchors, tipping their target audience toward nightlife, entertainment, and flirtation, and away from wholesome family shopping trips.

As *Los Angeles Magazine* wrote, admiringly,

> In the late '80s Jerde rebuilt Del Mar Plaza as an Italian village. [Jerde] pried the lid off Newport Beach's enclosed Fashion Island, introduced colonnades and side streets and sidewalk cafes. For Euro-Disney he designed a "utopian suburb" with the density of Paris. His plans were scrapped, but he cribbed his EuroDisney ideas for CityWalk. "It's a great simulacrum of what L.A. should do," he says of his most controversial work. "This isn't the L.A. we did get, but it's the L.A. we could have gotten—the quintessential, idealized L.A."

Universal CityWalk, built in 1993 and designed by Jerde's firm, has a multiplex at one end and a Universal Studios theme park at the other, the two cinematic venues connected by a multilevel "street" of restaurants, shopping, and other entertainment venues. Originally CityWalk was to be just one street in a vast, Universal Studios–funded neighborhood, with other newly built streets themed around nightlife, shopping, and an artificial canal. Management and ownership shuffles at the studio meant that only the first

Universal CityWalk, Los Angeles, California, Jerde Partnership, 1994. (JERDE)

"walk" got built. CityWalk combines the stylings of twentieth-century L.A. architecture—including signs salvaged from demolished supermarkets, and references to Venice Beach and the Bradbury Building—with postmodern stripes, neon lights, and high-tech painted-metal elements. "The aesthetic of the 2010s seems more minimalist and tasteful, which can border on boring," commented Scott Gairdner, cocreator of a twenty-four-plus-hour 2019 podcast on CityWalk. "But the '90s and early 2000s have all the aesthetics yelling and screaming at each other."

A three-dimensional King Kong pops up at the halfway point, as the straight pathway changes to a semicircle between the stores, luring unsuspecting Fay Wrays farther down the route. Jerde always claimed *Blade Runner* as his inspiration: Ridley Scott's science fiction classic also makes an artifact out of twentieth-century L.A. In a 1998 lecture to students at the Southern California Institute of Architecture, Jerde described CityWalk's architecture as "a metaphorical LA," a visual answer to the futurist's question of what would happen "had LA kept going and gotten the density you find in other cities."

But while the aesthetics screamed fun, all the oversize gorillas in the world could not distract from the same governance questions found on other pedestrian streets. Observers saw CityWalk as a sanitized, "poverty-free" promenade that included a Los Angeles County sheriff's substation and on-site parking—a "walk" in name only, given that it was a branded, policed, and car-friendly space. Mike Davis, whose jaundiced take on the public realm in Los Angeles, *City of Quartz*, was published in 1990, was quoted describing the complex as an "ominous parallel universe" in a 1993 *Mother Jones* article: "MCA [Universal] executives have always stressed the most popular parts of L.A. are now too dangerous; the city scene is a criminalized Third World. So now they go off the real world to simulators."

In the *Harvard Design School Guide to Shopping*, Daniel Herman proposes the term "Jerde transfer" to follow on the "Gruen transfer." While Gruen pitched his malls as refuges from the chaos of the suburbs and downtrodden downtowns, lulling shoppers into a receptive state, Jerde introduced new chaos. "Jerde claims he is not interested in shopping. What really interests him is theater. He throws large amounts of architectural matter at the shopper: countless turns and counterturns, unlikely ramps stuck to soffits, thresholds over thresholds that dislodge the visitor of certainty, sending the 'keyed-up' over the top and into a drone state of consumption," Herman writes. The "fun house logic" of Horton Plaza or CityWalk breaks the visitor down by confusing her senses spatially, then luring her in to shop with sales, displays, and signs.

$$\rightarrow$$

During the 1970s a widening split developed between the commercial and academic branches of architecture. Malls ended up on the wrong side of the tracks: Good architects design museums; bad architects design malls. Jerde was highly sensitized to this split. In his 2002 *Los Angeles Magazine* profile, Jerde contrasted himself with Frank Gehry, an architect who made his career in L.A. at the same time, but who is today heralded as a genius rather than a sellout. Architect Rem Koolhaas even referred to Jerde as Gehry's evil twin.

And yet the early years of their careers were quite similar. Gehry worked for Gruen Associates and contributed to the design of Midtown Plaza in Rochester, as well as designing several California J. Magnin stores with other collaborators. Gehry designed a mall: Santa Monica Place, a Rouse project just off the Pacific Ocean, building on a 1960s Gruen master plan for the city that suggested pedestrianizing Third Street. Gehry and Rouse's first proposal was for a mixed-use neighborhood, with new low-rise retail buildings facing Santa Monica's existing streets and camouflaging the taller hotel and office towers inside the blocks, far less of a fortress than Midtown Plaza. What ended up getting built was closer to the classic shopping mall formula of two department stores and an interior street. Gehry's hand can be seen primarily in the parking garages—which were wrapped in what would become his signature chain-link fencing and emblazoned SANTA MONICA PLACE in two-story letters—and in moments like the entrance, a portal made of deconstructed and asymmetrical architectural elements.

Santa Monica Place, Santa Monica,
California, Frank Gehry and Associates,
1980. Renovated 2010. (Santa Monica
History Museum, Outlook Collection)

Gehry's Santa Monica design was cool and monochromatic, whereas Jerde's creations were hot and complex. Both architects were trying to create an enclosed urban mall that didn't ignore its location and was crossed by a diagonal pedestrian way, with pop-out spaces to pause and gather. As Crawford writes of the contrast in their styles, "Both utilize a profusion of bridges, terraces and screenlike elements with punctured openings to further complicate the space." Gehry, in what would become a signature move, also pushes the interior structure through the outside walls, taking "breaking up the facade" literally. The overall whiteness acted as a kind of camouflage, at least to critics, who read Gehry's mall as closer to high art than any of Jerde's projects. Consumers were less enthralled, and Rouse eventually added back in color, graphics, palm trees, and other elements of a typical mall. In 2010, Jerde Partnership was hired to do an extensive renovation, removing the roof and completely redesigning the interior.

After Santa Monica Place, Gehry swore off all commercial projects. In Paul Goldberger's biography of Gehry, *Building Art*, he relates a conversation between Gehry and Matt DeVito, chief executive of the Rouse Company, soon after the completion of Santa Monica Place in 1980.

> "Frank, you don't like Santa Monica Place, do you?" DeVito asked him.
>
> Frank did not want to offend DeVito, whom he genuinely liked, but he did not want to lie to him, either. "No," he said.
>
> "Why are you wasting your time and energy fighting with commercial developers when you really have a different mission in life?" DeVito asked. "Why don't you just do what you're good at?"

Goldberger positions Gehry's split from Rouse, and larger refusal of development work, as that of an iconoclast. By 1980, Rouse had already successfully teamed with the Thompsons and turned much of his company's attention toward festival marketplaces and adaptive reuse. "Benjamin Thompson was an architect more sophisticated than a typical shopping center architect but with none of Frank's desire to push the boundaries of architecture," Goldberger writes. While it is true that Ben Thompson never deconstructed anything, this definition of "pushing the boundaries" is largely aesthetic; what the Thompsons, with Rouse money, did to and for cities went distinctly against the grain, and his ground-up designs in Baltimore and South Street Seaport were striking examples of postmodernism in their time. Reading Goldberger (who, as a *New York Times* critic, praised Horton Plaza), you can see why Jerde, Thompson, and a raft of other commercial architects chafed at the hierarchies of the architecture profession.

Jeffrey Meikle provided a corrective to this attitude in his 1981 essay "The Malling of the Mall," which collects critics' takes on I. M. Pei's East Building on the National Mall in Washington. The East Building is the triangular, Tennessee marble–clad wing of the National Gallery, intended to hold the nation's collection of modern and contemporary art, and one of the first additions to the Mall in a modern style. It garnered immediate praise and then, as it got used, was criticized as partaking too much of the design of the shopping mall, with its central top-lit atrium (perfect for people-watching) and underground concourse with a fountain, moving sidewalk, and café/ food court popular with families. Pei, who had a long career in commercial design, would likely have had no issue with the comparison, but others weren't so generous. How could mass culture positively influence high culture? Martin Filler, discussing the East Building in a critics' roundtable for *Progressive Architecture*, outlines the building's effect succinctly:

> For in resembling nothing quite so much as the poshest of suburban shopping malls, the atrium of the East Building meets its visitors more than halfway in providing an experience that supplants the purported one of the building, much as the Pompidou Center, and not the art within it, has become the real tourist attraction . . . The building represents . . . the enshrinement on the mall of the atrium idea, the first resort of the architect who wishes to create "excitement" among the public.

Meikle points the snobby critics toward the past, where the arcade, the train shed, the exhibition hall, and eventually the museum all used glass roofs to cover a crowd. "Museum keepers have always to a certain extent acted as commercial showmen. It is a credit to the cultural shrewdness of the developers of the enclosed shopping mall that I. M. Pei adopted its major elements, however unintentionally, for a late-twentieth-century art museum."

Many histories of the mall begin with the Galleria Vittorio Emanuele II in Milan, built from 1865 to 1877 on that city's central piazza. On the east side of the piazza, the many-spired Gothic duomo, the religious crown of the city. On the north side, the neoclassical palace of shopping, the commercial pendant to all that religiosity. Northern Italy is hard and gray and business-like in a way that Rome could never be, and Milan is the capital of the Italian fashion industry, so it makes sense that shopping has both pride of place and pride of architecture at the city's center. While far from the first glass-roofed shopping arcade, this galleria became an international model, bestowing its name (easier for Anglophones to say than the French *galerie*) and its look—long glass barrel vault—on the second generation of shopping malls. The first generation tended to architectural blandness, and Gruen and his competitors found that exuberant exterior architecture didn't pay. The second generation, as Jerde realized, needed a way to separate themselves from the herd.

Jerde did this through flamboyance, both in exterior packaging and interior amenities. The idea was Italian hill town, or Hollywood soundstage, or oasis in the Midwestern tundra, as the location suggested. Other designers and developers chose more restrained approaches to making places people would remember and return to. For them, the Galleria Vittorio Emanuele provided a classic and *classy* point of reference, easily adapted to modern

Winter Garden at the World Financial Center, New York City, Cesar Pelli & Associates, landscape architect, Diana Balmori, 1988, restored 2002. (Pelli Clarke Pelli)

building technology that favored glass in all things. Jerde had nothing but disdain for the Galleria-ists, saying, of Los Angeles rival (and onetime Gruen design partner) Cesar Pelli that he "produc[es] buildings like a mayfly on steroids." Pelli designed the Winter Garden at the World Financial Center and a glass addition to the Museum of Modern Art at the same time—and his escalators were duly criticized as being too mall-like.

The first arcade in Europe was the Galeries de Bois in Paris, 1786. The first arcade in the United States was in Providence, Rhode Island, 1828. But these were relatively narrow, modest productions, with glass roofs spanning a distance no greater than that of a typical street. These "passages" became important gathering places and social nexuses in the same manner as department stores, their contemporaries, adding a layer of safety and clean-liness to the often anarchic and dirty street. They gestured at a future, more advanced city, employing new engineering technology to provide cover from weather and circulate air.

The combination of modernity and commerce was made explicit in the body of the Crystal Palace, the modular, cast-iron and plate-glass structure erected in London's Hyde Park to house the Great Exhibition of 1851. The glass enclosed 990,000 square feet of interior space, 1,851 feet long and 128 feet high, displaying technological wonders from around the world. It was the creation of Joseph Paxton, the gardener and landscape architect already internationally known for his design of one of the first public parks, at Birkenhead. In the Crystal Palace, Paxton fused the architecture of the conservatory—he had built several large, modular glass houses for the Duke of Devonshire at Chatsworth—with the urban strength and scale of the new iron train sheds.

Louise Wyman writes, "The Crystal Palace transformed the arcade concept from a glass-covered street to a glass building and a container of landscape." The street of the original arcades widens and relaxes to accom-modate plants, benches, cafés. It's impossible to imagine a mall without a central court and social spaces, and the Crystal Palace was the first to demon-strate that particular combination of qualities and to add desire on top. As Susan Buck-Morss writes in *The Dialectics of Seeing*, for those touring the exhibition, "the Crystal Palace blended together old nature and new nature—palms as well as pumps and pistons—in a fantasy world that entered the imagination of an entire generation of Europeans." The Crystal Palace eventually traveled to New York, where its architecture and contents provided a preview of the range of products and fantastic setting that first the department stores and then the malls would make commonplace. Shopping was the entertainment, when dressed accordingly.

As malls in America attempted a return to the city, a significant number adopted the major architectural move of the Galleria Vittorio Emanuele and its smaller brethren—the blocks-long steel-frame glass roof—as well as the name. There was Philadelphia's downtown Gallery, developed by Rouse, and many others that adopted the barrel vault, including Pelli's masterpiece, the Winter Garden. The American Galleria that most closely apes its ancestor is in Houston, at the center of the city's Post Oak neighborhood. Its architect was Gyo Obata, of the St. Louis megafirm HOK, who had also designed the National Mall's other 1970s modernist addition, the Air and Space Museum. The festival marketplaces and pedestrian malls of the 1970s demonstrated that urbanism could be manufactured whole cloth, through renovation

Neiman Marcus at The Galleria and Post Oak Tower, Houston, Texas, Hellmuth, Obata and Kassabaum (HOK), and Neuhaus & Taylor, 1969–1971. (HOK)

and rebranding; Houston's Galleria, built out in phases from 1970 to the present, demonstrated that a charismatic shopping center could spawn an entire mixed-use neighborhood, like Gruen's original plans for Southdale had intended, down to the high-density towers and forbidding local streets.

"It is because of the Galleria that Post Oak Boulevard replaced Main Street as the main shopping street of Houston in the 1970s," notes *SAH Archipedia*. "It is a regional shopping mall that so concentrated segments of the retail market that it could attract and support additional uses (such as hotels and office buildings) to become the kind of urban magnet that American downtowns had been from the 1870s to the 1970s." The authors add, "The Post Oak district was developed in the Galleria's image as an urban center that efficiently eliminated public space, public institutions, and their mixed constituencies to concentrate on consumerism." In other words, like Disneyland, like the pedestrian malls, like CityWalk, an attempt to create public life on private land.

The developer behind the Galleria was Gerald Hines, a trained engineer who turned a one-man development company into an international colossus. By 2020, the year of his death, the Hines company had built more than nine hundred projects around the world, including striking office buildings designed by Pei, Pelli, and Gehry. One of the best known is Pennzoil Place in downtown Houston, a sharp-edged two-tower complex designed by Philip Johnson and partner John Burgee and completed in 1976. "Corporations are today's equivalent of the Medici, or they can be," Hines said at the time of its completion. "What we've tried to do is create a way in which they can make some sort of real contribution to the quality of the city and yet not get sued by their stockholders. That's where Pennzoil will convince people—not because it's good architecture, but because it pays." Before and during the Pennzoil project, Hines was working with Obata to develop a new Medici-like prototype for the shopping mall. With the Galleria, as Richard West wrote in *Texas Monthly* in 1980, "Hines correctly predicted Houston's fantastic growth and realized that the sprawling city had to be cut down to several 'nodes,' human gathering points along the road, cosmopolitan islands of business and pleasure."

The first phase of the project was six hundred thousand square feet, a long dumbbell- or I-shaped building, on three floors, with a department store at either end and an ice rink on the lowest floor. The roof was glass, and long, open balconies allowed shoppers to look down on the rink, which was said to be inspired by the one at Rockefeller Center. Ice rinks soon became a standard amenity for top-tier malls. What better way to demonstrate victory over weather than winter in a hot climate? Along with taking one of New York's touristic icons as its centerpiece, the Galleria also looked to New York for its mixed-use amenities: a twenty-two-story Post Oak office tower, the four-hundred-room Houston Oaks Hotel, and the twenty-five-story Old Transco Tower. In 1971, the University Club moved into the fourth floor of the mall and added a running track around the outside of the skylight. Later phases, beginning in 1977, would add more mall and more towers, new residential units, and more offices and hotels, along with movie theaters, a bowling alley, and the all-important food court lining the sides of the ice rink. Meanwhile, outside the sprawling, connected indoor space of Gallerias I through V (completed in 2006), other enterprising developers added lower-rise multifamily housing and office parks.

West's *Texas Monthly* piece, titled "My Home, the Galleria," satirically suggested that life might be lived entirely inside the mall, as on a space station:

> It was after watching the ice skaters in the Galleria on the first scorching day of the year that Henry P. Upchurch decided he would never again endure a Houston summer or drive through city traffic. As he walked to his car, a wave of heat rising from the asphalt hit him like a blast from a smelting furnace. His shirt stuck to his back. His glasses fogged over and perspiration stung his eyes. He blistered his hand when he gripped the steering wheel. He waited in line thirty minutes before the West Loop–Westheimer traffic light granted him the privilege of joining the frantic freeway world of cloverleafs, lane changers, tailgaters, screaming sirens, honkers, and weavers. A week later Henry quit his job, sold his car, gave away his umbrella, checked into the Galleria Plaza hotel, opened an account at the Galleria Bank,

and became the first full-time resident of the world's first four-level self-contained city . . . The Galleria reminded Henry P. of the best of Manhattan and Las Vegas, where luxury was the common lot, where night and day blurred, where there was no need for clocks.

The mixed-use strategy that so many urban malls forgot works here, albeit for a high-dollar clientele that primarily arrives by car. In his obituaries, Hines got more notice for the stand-alone skyscrapers he developed, but his greater legacy may be his interest in tweaking the development formulas for the mall.

More recently, the collective density of development in the area around the Galleria, referred to as Uptown Houston, has spurred attempts to retrofit the outdoors for pedestrians. What was suburban has become urban, by virtue of all that building and Houston's ongoing expansion outward. Historically, new development had been set back twenty-five feet from Post Oak Boulevard, and that margin filled with parking, creating individual buildings, widely spaced, with few connections between them. In 1995 the district commissioned the local office of landscape architecture firm SWA to design a streetscape program, with narrow sidewalks lined with trees for shade, landscaped plazas at major intersections, and other visible signs of walkable city life. The elements that first the urban passages, then the Milanese Galleria, and then the Houston Galleria offered as a seed for the district—things to look at, temperature control, a protected environment—now returned to their original environment, the city street.

The Houston Galleria became, in a word, a world. A world with pleasures, to be sure, but primarily a world of work. As Jerde's projects began to achieve urban scale, he did not deviate from his idea that the center of city life was fun. "In America the last vestiges of community are a parade, a football game and a shopping center," Jerde has said. At the Mall of America (MOA), completed in the Minneapolis suburb of Bloomington, Minnesota, in 1992, he had the opportunity to design all three at once.

Inside the Mall of America was to be a perpetual carnival. What it replaced was a stadium: the original home of the Minnesota Twins and Vikings, who left for greener fields at the Metrodome downtown in 1982, leaving seventy-eight acres. (The same movement back to the city that encouraged the development of urban malls spurred a wave of urban stadiums.) The land was purchased by Bloomington Port Authority, which chose the mall bid over developers of office parks, residential enclaves, and a convention center. The project was always controversial, thanks to its $650 million cost and the public subsidy of the infrastructure serving the mall. The original pitch, called the Minnesota International Center, included eight hundred stores, twice the eventual number at opening, plus a theme park called Fantasy World, a convention center, two office towers, and an eighteen-story hotel—along with a twelve-story roller coaster, an eighteen-hole golf course, an ice rink, and an indoor lake, which visitors could tour by submarine. "Can you imagine, in January, you walk out of your house and you come and do surfing? This is what we're proposing for you today," Nader Ghermezian, part of the Iranian Canadian family that developed the MOA, said in 1985. The Minnesota International Center would have been more: more space, more attractions, more worlds. Just being the Mall of America was, in some ways, a comedown from the fantasy.

The Mall of America was one of a series of VERY BIG MALLS dreamed up in the 1980s. The impetus, again, was weather. Triple Five Group, an Edmonton development company founded by the Ghermezians, created the category as it developed the West Edmonton Mall (WEM) in the 1970s on the previously rural outskirts of their hometown. Albertan winters are long and cold, making existing indoor shopping malls an important part of the community landscape, and holiday escapes to warmer, sunnier climates are a prized local tradition. WEM provided both an escape from the weather and an escape from Canada under a single roof, with 800 shops, 110 restaurants, an ice rink, a lake, an amusement park, and a replica of Columbus's

Top, aerial view of the Mall of America, Bloomington, Minnesota, Jerde Partnership, 1992. *Bottom*, West Market. (JERDE)

Santa Maria floating in an artificial lagoon. The Fantasyland Hotel offered Polynesian and Hollywood rooms, and you could travel between parts of the mall in a horse-drawn carriage. Certain wings of the mall looked like streets in Paris and New Orleans, though the view from the high-rise hotel was of downtown Edmonton, not the Eiffel Tower. WEM, which opened in phases from 1981 to 1985, and received another steroidal addition in 1998, remains North America's largest mall at 5.2 million square feet, and was the largest in the world for its first twenty-four years of existence. As Nader Ghermezian said at the opening ceremony, "What we have done means you don't have to go to New York or Paris or Disneyland or Hawaii. We have it all here for you in one place, in Edmonton, Alberta, Canada!" Ghermezian used almost exactly the same line to sell doubtful Minnesotans on the idea, saying, at a 1986 news conference, "You will have all the shoppers from New York, Rome, Los Angeles and Paris coming here. I bring you the moon and you don't want it?"

There was no night sky at the Mall of America (been there, done that at Jerde's Fremont Street Experience in Las Vegas), but instead a vast rectangular skylight, crisscrossed and supported by white-painted open-frame steel girders. This was the type of ceiling system more often seen in convention centers and sports stadiums, and necessary to expose the mall's centerpiece, a seven-acre Camp Snoopy theme park, to hours of climate-controlled daylight. Around the theme park center, with its indoor roller coaster, tree-shaped spinners, carousels, windmills, and live trees and fake river rocks, the more ordinary assets of the shopping mall were arranged in a rectangle four and a half miles around, with a department store at each corner and a themed entrance at the center of each side.

As Deborah Karasov and Judith A. Martin write in their 1993 assessment titled "The Mall of Them All" in *Design Quarterly*, the MOA has actually absorbed and roofed "the usual shopping mall and smaller, peripheral malls, fast-foot outlets, multiplex theaters, and bars. Only the spaces that normally separate these businesses have been condensed; the four-to-six-lane highways have been replaced by forty-to-fifty-foot interior streets." And while the four entrances have been designed as if they were downtown, with distinct porticoes and a smattering of street furniture, most people enter from the mall's enclosed parking garages, connected by skyways, which flank and increase the buildings' bulk.

In the mall's initial configuration, each of the four internal streets was themed, decorated, and roofed differently. West Market had the familiar barrel vault of many galleries, and an international-market theme with carts and small sellers. North Garden had trellises and climbing vines, like the French Quarter transplanted to the cold north. South Avenue was posh; East Broadway, "high energy" and contemporary, with neon accents. To circulate between the four quadrants was to visit America's top tourist cities in a day. After dark, lights came on in Camp Snoopy's trees, and diners at the California Café could pretend they were outside; they could also get a drink or three on the so-called Upper East Side, a separate after-hours section of the mall featuring a comedy club, a Hooters, and the Gatlin Brothers' Music City/Grille.

Karasov and Martin find all the theming sadly wanting. "All are American experiences," they quote from the architects' promotional materials, but the impressions of other cities are twice removed, rendered in inexpensive and mundane materials, designed to make the long halls bearable but not memorable. "There is little to surprise or delight the sophisticated visitor," they write. "The color, texture, and fantasy that the Jerde Partnership brought to its Southern California projects, such as Newport Beach's Fashion Island or San Diego's Horton Plaza, are missing here," in favor of what they call a "familiar and nonthreatening" look. In trying to be all things to all Americans, the slightly wild joy of Jerde's work got lost. Or maybe it was simply too much space under glass.

It's also instructive to read the contemporary coverage of the opening. In Neal Karlen's analysis in the *New York Times*, "Gruen languishes in the rogue's gallery reserved for those pioneers of plastic consumerism who gave America everything from aerosol cheese to Astroturf." He cites consumer surveys, conducted in 1990, that suggest shopping no longer appeals as a leisure activity, with the monthly average time spent in malls dropping from twelve hours in 1980 to four in 1990. Big-box stores had begun to eat into mall sales and, as Karlen wrote, developers like Melvin Simon and Triple Five Group had turned back to Gruen's original destination idea: "They have tried to create a space that can make the megamall a destination, an idealized community, fun." You can hear the sneer. Meanwhile, 150,000 people showed up the first day and, through the mall's twenty-fifth anniversary in 2017, 42 million had visited. "I remember walking towards the entrance the morning we opened and seeing all these faces pressed up against the glass," Maureen Bausch, MOA's first publicist said at the anniversary. "That's when I knew for certain it was going to be super successful." Even Karlen admitted, "From the epicenter near Camp Snoopy, it felt like an ecstatic mall rave, the staccato ka-ching of thousands of cash registers serving as the high-frequency techno-beat for hundreds of thousands of Midwest shoppers."

In the more recent past, Triple Five attempted to relaunch the VERY BIG MALL for the twenty-first century with American Dream in New Jersey. Hobbled by financial problems, construction delays, and slow leasing, American Dream finally opened its first "Chapter" in October 2019, with an ice rink and a Nickelodeon-themed amusement park. A ski run opened that December. A planned March 2020 opening for the standard parts of the mall—department stores, restaurants, Asian American supermarket chain H Mart—was thwarted by the pandemic. Early reports made American Dream sound eerily absent, like a zombie movie waiting to happen, without the crowds that a full-dress opening would have brought in. In the *New York Times*, Amanda Hess referred to it as "a post-shopping mall," with half its space allotted to entertainment rather than retail. Jerde and the Ghermezians would beg to differ, even if it is now in both their interests for the entertainment mall to be seen as the *new* new thing. "No, it is not a mall," she concludes. "It's a performance piece ruminating on the corporate takeover of nature and society. The name—American Dream—is both unnerving and absolutely correct." But based on my visit almost eighteen months later, I would argue that the shopping mall was ever thus, a corporate takeover of what should by rights be public space, and that the privatization of what were once communal places and activities is at the heart of the original postwar American dream. American Dream just makes it bigger. In doing so, this mall physically and psychologically fractures the human relationships that once bridged the gap between shopping and sociability.

→

On December 20, 2014, two thousand to three thousand Black Lives Matter protesters stood beneath a pair of silvery multistory Christmas trees at the Mall of America and chanted, "Hands up! Don't shoot!" Protest organizers had been warned earlier in the week that they could be arrested and banned from the property for a year. Within moments of the beginning of the chants, the giant screen mounted between the trees announced in blue block caps: THIS DEMONSTRATION IS NOT AUTHORIZED AND IS IN CLEAR VIOLATION OF MALL OF AMERICA POLICY.

"While you're on your shopping spree, Black people cannot breathe," chanted the protesters in response.

Ultimately, twenty-five were arrested and charged with misdemeanors including trespassing. Protesters felt it was worth it: Where in Minneapolis could they get more attention than the Mall of America on the weekend before Christmas?

The battle over the public role of malls, often in conflict with the private nature of their ownership, has been playing out for eight decades, both in atriums and in the courts. In 1943, Grace Marsh stood outside the post office in Chickasaw, Alabama, and tried to hand out copies of the *Watchtower*, the official magazine of the Jehovah's Witnesses. Marsh was a minister for the church, and a tenet of their faith—embodied by the word "witness" in the name—was the promise to proselytize in person. On most other American Main Streets, with their laundromats and five-and-dimes, Marsh's witness would have been protected by the First Amendment, as handing out religious pamphlets is both an act of free speech and free exercise of religion. But Chickasaw wasn't just any Alabama town: It was built and owned by the Gulf Shipbuilding Corporation, and the officer who arrested her was not hired by the county or state but by Gulf. Marsh sued to overturn her conviction for criminal trespass, and her case made it to the U.S. Supreme Court in the winter of 1945–1946. In *Marsh v. Alabama*, the majority ruled in Marsh's favor.

"Ownership does not mean absolute dominion," wrote Justice Hugo L. Black. "The more an owner, for his advantage, opens up his property for use by the public in general, the more do his rights become circumscribed by the statutory and constitutional rights of those who use it." Because Chickasaw, located just outside Mobile, was open for business for anyone from the region, because its Main Street looked just like any other Main Street in the region, it had to be open to activities protected on any public sidewalk. The rights of the corporation, when the corporation was building urban infrastructure, did not trump the rights of the individual. Because of its attempt to define downtown—to codify an idea of the protections that Main Streets conferred—*Marsh* has become the precedent for sixty years of legal debate about what the mall owes to its shoppers.

Between Christmas 1943 and Christmas 2014, federal and state supreme courts returned, time and again, to the question of whether privately owned shopping malls, representing the middle to late twentieth-century equivalent of the company town, could be spaces of protest. Supreme Court justice Thurgood Marshall was among the first to understand and defend the central role malls would play in American public life. Downtown wasn't just for business; it was a platform for free speech and free assembly, he argued, connecting his work as a civil rights lawyer for the NAACP to his work as a liberal justice on the Supreme Court. If business moved to the suburbs, speech ought to go with it.

The first of these cases was *Amalgamated Food Employees Union v. Logan Valley Plaza*, for which Marshall wrote the majority opinion in 1968. Logan Valley Plaza was a neighborhood shopping center, anchored by a Weis supermarket and a Sears store, that opened in Altoona, Pennsylvania, on December 8, 1965. The supermarket hired nonunion workers to stock shelves and run checkout counters, setting up a conflict with the local Chapter of the Amalgamated Food Employees Union. A week after the shopping center opened, union members began picketing the pavement outside the entrance to the supermarket. The owners of the plaza and Weis sued to prevent ongoing pickets, shunting the protesters to berms along the public roads feeding the parking lot.

The Pennsylvania Supreme Court upheld the rights of the owners, and the charges of trespassing on private property; the U.S. Supreme Court disagreed. "We start from the premise that peaceful picketing carried on in a location open generally to the public is, absent other factors involving the purpose or manner of the picketing, protected by the First Amendment," Marshall wrote. "The shopping center here is clearly the functional equivalent of the business district of Chickasaw involved in *Marsh*."

In subsequent Supreme Court cases, *how* embedded the mall had become in the town's public life became a recurring topic. In *Amalgamated*, the shopping center's proximity to public roads, and the lack of sidewalks on those roads, came into play. If the shopping center was inviting the public in, and using publicly funded infrastructure for access, it could not then pick and choose which members of the public were allowed to use its spaces. It also could not screen out public protest through design by forcing picketers onto berms never intended for occupation.

Justice Marshall foresaw that ongoing suburban development would create only more situations like that of the Amalgamated union workers: a built environment that limited protest through its form. While businesses that remained downtown, served by public sidewalks and streets, would remain open to protest, were Logan Valley to win in the case, businesses in the suburbs could wall themselves off "from similar criticism by creating a *cordon sanitaire* of parking lots around their stores," Marshall wrote.

The economic development of the United States in the last 20 years reinforces our opinion of the correctness of the approach taken in *Marsh*. The large-scale movement of this country's population from the cities to the suburbs has been accompanied by the advent of the suburban shopping center, typically a cluster of individual retail units on a single large privately owned tract. It has been estimated that, by the end of 1966, there were between 10,000 and 11,000 shopping centers in the United States and Canada, accounting for approximately 37% of the total retail sales in those two countries . . .

Without this decision, suburban businesses could wall themselves off from workers' challenges on multiple fronts—including minority discrimination.

It was not difficult in the context of 1968 for Marshall to imagine other kinds of protest that might take place on mall grounds, over employment, over civil rights, over war. By the late 1960s, downtown pedestrian malls and early adaptive-reuse projects like Ghirardelli Square had already begun to blur the boundaries between business interest and public interest in existing downtown areas, while civil rights protests were dominating city streets and university campuses.

Writing for the minority, Justice Byron White reacted negatively to Marshall's characterization of Logan Valley Plaza as equivalent to the Chickasaw downtown. "The invitation is to shop for the products which are sold," he wrote, and only to shop. But the architects and developers of the shopping mall had always planned around central greens, sculpture, and covered walks. Neither the Gruen transfer nor the Jerde transfer would be possible if what happened in malls were just shopping.

Four years later, a more conservative-dominated Supreme Court reversed course. Marshall, writing for the minority in *Lloyd Corp., Ltd., v. Tanner*, painstakingly describes all the ways that the Lloyd Center, a Portland, Oregon, shopping mall, engaged with the public economically and programmatically. In 1954, when the owners of the Lloyd Center acquired the land from the city of Portland, for example, the city council called it "a general retail business district" when agreeing to de-map eight acres of public streets. The mall owners offered the Girl and Boy Scouts and American Cancer Society free use of the on-site auditorium and allowed charities to solicit donations for veterans at Christmas. Political use was forbidden, except when the mall invited the 1964 presidential candidates to speak there, arguing "that our convenient location and setting would provide the largest audience [the candidates] could attract in Oregon." Marshall creates a chain of evidence establishing that the Lloyd Corporation was open to political speech and public meetings, but only when the owners got to choose the participants. Marshall wrote,

> For many persons who do not have easy access to television, radio, the major newspapers, and the other forms of mass media, the only way they can express themselves to a broad range of citizens on issues of general public concern is to picket, or to handbill, or to utilize other free or relatively inexpensive means of communication. The only hope that these people have to be able to communicate effectively is to be permitted to speak in those areas in which most of their fellow citizens can be found.

For a moment, a justice sounded very much like an architecture critic. Marshall's argument here recalls a significant moment in Charles Moore's "Public Life" essay. One of Moore's tests, as he searches for centers in Southern California life, is to ask of towns, Where would protest need to be to get attention? Marshall thinks it would have to happen at the mall. Moore thinks it would need to be either the freeway (where Black Lives Matter protests would also occur) or Disneyland. Moore writes, "Of course Disneyland, in spite of the skill and variety of its enchantments, does not offer the full range of public experience. The political experience, for instance, is not manifested here, and the place would not pass our revolution test."

After *Lloyd* and a similar anti-protest decision in the 1975 case *Hudgens v. National Labor Relations Board*, the debate about the publicness of the mall moved to the states. In 1980, in *Robins v. Pruneyard Shopping Center*, the California Supreme Court affirmed that the California state constitution protects free speech and petitioning in shopping centers even when they are privately owned. The U.S. Supreme Court agreed and, as Jennifer Niles Coffin writes in "The United Mall of America," "extended an express invitation to state courts to interpret the free speech provisions within their state constitutions more broadly than the First Amendment by granting protection of speech in shopping malls." Today, only a handful of states, including California, Colorado, Massachusetts, New Jersey, and Oregon, affirm the right of free speech in shopping malls.

The Minnesota Supreme Court first reviewed the question in 1999's *State of Minnesota v. Wicklund,* which considered the rights of antifur protesters at—where else?—the Mall of America. Literature about the MOA had promoted the complex, which by the 1990s had grown to 4.2 million square feet, as having "city streets," serving as a "town square," and acting as a "city within a city." So, too, had the mall's construction been funded by $105 million in tax-increment financing bonds for site preparation, new roads and utilities, and access ramps and pedestrian bridges. Its 1999 amenities included a public school, a branch of a private university, and a police substation, while local police officers were paid time and a half to serve as mall security. Nonetheless, the court ruled in favor of the mall's owners and rejected the rights of protesters to picket Macy's for selling fur.

The most eloquent defense of the mall's public role came from New Jersey chief justice Robert Wilentz, writing in 1994 for the majority in *New Jersey Coalition Against War in the Middle East v. JMB Realty Corp.* The defendants, in this case, were ten large regional malls in northern New Jersey that sought to prevent leafleting by protesters against the Iraq War. He demolishes the idea that a shopping center in 1990s New Jersey could be just for commerce:

> As the owners of land-based shopping malls who have, by design and demographic accident, replaced the traditional town square, profit from the human need for physical community, they should also be required to pay the minimal cost of providing a space for real public discourse, unmediated by corporate sponsorship.

Justice Wilentz's opinion itemized the many ways the New Jersey shopping malls had already taken over the traditional role of the commons, but his examples weren't even the most extensive listing of how public facilities and private profits had become intertwined. In case after case, state courts

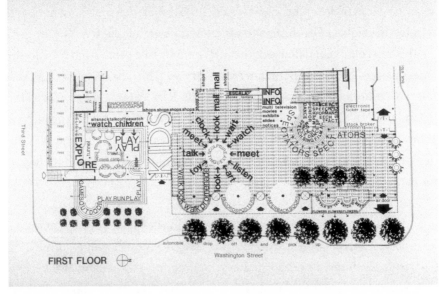

Top, the Commons, Columbus, Indiana, Cesar Pelli for Gruen Associates, 1973. Demolished 2008. (Gruen Associates) *Bottom*, verbal plan of the Commons. (Pelli Clarke Pelli Architects)

found that the common areas of malls—atriums, hallways, landscaped walkways, and food courts—had become the town square, both through adjacency to public services and through a lack of alternatives. If you needed to see people, you had to go to the mall.

The recognition that the mall had become the equivalent of the town square provoked the building of a few experimental shopping centers intended to be more self-consciously public. The most interesting of these is the Commons and Courthouse Center in Columbus, Indiana, completed in 1976. The project connected a privately owned shopping center, which included a Sears and a two-screen cinema, to a city-owned two-acre indoor space, with a free indoor playground, mixed seating, a performance stage, and an exhibition gallery. These varied uses were all wrapped in one of architect Cesar Pelli's signature glass skins, this one whiskey-colored, rising to several triangular peaks. The Commons met the challenge of urban messiness from a different angle, adding a public garden to a shopping mall under the aegis of progressive urban planning.

In the 1976 *Progressive Architecture* story "Piazza, American Style," critic John Morris Dixon set the scene: "From its seedy downtown to its highway commercial strips, Columbus looked all too much like any Midwestern town of about 30,000." But Columbus, Indiana, was not just any Midwestern town. Starting in 1954, the Cummins Foundation—underwritten by the town's largest employer and its visionary chairman and CEO, J. Irwin Miller— offered to pay the architectural fees for new public buildings if their designers were chosen from a list of distinguished national practices. The result was a postwar building boom in superlative modern architecture, from schools and fire stations to the post office and city hall. Eero Saarinen, a close friend of Miller's, designed two churches, a bank, and two houses for the Miller family, and advised on the list of architects for public commissions. Pelli already knew Miller and the town well from an early-career stint in Saarinen's Detroit-area office.

By the early 1970s, it seemed that business on Washington Street, the town's main retail strip, would be eviscerated by competition from suburban malls. Miller's Irwin Management Company tasked Pelli—by this point

L.A.-based and working for Gruen Associates—with creating a commercial building that would match the adventurous spirit of Columbus's midcentury buildings. The Commons (which soon became the accepted name for the entire two-block, 240,000-square-foot complex) set out to be a different type of mall. Rather than enclosing a central atrium in layers of shops, it put its two-acre public space out front on Washington Street, and used the movement of children in an elaborate indoor playground and a specially commissioned kinetic sculpture, Jean Tinguely's *Chaos I*, to draw people in. On the project's most trafficked corner, a fifteen-foot-wide "air door" was intended to stay open during business hours so that residents could flow seamlessly from the exterior to the interior sidewalk.

"This is not a mall," Pelli told interviewer Michael J. Crosbie. "It is more like a downtown living room."

> Miller asked what would happen in this space. I told him that I wanted it to function for late 20th century America like a piazza functioned for 17th century Italy. Mostly it would be a great place where people would come, read the paper, have a cup of coffee, meet with friends. But occasionally something will happen there that will bring in people from the whole town.

It sounds much like the bustling plazas that inspired Ray Bradbury's visions of "Somewhere To Go." A "verbal plan" for this public room describes those activities in detail. The blueprint shows half-round banquettes by the front door overlaid with the words "sit talk sit talk" and "watch sit." The playground, carpeted in green artificial turf and including a red fiberglass "play tank," is filled with action verbs: "explore," "crawl," "climb," "run." *Chaos I* is a nexus for activities for the old and young: "toy," "talk," "clock," "art," "look." Stretching off to the west, down the spine of the commercial part of the Commons, it reads "mall mall mall," "shops shops shops." This verbal plan offers excellent shorthand for each of Pelli's signature public rooms, with the proportion of art to play, shops to sitting, talking to looking, changing in each case.

The financial arrangement was also different: Irwin and his wife, Xenia Miller, along with Irwin's sister, Clementine Tangeman, paid for the construction of the public part of the Commons, including the Tinguely sculpture, while a private mall developer coordinated the tenants for the larger commercial space. The donors also agreed to make up deficits for the running of the space through 1977, hoping that the programming, kiosks, and rental fees could support its care and maintenance. This proved to be wishful thinking. The space was never self-supporting, and free-and-easy use of the playground conflicted with closures for performances, while the supposedly flexible lighting systems and projection screens proved difficult to manage. Like many all-purpose spaces, the Commons attempted to serve so many masters that it served none of them well—except for generations of children who remember *Chaos I* and the chaos of the playground with deep fondness. When the Commons was torn down in 2008 and replaced with a blander, more community-center-like building, one element that was replicated was a free indoor play structure.

But the idea of a mall without the mall, an atrium without a ring of shops, an interior space that's intended for a public regardless of ability to purchase, has proved durable despite the Commons' limited tenure. Pelli revised and glamorized the idea for the Winter Garden at the World Financial Center, which, while privately owned, has come to function as a true commons for those who live and work in Battery Park City since its opening in 1988. The 120-foot-high glass room, softened by sixteen 45-foot-tall palm trees selected by Pelli's partner, landscape architect Diana Balmori, was originally designed to link four new office towers built by Olympia & York. The Winter Garden was damaged by falling debris from the World Trade Center on September 11, 2001, and served as a triage center in the immediate aftermath of the attack. Brookfield Properties spent fifty million dollars to reopen the Winter Garden a year later, a testimony to lower Manhattan's resilience and the important role the forty-five-thousand-square-foot space had come to play downtown.

In late 2019, the Dutch city of Groningen opened the Forum, a €101 million project, envisioned as ten public squares stacked on top of one another and connected by escalators. As the *Guardian* put it, "It's a new-look department store that doesn't actually sell very much," paid for by the city. The Forum contains a six-screen cinema, a museum of comics, cafés, a rooftop restaurant and bar, and an auditorium and exhibition halls, along with a library of books for rent that spans several floors. One floor is cut out to support a room-size net, combining lounge space and playground. Designed by up-and-coming NL Architects, a firm based in Amsterdam, the Forum has the spare, crisp aesthetics of many new libraries and museums, with a minimum of messages. You are made welcome, the architects say, by no lines, no advertising, no security, and no expectation of purchase. Sit where you want. The architects even use the same language as Pelli, telling *Dezeen*, "We hope it will become a kind of living room for the locals."

The promise of shopping malls was that commerce would support community. But experiments like the Commons, and now the Forum, have proved possible only in societies or localities with robust public or philanthropic funding for public space. Architects like Jon Jerde, at one end of the aesthetic spectrum, and Cesar Pelli, at the other, spent the 1970s and 1980s trying to expand the template set by Gruen into something truly urban and truly communitarian over the armature of commerce. Adding entertainment, adding a specific sense of place, adding the scale and mixed-use amenities of a "real" city—all aimed to revivify what some saw as the fading market for malls in the 1980s. The simple narrative of shops arranged around a village green developed into light shows, hill towns, and skylights worthy of the Great Exhibition: the world under glass. With that came worldly expectations, still unmet, that the mall might replace the Main Streets it sent under.

Country Club Plaza, Kansas City, Missouri, c. 1945, designed by Edward Buehler Delk, was one of the first planned suburban shopping centers in the United States. (Missouri Valley Special Collections, Kansas City Public Library, Kansas City, Missouri)

Northland in Southfield, Michigan, completed in 1954, was Victor Gruen's first attempt to build a suburban Main Street. *Totem* by Gwen Lux, a sculpture in the shopping center's North Court, served as a popular meeting spot. (Gruen Associates)

"Every day will be a perfect shopping day" at Southdale, opened in 1956 and considered the first enclosed shopping center in the United States. The central atrium was named the "Garden Court of Perpetual Spring" and featured an aviary. (Gruen Associates)

Raymond and Patsy Nasher and their three daughters on opening day of NorthPark Center, Dallas, Texas, August 19, 1965. (Nancy Nasher is at center.) The shopping mall, one of few still under family ownership, remains one of the country's most beautiful and most profitable. (NorthPark Center)

Lawrence Halprin & Associates's playable fountain, located just outside the Neiman Marcus at NorthPark, was soon joined by dozens of other modern artworks purchased by the Nashers. (NorthPark Center)

Developer James Rouse and designers Ben and Jane Thompson teamed up to re-develop historic Faneuil Hall and Quincy Market in Boston, Massachusetts, which created a vogue for "festival marketplaces." (Photograph by Steve Rosenthal © Historic New England, from the Steve Rosenthal Collection of Commissioned Work at Historic New England)

Rouse and the Thompsons collaborated again on Harborplace, opened in 1980, and built from scratch as part of a massive redevelopment of Baltimore, Maryland's Inner Harbor. (Photograph by Steve Rosenthal © Historic New England, from the Steve Rosenthal Collection of Commissioned Work at Historic New England)

Even as Victor Gruen and his associates were building new town squares for the suburbs, they proposed big changes to save center cities, including the pedestrianization of downtown Fort Worth, drafted in 1956. (Gruen Associates)

While most malls serve as de facto public space, the Commons in Columbus, Indiana, included a community playground, a flexible exhibition space, and a kinetic sculpture by Jean Tinguely, *Chaos I* (1974). Demolished 2008. (Gruen Associates)

California architect Jon Jerde treated the mall as an entertainment destination, and shopping as a sideline, beginning with the outdoor Horton Plaza, built in downtown San Diego, California, in 1985. Partially demolished 2020–2021. (Photograph by Stephen Simpson; JERDE)

More sober malls, built in the 1970s and after, took their name and their design from the glass-roofed Galleria Vittorio Emanuele II in Milan; this one is in Houston, Texas, designed by Hellmuth, Obata and Kassabaum (HOK), and Neuhaus and Taylor, 1969–1971. (Photograph by Bob Rowan/Getty Images)

Cher and Christian on the escalators, *Clueless* (1995). The quintessential 1990s teen movie shot a key scene of adolescent belonging at Westfield Fashion Square, Los Angeles, designed by Welton Becket & Associates and Burke, Kober, and Nikolai, 1962. Enclosed 1990. (Paramount Pictures)

Owings Mills Mall outside Baltimore, designed by RTKL Associates Inc. in 1986, was cannibalized by a bigger, newer mall and demolished in 2016. (Abandoned America/Matthew Christopher)

Hudson Yards's "vertical retail center" opened in 2019 on Manhattan's Far West Side. The design, by Kohn Pedersen Fox (KPF) and Elkus Manfredi, ignores many of the lessons of community gathering space and food-as-magnet pioneered by horizontal malls. (Photograph by Max Touhey)

The developers of the Mall of America hoped for another hit with the three-million-square-foot American Dream in East Rutherford, New Jersey, which opened just before the pandemic and includes a skating rink, a ski slope, a theme park, and this Dreamworks Water Park. (Photograph by Ross Mantle)

Chapter 5
Whose Mall Is It Anyway?

N ineteen-fifties depictions of adolescence had teens strolling Main Street and hanging out at the soda shop. Nineteen-nineties teens got dropped off at the mall and hung out at the food court. A popular parenting manual by Anthony E. Wolf, first published in 1995 and updated in 2002, was titled *Get Out of My Life, but First Could You Drive Me and Cheryl to the Mall?* For children growing up in car-dominated landscapes, the mall offered the first opportunity for independent movement, the first opportunity for independent consumption, and the first opportunity to make their own money, through entry-level retail jobs. Teen purchasing increased by almost 43 percent during the 1980s and, pre-online gaming and internet shopping, there was only one place to spend it. In *The Malling of America*, published in 1985, author William Severini Kowinski asserts, "Teenagers in America now spend more time in the mall than anywhere else but home and school." I was one of those teens: searching for my own style at the Gap and my own reading material at B. Dalton, meeting up with friends at the multiplex and fretting over whether we would be allowed into R-rated movies, nervously ferrying my babysitting charge to the mall soon after I got my driver's license. Other friends born in the 1970s worked the wrapping counter at Christmas, skated the parking ramp, learned to fold better than any machine. The mall was our practice city, training wheels for the real world.

In this period young adults' "appropriation of the mall was so ubiquitous that it gave rise to a designation that linked the teen generation with a building typology—mall rats (males) and bunnies (females)," writes Susan Nigra Snyder. "For white, middle-class teenagers, the mall became a parent-approved, safe alternative to declining downtowns," a place to see and be seen while riding the escalators and overlooking the atrium. While downtown Chapel Hill then, and downtown Durham today, offered food and films and window-shopping, our parents felt better if we were at the mall, where the threats of cars and crime were less, and our limited budgets could buy us more. Pre-pandemic, my tween niece wandered the Streets at Southpoint with her friends while her mother whiled away the time at a café—there if needed, but out of sight.

At the mall they (and I) found an "alternate world" in which good teens held the center—the atrium—and troublemakers held the edges: the underlit halls outside the video game arcade and the edges of the parking lot. They (and I) didn't have to buy anything to be there, though we could peruse the trappings of different identities available for sale. But teens who didn't conform to mall managers' ideas of good behavior, or store owners' ideas of good consumers, soon realized they were under surveillance. The structures that allowed parents to feel safe dropping off their teenagers—including enclosure, lighting, and public-facing spaces, as well as private mall security—were also used to corral and criminalize them.

Teens weren't, and aren't, alone in their desire for a gentler public realm. While teens and their parents use the mall as a dry run of independence, the same features also provide an ADA-accessible option for people with different limitations on their mobility. Car-dominated landscapes provide scant protection for older adults in need of exercise and socialization, isolating people in single-family homes and neighborhoods with limited sidewalks and public parks. This lack of infrastructure, combined with infrequent curb cuts, benches and bathrooms, can also make it difficult for people with physical disabilities to navigate independently. Malls, created to fill in the blanks between highway systems and residential enclaves, now fill in a blank for senior citizens, with early hours set aside for another group named after the building: mall walkers. Protection from weather, protection from traffic, smooth surfaces, automatic doors and elevators, and abundant bathrooms make malls an improvement on the outdoors for those who can ill afford a trip or an expensive gym. After their exercise, convenient food options serve the purpose of the sidewalk café.

The appropriation of the mall's various spaces by these temporally, racially, and economically diverse groups has often created a conflict, however, between the commercial imperative and the people who want to use them every day. When the ideal mallgoer of the 1950s was a young married woman, ready to stock her new suburban single-family home, mall owners understood that to get the women to spend more time (and more money), you also had to provide space for her children. Victor Gruen and Elsie Krummeck's design for Milliron's department store in Los Angeles included a nursery on the top level, just off the rooftop parking lot, and the first wave of suburban malls also catered to the mothers of small children. In *Operation Shopping Centers*, a 1961 handbook for developers published by the Urban Land Institute, the Old Woman in the Shoe nursery at Park Central Shopping City in Phoenix is labeled "best in class," with a four-room cottage erected in the corner of the mall parking lot, each room set up for a different age group. Payment for the service was like a parking validation: spend more than three dollars at any store in the mall and get one free hour of babysitting.

Those baby boom babies would become teenagers, and initially the mall also wanted to be the place to be for older children. *Operation Shopping Centers* suggests that malls throw teenage block parties (moving a neighborhood social event to privatized space), sponsored by record companies that could supply recording stars, entice local DJs, and offer soft drinks and hot dogs to the crowd. At the nursery, and the corporate block party, the parental credit card hovered in the background. These events were less about what teens wanted and more about how to corral their energy and channel their consumerism.

Adolescent moods and adolescent enthusiasms wouldn't stay put. By the 1980s cultural change had begun to break down those fences. Women were more likely to be working during the day—at the mall or elsewhere—than to be looking for a space to spend their free time. Older children were more likely to be dropped off for supervision by the mall as an entity than to be signed into a nursery or signed up for organized activities. Teen media of the era, particularly movies, included scenes of strolling the mall over and over again, from *Bill & Ted's Excellent Adventure* to *Fast Times at Ridgemont High* to *Smooth Talk* to *Valley Girl*, scenes that would be referenced and replayed in 1990s and 2000s teen entertainment including *Mallrats, Mean Girls*, and *The OC*. Arcade games replaced sock hops, food courts replaced tea parties. New mall policies, including curfews and parental escort rules, would attempt to cage the mall rats and police their spending. The vulnerable people who most needed the mall were a challenge to its conventions.

A stepped, centralized seating area appears, in one form or another, in most malls built in the 1980s. Sometimes there's a fountain. Sometimes there are plants. Sometimes there is a sculpture. If the mall is multilevel, skylights illuminate the space from above. Escalators traveling between floors make for easy, surreptitious people-watching. Is my friend hanging out at the mall? Is my crush? This is the atrium, the most important interior space of the mall for the adolescent both architecturally and psychologically.

The earliest indoor shopping malls, with their I-shaped, bowling-alley forms, had no centralized place where groups could gather, nor much need for one. But by the early 1970s, and the advent of more complexly laid-out malls in T-, X-, or O-shapes, patrons might wander forever, missing each other in the long, low-ceilinged identical halls. Hence the atrium, which has its own storied architectural history: Ancient Roman houses were centered on open-air or skylit spaces, which provided daylight and breezes to the rooms surrounding them. These courts often had an impluvium, or fountain, to catch rainwater from the roof, as well as furnishings for outdoor entertaining. In the shopping mall, the atrium serves a similar function, opening up the middle of a building lined with windowless shops; letting in light, water, and plants; and furnished like a living room. The atrium was the center of the social life of the Roman domus and so, too, has it been the center of mall sociability. Gruen envisioned Southdale as an ersatz town green and, indeed, some of that civic sensibility remains in the symmetry and greenery of mall atriums. But the theatrical aspect of circumnavigating, posing, or performing in that centralized space makes this green seem more like the gossipy New England of Peyton Place than the buttoned-up town squares of earlier American depictions.

In the 2008 book *Hanging Out and the Mall*, consumption scholar Jennifer Smith Maguire describes teenagers perched along the second-floor railings around the atrium of the pseudonymous Mountain Mall in Ontario, Canada, grouping themselves to take advantage of the lookout at peak times after school and on Friday and Saturday evenings. Other teens describe choosing a spot on one of the benches in the middle of the mall, where they can see the maximum number of people walking by. The teen gossips comment on the other patrons, creating an intimate bubble of gibes and put-downs within the white noise of other conversations and the mall's Muzak.

Shopping at Old Orchard Mall in *Mean Girls* (2004). Shot at Sherway Gardens Mall, Etobicoke, Ontario, 1971. (Paramount Pictures/Photofest)

A friend who works with Bronx teens told me that his students like to take the subway to Bryant Park in Manhattan: That open green space, surrounded by national brand-name stores, with coffee kiosks on the corners and a carousel, serves as their stand-in for a suburban mall.

The importance of the mall's central atrium to teen life is reflected in the way teens occupy malls on film. In *Clueless*, director Amy Heckerling's 1995 update of Jane Austen's *Emma*, heroine Cher Horowitz (Alicia Silverstone) shares the self-delusion and queen-bee fashion sense of her nineteenth-century counterpart. Where Austen's heroine encounters strangers on the high street and in millinery shops, Heckerling's frequents Westfield Fashion Square and Contempo Casuals. Westfield Fashion Square is a long, narrow, three-story mall, topped with a glass barrel vault and featuring indoor palms. The scene begins with Cher and Christian (Justin Walker, in the Frank Churchill role) riding up the escalators, the symmetry of their bodies reflecting that of the mall rising around them. The movie audience is in front of them, but the mall audience is all around. Cher and Christian are mirror images of each other, self-centered and vain; she sees him as a potential love interest, but his eyes stray elsewhere—she's too caught up in her match-making to realize that her ideal shopping companion might also be gay.

As they reach the top of the escalator, they are distracted by shrieks: Tai (the Harriet Smith analogue, played by Brittany Murphy) is being dangled over the mall's glass railing by a couple of guys Cher dismisses as "generic." Christian saves her, shoving one flannel shirt in the chest. The benign audience for the runway that the escalators provide turns more sinister. The exposed areas of the mall are where strangers from different classes—the fashionable and the generic—come in close contact. That can provide the frisson of flir-tation (finding your crush in the food court) or turn to violence (taking teasing to a threatening place). The stakes are raised by the sense of performing for an audience. Later, Cher and Tai offer up very different accounts of what happened that day at the mall, as if they've been watching different movies.

The interaction of teen drama and the big architecture of the mall crops up again and again in media. "In '80s teen movies like *Weird Science*, the mall functions as a microcosm of society similar to a primate cage or a prison yard," write the authors of an *A.V. Club* roundup of fifteen pivotal mall scenes. *Smooth Talk*, a darker and more reflective take on teens trying out adulthood, "is freshest and most enjoyable—when Connie and her girlfriends hang out at the mall, talking obliquely but companionably about what they're going through, and delighting in their ability to tease and confuse their male peers. It's a wide-open public laboratory in which they can experiment in relative safety." In Smith Maguire's analysis, the mall represents the adult world. Children are taught how to navigate it by accompanying their parents (most often, their mothers) on shopping trips. It is a leap toward self-determination to go alone. "Entrance without the assistance of one's parents is the first step" to adulthood. The *A.V. Club* roundup doesn't even mention 2004's *Mean Girls*, which was based on a nonfiction book by Rosalind Wiseman about teen girl behavior and includes a scene of literal primate behavior. "Being at Old Orchard Mall kind of reminded me of being at home in Africa by the watering hole, when the animals are in heat," Cady (Lindsay Lohan) comments in a voiceover, watching coiffed teens in lowrider jeans and hoodies chirp at, groom, and pounce on one another at Old Orchard's central fountain.

Mimi Ito, director of the Connected Learning Lab at the University of California, Irvine, and cofounder of the nonprofit Connected Camps, told me she wishes there were more digital places like the mall. "Think about kids eight to thirteen," Ito said. "You start letting kids go to some places without adult supervision. You go to the corner store, you walk to school, you go to the mall—these are rites of passage." But online, "once you are thirteen, you check off a box, good luck with that," and you are treated as an adult rather than a young person who might need help navigating the world.

Adolescents try on grown-up behavior through their interactions with one another, through the clothes they buy, and through the media they consume, sometimes literally, at the mall. It comes as no surprise that, as teens shop for CDs of their favorite bands, adults also shopped for teens to put in those bands. As long as there has been mass media, there have been teen stars, from Lana Turner, discovered at the Top Hat Malt Shop in 1937 and then shuffled into films that saw her, a pouty sixteen-year-old, flirting at cinematic soda counters, to the faux-teen stars of *Happy Days*, a television show set in the same nostalgic past but filmed in the 1970s. By the 1980s, the mall was the accepted space of adolescence, with Orange Julius instead of milkshakes. To be discovered by a talent scout and adopted as a teen dream—one day you were spotted in the atrium, and the next brought back to perform there.

A 1987 *Los Angeles Times* article on Tiffany, the red-haired singer known for "I Think We're Alone Now," made the thin line between star and audience explicit.

> Chances were that Tiffany Darwisch was going to do what most 15-year-olds do during the summer—go to the mall. So, when offered an expenses-paid trip to malls from coast to coast, she could not say "yes" fast enough . . .
>
> "We wanted to take her to where her peer group hangs out all summer long—shopping malls," Brad Schmidt said excitedly. "If 'Tif [*sic*] is going to make it, she's going to do it first among 12- to 18-year-olds, and what better place to expose her than in America's playgrounds, the malls."

In a 2012 interview looking back on her career, adult Tiffany remembered initially being booked in East Coast clubs, singing her songs, and then being stuck, unable to drink and unable to hang out afterward with the audience. Her label was thinking of dropping her, until one day Larry Solters, an executive at label MCA, was at the mall with his own daughter.

> You see all these little kiosks that they set up with hair stuff and hair shows and applications of makeup and makeovers. He probably was walking by one of those and thought, "Well, what about somebody singing in the mall? This is where young girls hang out." When they presented it to me, I thought it was great, because that's exactly where I *did* hang out. My girlfriends and I, that was the safe place to be.

Every subsequent decade has repurposed the Tiffany template. Ten years later, Britney Spears's management would send the eighteen-year-old out wearing pigtails and a plaid schoolgirl skirt, and backed by two dancers, to promote her debut album, . . . *Baby One More Time*, with a thirty-minute, L'Oréal-sponsored set performed right in the middle of a mall. Ten years after Britney, the teen stars of the *Twilight Saga*, the movie adaptation of the bestselling young adult series set in a world of vampires and werewolves, were sent on a fifteen-city nationwide tour of shopping malls, supported by Hot Topic and Nordstrom.

Hot Topic, a store founded by Orv Madden in Southern California in 1989, had proved surprisingly agile in keeping up with changing teen trends. Its first location, in Montclair, sold "skulls, crucifixes, spike bracelets, pyramid belts and other hard-to-find stuff in the mall." The next year Madden and his first employee, Cindy Levitt, added "the rock wall" lined with band T-shirts, and by 1991, Hot Topic became known as "the loudest store in the mall," according to the official company history. Since then, Hot Topic remained hot by absorbing fandom after fandom, punk into anime, *Twin Peaks* into Care Bears when rave culture picked up on nostalgia for the sweet. While urban teenagers might have been able to find studded chokers and Manic Panic, Hot Topic brought these commodified elements of rebellion closer. "People definitely associate us with 90s fashion," Levitt told *i-D* in 2017. "We also represent the subversive, the anarchistic, the left of center." The *Twilight* films proved a perfect fit: Glowing, sexy shapeshifters pushed parental buttons, while the young stars and PG-13 rating kept things safe, just like the mall.

A 2008 *New York Times* profile of dreamy vampire and *Twilight* star Robert Pattinson ran under the headline "The Vampire of the Mall," and featured coverage of Pattinson's visit to a Pennsylvania Hot Topic. David Carr wrote,

> There are times when the limitations of the printed word come into focus, like when there is a need to convey how it sounded when

Robert Pattinson, who stars as the vampire heartthrob Edward Cullen in the forthcoming movie "Twilight," stepped onto a riser at the King of Prussia Mall outside Philadelphia on Thursday evening in front of more than 1,000 mostly teenage girls.

At King of Prussia Mall, it was just screaming. At other locations, fans ended up with broken bones, spilled copious tears, and asked Pattinson to bite them. Within the alternate reality of the mall, even vampires had braces.

$\rightarrow$

Was Caroline Knutson "the original mall walker"? It is hard to say for certain, as mall walking is a sport without a federation. It's an activity dominated by a population the media often ignores, and it primarily occurs before official store-opening hours. What Knutson was not was a teenager: In her fifties, and overweight, she sought out the mall for some of the same reasons young adults did. She needed a safe space where she could be independent but also protected.

The term "mall walking" first entered the official lexicon in 1985, thanks to an article in the *New York Times*. When Knutson began walking laps at Salem, Oregon's Lancaster Mall in 1982, she felt like she was onto something. She had signed up for TOPS—Take Off Pounds Sensibly, a nationwide nonprofit wellness group—and it provided new friends as well as a new routine. She chatted, shopped, and exercised, on dark winter mornings as well as light summer ones. Back then she drove herself to the mall and walked without assistance. By 2013, when the Salem *Statesman Journal* caught up with her, she was vision impaired and using a rolling walker. Her daughter had to drop her off, but she still showed up most weekday mornings at the mall. Now she made one half-mile loop of the mall rather than six to eight. "Asked how she navigates the mall with such poor vision, she chuckles through her response: 'I've walked there since 1982. I know that mall.'" After heart surgery in 2003, a doctor suggested she get on a treadmill. *"I'm a mall walker!"* Knutson's daughter remembers her mother proclaiming.

What began as an inexpensive way to lose weight became part of Knutson's identity and—despite the death of her husband and another daughter, despite changes in walking companions, favorite stores, and her own deteriorating health—a treasured thirty-year routine. The mall, in its quiet early hours, provides affordances most cities and suburbs cannot: even, open walkways, consistent weather, bathrooms, and benches. The mall is also "safe," as Genevieve Bogdan told the *New York Times* in 1985; the Connecticut school nurse was "apprehensive about walking alone outdoors early in the morning before work."

In 2015, the Centers for Disease Control and Prevention sponsored a resource guide on mall walking, citing the importance of regular physical activity for all adults and the low barrier to entry with a walking program. "It is an activity that requires little or no specialized skills or training," says the report, does not require expensive equipment, and can be tailored to people with varying levels of mobility, including those who use assistive devices. Despite the low economic and physical barriers to entry, however, the CDC report acknowledges major environmental barriers to walking outside: "street layout, sidewalk conditions, proximity of desirable destinations, perceived safety from traffic, and crime, all influence walking-related physical activity." These factors are especially discouraging to middle-aged and older adults with physical or cognitive disabilities, as is extreme or inclement weather. In many places, the outdoor built environment presents too much of a challenge for daily exercise for any but the young and nondisabled—and the report doesn't even mention gender-related crime. The authors' solution is to identify a widely distributed, weather- and traffic-protected, constantly surveilled and accessible alternative: the mall. Whereas most cities and suburbs don't provide "level surfaces, benches for places to rest, water fountains for availability of free water, and accessible restrooms," malls do.

For teens and older or disabled adults, the mall appears as a ready-made ersatz city, a theme park of urbanity even without the simulated New Orleans latticework of destination shopping experiences like the Mall of America. The mall was always intended as a protected space, its stores and spaces targeting suburban women and children at home during the day and isolated from walkable downtowns. For the more vulnerable among us, malls' privately owned and privately managed amenities offer an on- or off-ramp from the real world, sometimes literally. Skateboarders and wheelchair users both appreciate the fact that most malls were built to include ramps, escalators, and elevators, or have been retrofitted to do so. At Grossmont Center, a mall in La Mesa, California, the parking lot features signs giving the step counts from your parking spot to Target, Macy's, and the movie theater. Few cities can say the same. On Twitter, city planner Amina Yasin praised malls as spaces that accommodate many racialized and even unhoused senior citizens, offering free and low-cost-of-entry access to air-conditioning, bathrooms, and exercise, while throwing up her hands that "white urbanism decided malls are evil." Gabrielle Peters, a writer and former member of the city of Vancouver's Active Transportation and Policy Council, responded with her own thread on some ways malls offer better access for people with physical disabilities than city streets: dedicated transit stops, wide automatic doors, wide level passages, multiple types of seating, elevators prominently placed rather than hidden, ramps paired with stairs, public bathrooms, and so on. "There's a lot wrong with malls in terms of accessibility and because they are private property and the whole consumerism thing," she wrote, "but the mall also has a lot to teach urbanism." The CDC guidelines also address connections to public transportation. In planning a mall walking program, they counsel, organizers need to be cognizant of how members will reach the mall. "Many malls are isolated from the communities they serve by highway and roadway barriers, and access to the malls by walking or biking are not options." They suggest adding transit stops, subsidizing community transportation options, and encouraging carpooling as means of filling in a long-standing gap.

But it isn't only the ease of exercise that has made mall walking programs durable. The CDC program guide highlights five successful programs and includes testimonials from leaders and members. Walkers mention checking in on one another, if someone has been out of town, as well as sitting together at Starbucks afterward for coffee—one way in which accommodating a free, before-hours program actually helps some of the businesses in the mall. "Well, I know where to go shopping for my wife for her birthday, because I window shop while walking," one seventy-six-year-old Bellevue, Washington, walker told the authors. The same mall, Bellevue Square, even changes the music to Frank Sinatra while the walkers are making their rounds.

Ethnographer Elijah Anderson's book *The Cosmopolitan Canopy* describes the de facto senior center that formed on weekday mornings in the lower-level food court at the Gallery, the central Philadelphia mall that functioned as a hub for the city's lower-middle- and working-class Black population. At the food court, where communal tables are ringed by fast-food outlets, the best seats were along the corridor leading to the court itself, the better to "watch the action." Anderson, sitting in for a day, observes the largely male population commenting on ladies' dress and appearance, reading the paper, and, in one case, getting served coffee by a woman acting as mall "wife."

The food court at the Gallery, like the Bellevue Starbucks, offered a relatively low-cost way to hang out after the transit trip or mall walk. While public libraries and senior centers offer free public seating, they have neither the proximity to shopping, nor the proximity to the action that a mall offers. Like teens hanging out in the atrium, the seniors in the food court can observe without penalty and be a part of community life that can be overwhelming in truly public spaces. After police officers removed elderly Korean Americans from a McDonald's in Flushing, Queens—managers claimed the group overstayed their welcome, buying only coffee and french fries—sociologist Stacy Torres wrote in the *New York Times*, "Centers offer vital services, but McDonald's offers an alternative that doesn't segregate people from intergenerational contact. 'I hate old people,' one 89-year-old man told me."

When the Gallery closed for an upgrade in 2015, the de facto senior center got broken up. When the Lincoln Mall in Matteson, Illinois, closed that same year, the Lincoln Mall Milers feared the same fate for their walking group. "This is a family," Nancy Dornhecker, the community outreach coordinator of University of Chicago Medicine Ingalls Memorial Hospital told

Racked in 2018. "They are a very tight-knit group. I know when someone gets sick or when a loved one passes away." The Milers didn't want to join one of the two other mall walking programs Dornhecker coordinates, as those malls were farther away. Instead, they moved themselves to the Matteson Community Center, where Dornhecker has to provide the coffee and bagels. Group members sometimes drive elsewhere to get lunch or see a movie after their walk, but it isn't as convenient as having shopping options literally at your feet. "They would know when the sale signs go up," Dornhecker said. "They would call me and say 'this would look cute on you' and put it on hold for me so I could come after work and see it."

As malls closed in the spring of 2020 because of Covid-19, mall walkers across the country were forced back outside, battling weather and uneven sidewalks in their neighborhoods, missing the groups that easily formed on the neutral ground of the mall. One New Jersey couple took to walking the parking lot of the mall they once traversed inside, drawn to its spaciousness and their sense of routine. As malls reopened in the summer and fall with social-distancing and mask-wearing policies, some malls suspended their programs until the pandemic's end, while others curtailed the hours. Florence Henderson of Fox Chapel, Pennsylvania, wrote plaintively to the Pittsburgh *Tribune-Review*, "The mall walkers who have been walking at Pittsburgh Mills for years would like to see the mall open a little earlier in these colder months. It is such a wonderful, well-maintained mall where we have made such great friendships."

If the atrium is the catwalk of teen life, and the food court the mall walkers' tearoom, the arcade is the cave: a space where teens can lose themselves. In Ray Bradbury's essay "The Aesthetics of Lostness," mentioned in chapter 4, he suggests branding the top level of some future mall THE ATTIC, and stocking it with quirky shops that would attract mostly children.

As an Old, his conception of what kids might like seems antiquated. Toys? Magic tricks? No. Paranormal films? Yes. But versions of all these otherworldly objects do come to take up space in the "half-lit and fully exciting" realm of the video game arcade, where 8-bit villains stalk the unwary and pinball machines light up like a child's plaything. Because arcades were such a draw for teenagers, they were generally tucked away in the equivalent of the mall's "attic," either down a side corridor, grouped with other teen-centric businesses, or in lesser real estate on a mall's second or third level. Teens would seek out the arcades, and up there the lights, sounds, and clientele would not disturb the mall's middle-aged, income-earning prime customers.

The arcade gave teens their own place at the mall, but its less than prime position served as an indication of the ambivalence with which, over time, parents, store managers, and mall owners came to regard the presence of teens.

Malls and arcades grew up together during the great shopping center boom of the 1970s and 1980s. Initially, video game machines were stand-alones, installed on the way to the restrooms in pizza places, laundromats, and bars. But as they became more popular, and new games were added, the machines started to require their own spaces. "Gaming" became a destination activity in and of itself, rather than a stop in the middle of another social gathering. But what kind of social activity was gaming? The original Chuck E. Cheese, which opened in San Jose in 1977, was the invention of Atari founder Nolan Bushnell. He and partners Al Alcorn and Ted Dabney had created the runaway arcade hit *Pong* in 1972, a game so popular that it was soon generating the then unheard-of sum of forty dollars per day per machine. This gave Atari the capital to produce more games and turn arcades themselves into moneymakers. With Chuck E. Cheese, Bushnell tried to code gaming as family-friendly, multigenerational, safe fun. Five thousand arcades were added to malls between 1980 and 1982, doubling their existing number, and thousands more would arrive through the rest of the decade. Initially, reporting on arcades fell into the pattern Bushnell imagined; media coverage framed them as social and diverse. "Look at all these people together—blacks, whites, Puerto Ricans, Chinese. This is probably the one place in Boston where there are not hassles about race," eighteen-year-old

Martha Abrams, a regular at Boston's Teddy Bear arcade, told *Newsweek* in 1981. The arcade business hit its peak in 1989, and then underwent a long falloff through 2013. By then gaming had permanently gone into the home.

In his 2013 essay "Arcade Addicts and Mallrats," historian Kyle Riismandel chronicles the transformation of arcades and the malls around them from safe spaces *for* teens into spaces that must be protected *from* teens. A mother interviewed for a 1988 newspaper article sums up the dilemma: "Part of me says when you get a lot of kids together it's not a healthy thing. The other part says they have to have someplace to go that's not on the street corner. At least it's well lit. I know she won't get raped." Wheaton Plaza in Montgomery County, Maryland, is a good example of this transition. In 1981, when the *Washington Post*'s Bob Levey dropped in, the mall was serving its second generation of teens as one of few regional shopping centers in this D.C. suburb to which kids could walk from residential neighborhoods. Paul Quinn, a county policeman who grew up a mile away, said, "This place is the ball field and the dance hall and the Saturday night date I used to know all rolled into one . . . (It's) a neighborhood center for neighborhood kids, almost a neighborhood itself." Steve Rader, a teen in 1981, echoed him, "This is like a community of friends for me. This is where I feel comfortable." Three new youth-oriented clothing stores have replaced options serving older customers, and several stores offer half-price specials for those celebrating their sweet sixteens.

But all is not well at Wheaton Plaza. Lot 19, at the northwestern edge of the shopping center, has become a nighttime party spot with underage drinking and vandalism. The center's owners have increased security, adding two additional guards, and Time-Out, the on-site arcade, has spent thirty thousand dollars on its own security. Riismandel writes, "The presence of the 'good' teen, like Steve Rader, alongside the drinking rabble-rousers in the parking lot highlighted the tenuous position of suburban teens in public. They were both dangerous to the primary purpose of the mall, selling goods and services, and vital to the shopping center's ability to make money, as more of them flocked to malls as largely unsupervised social centers."

In October 2020, when American couldn't go to the mall, and people of all ages found solace in playing video games from their sofas, Twitter account Boston Radio Watch resurfaced a hysterical TV report on the terrors of game-addicted teens. "The way officials tell it, Boston has become the victim of an electronic blight," reported CBS Boston reporter Steve Young in 1982. "With fewer than six hundred thousand people, the city has four to five thousand video games, not just in arcades but also in drugstores, pizza parlors, super-markets." What were they afraid of? That games were addictive, a waste of time and money, and that hanging out at the arcades, as well as the shopping centers in which they were located, would lead to bad behavior, including sex and drug use. In the CBS Boston report the then commissioner of licenses, Joanne Prevost, refers to arcade rats "terrorizing" senior citizens and making adults uncomfortable with their "fast remarks."

Boston city officials responded to reports by limiting arcade games to commercial and industrial districts, one of several cities and suburbs to enact arcade-specific legislation in the 1980s. Bloomfield, New Jersey, passed legislation mandating professional security by off-duty police officers if owners had more than twenty machines in one location. (The police officer requirement was eventually struck down by the New Jersey Supreme Court.) Vienna, Virginia, limited establishments to no more than three machines; Palm Springs, to no more than four. Some communities limited arcade access to those over seventeen, while Bradley, Illinois, prohibited children under sixteen from playing video games at arcades in malls altogether. The White Plains Galleria simply banned arcades. "Arcade panic" was nationwide.

As a result, malls overhauled security, hiring more professionals and adding video surveillance. They wanted the teens for their pocket money, but they also needed to protect themselves from real petty crimes like shoplifting as well as the negative perceptions of adolescent groups. Shoplifting, loitering, drinking, and vandalism were mall owners' top security concerns, reported *Shopping Center World* in November 1978, all crimes predominantly associated with teenagers. By 1994, the number of private security personnel nationwide outstripped that of public law enforcement, as new-built malls hired new-badged mall cops. The total number of security guards increased by 300 percent between 1969 and 1988 and, as Riismandel found, spurred the output of a reported 1,200 volumes on private security. By the end of the 1980s, nearly all malls also had a layer of less visible but more effective security in the form of closed-circuit TV cameras. Over the decade, the technology grew cheaper and more effective, capturing images of misbehavior clearly and providing recorded evidence for future prosecution. In addition, the camera allowed a smaller number of personnel to watch a larger area; malls still found visible cops to be a useful deterrent. "Initiated in large part by the presence of disruptive teens, this advance changed the very nature of mall space as patrons understood they were likely being watched," Riismandel writes. This "might have enhanced a sense of safety for some but discouraged free association and expression in the heavily policed, quasi-public space of the mall."

Arcade panic wasn't even a new phenomenon. "Amusement arcades" stocked with coin-operated machines proliferated throughout the first half of the twentieth century. The same, largely Chicago-based manufacturers made jukeboxes, pinball machines, and gumball dispensers as well as slots—machines used in many municipalities to get around the prohibition of gambling. Pinball, in particular, was examined closely. Was it a "game of skill" or a "game of chance"? Pinball won its place in the hall of moral panic thanks to New York City mayor Fiorello La Guardia, who, on January 21, 1942, ordered the seizure of thousands of machines and banned pinball from the five boroughs. To La Guardia, those who profited from pinball were "slimy crews of tinhorns, well dressed and living in luxury on penny thievery." He posed for news photographers swinging a sledgehammer into a confiscated machine; two days later, the "shiny trimmings of 2,000 machines" had been virtuously stripped and shipped off to munitions factories to aid the war effort. Pinball remained illegal in New York City until 1976.

Meanwhile, game manufacturers continued to innovate, making design changes that differentiated pinball from slots. In 1947, D. Gottlieb & Company debuted the "flipper" mechanism now commonly associated with the pinball—those two-inch-long bats that allow players to flip the ball back up the pin field—which more clearly delineated it as a game of skill. In the postwar era, Laura June writes for the *Verge*, "the quickest route to proving your rebel status in America was to be seen within a few feet of a pinball machine. That cliché would later be reinforced in the form of the leather jacket-wearing, authority-bucking pinball wizard The Fonz from *Happy Days*." The original, hyperfocused "pinball wizard" was the eponymous hero of the Who's rock opera *Tommy*, released in 1969. Parents' groups continued to organize against pinball arcades, fearing "zombified," disconnected children unable to "think logically" as the pinball racket "bleeds millions of dollars from youngsters each year." *Better Homes and Gardens* threatened parents in October 1957: "Act now to keep your child from being victimized!"

In November 1982, U.S. surgeon general C. Everett Koop gave a speech on domestic violence and child abuse. In the Q&A that followed, an audience member asked a question about the effects of video games on children. Koop replied that, while there was no scientific evidence of harm, children were becoming "addicted . . . body and soul." His remarks made headlines, despite a follow-up statement intended to curtail parental panic. Psychologists questioned the ability of players to separate games from reality, while physiologists diagnosed "*Pac-Man* elbow" and "*Space Invaders* wrist." The language of vice was once again applied, by figures in government, to activities that had initially been represented as good, clean fun. The video game arcade, like the amusement arcade, was transformed from a wholesome teen hideout into a den of iniquity. Rochelle Slovin, founding director of the American Museum of the Moving Image, wrote after the museum curated its first show on video games in 2001,

> The video game arcade of the 1980s moved from being a way to contain public teens to being understood as another home to teen misbehavior that helped legitimate the expansion and professionalization of shopping center security. In turn, the increased policing of suburban public space not only facilitated the movement of video games and their players into the home but also virtually erased the suburban arcade in the 1990s.

The same panic would come for home video games too. Maaike Lauwaert writes in *The Place of Play: Toys and Digital Cultures*, "Reluctant to let children play outside unsupervised and lacking the time to accompany them regularly, parents tend to keep their children safely indoors." As digital toys came to dominate the market in the 1980s, parents began to fear their children turning into "couch potatoes." "Computer games not only over-domesticate child and play," Lauwaert writes, "they also frustrate the private room as sanctuary," inviting peer pressure and strange adults into the home through online gaming communities. The popular press claimed Nintendo and Sega Genesis consoles were as addictive as *Pac-Man* and *Space Invaders*. A March 1989 story in *Newsweek* asserted that "Nintendo has led people to do crazy things," and "Nintendinitis" was added to the list of physical ailments resulting from gameplay.

In 2020, as people found themselves in their sixth month of quarantine, and sales of video games, gaming systems, and even gaming chairs grew exponentially, it was hard to reconcile these fears with the reality—the size and reputability of the business that games have become, as well as their majority-adult audience. The kids kicked out of arcades in the 1980s are now spending thousands on at-home systems, as well as visiting arcades with a distinctly over-twenty-one clientele. The media transition from "adults just don't understand" to "adults play too" happened during the 1990s, as younger writers at news magazines, some of whom had grown up with Atari at the arcade and/or Atari at home, took over the beat. As Spencer Buell wrote in *Boston* magazine, of that dramatic CBS Boston report:

> Imagine explaining to one of these concerned citizens that the owner of the New England Patriots would one day have in his portfolio a professional e-sports team, which (pre-Covid) was competing for crowds of thousands in arenas. Or that, in the jaws of a pandemic, video games would emerge as one of the few remaining safe ways for teens to unwind and socialize with friends without spreading a deadly virus? Or that these machines would be so beloved by '80s

kids, they'd build trendy arcade bars like Boston's A4cade and VERSUS so adults could relive those cherished memories while sipping craft beers and cocktails?

$$\rightarrow$$

In *Hanging Out and the Mall*, Smith Maguire describes the relationship of teens to malls as ambivalent. "Malls target teenagers with age-specific clothing stores, music stores, and so forth, to attract a population with spending potential and a seeming propensity for group shopping." But then: "Lured as a niche market and represented in the commodities as desirable, teenagers answer the call of the mall only to be treated with suspicion, (particularly if they are in groups) by the same adults who covet youthfulness." Arcade panic targeted teens in what should have been a safe space, offering them inexpensive fun and then slapping them on the wrist for enjoying it. Other forms of mall surveillance targeted teens for their mere existence. If you scroll through lists of classic mall scenes with a more critical eye, it is easy to spot one similarity: Most are centered on young, blond, white teenagers. When teens of color go to the mall, things go down a little differently.

In 1989, issue 244 of *The Uncanny X-Men* introduced a new character, Jubilation Lee, one of vanishingly few Chinese American characters in comics. First seen at the Hollywood Mall, a young woman with spiked black hair and big hoop earrings is putting on a light show, sparks and stars and bursts of light emanating from her palms. "Pieces of raw energy," she says, "that come when I call." Mall security is suspicious and begins to chase her. Skateboarders, fellow instruments of chaos, cut them off, while she slides between the legs of one mall cop and leaps off the second-story balcony into the atrium. "It's fifty feet to the main floor!" says one. "Good riddance," says the other. "I'll have you know," Jubilee says, while gracefully plunging through the mall's large Calder-esque mobile, "I attended Beverly Hills Prep! . . . And I was an absolutely aces gymnast!" Her mutant powers allow Jubilee to escape; most minority characters aren't so lucky, as seen in sitcoms from *The Fresh Prince of Bel-Air* in the 1990s to the more recent *Everybody Hates Chris* and *Mixed-ish* (both set in the 1980s). They repeatedly end up in mall security offices that all seem to be staffed by the same white, middle-aged, and mustachioed cop.

Everybody Hates Chris was a sitcom loosely based on comedian Chris Rock's adolescent years. In the segment "Shopping While Black," a teenage Chris goes to a department store to buy his mother some perfume for Mother's Day. "The problem with going to department stores," he says in a voice-over, "is every time a Black person enters, they get followed. It doesn't matter if you were a baby wearing diapers"—a toddler in a cute pink dress crawls under a rack of clothes, pursued by security guard with walkie-talkie ("She's on the move")—"or a senior citizen wearing diapers"—a grand-mother in a wheelchair passes by. A Black security guard is racially profiled by his own colleague: "What do you mean I'm on the move, I work here!" In a 2020 episode of *Mixed-ish*, lead character Rainbow (Arica Himmel) is taught a lesson in how the world sees her—as Black, not mixed—when she and three friends are falsely accused of shoplifting by "clearance rack Tom Selleck," after meeting up at a lip-synch studio at the mall. When her white dad comes to pick her up, the guard falls all over himself to apologize, but Rainbow, in full after-school-special mode, refuses to take advantage of her (half) white privilege and leave without her friends.

Detroit writer Aaron Foley relates a real-world version of the oppositional relationship between teens and shopkeepers in his requiem for Victor Gruen's Northland, the architect's first major shopping center and "a place where, if you were a teenager in Detroit in the late '90s or early 2000s like I was, you likely spent a lot of time." While Detroit observers tend to draw a color line across the city with Black residents south of 8 Mile and whites up north, Southfield, the inner-ring suburb in which Northland was built, was an exception: middle-class and integrated, as was the mall. Rents at Northland were low enough that independent minority store owners could set up beside national brands like Stride Rite and the Gap, Foley writes, including boutiques like Sun's that catered to the prevailing teen taste for "oversized T-shirts, baggy jeans and fresh kicks." It was to Sun's that he went, mother and grandmother in tow, to buy a particularly coveted Sean John shirt. When they reached the checkout,

> the customer was causing a ruckus over, I don't know, a shirt not being in his size or something, and they exchanged heated words. The customer left, and the checkout guy said "stupid [n*****]" under his breath just as we laid the shirt down.
> "What?" my mother and grandmother said in unison.
> "Oh, no, not you—to him," he said . . .
> "Do you still want the shirt, Aaron?" I remember my grand-mother asking.

The decision should have been easy—to walk away—but, Foley writes, "I really just wanted the shirt." He remembered the racist incident, rather than what happened to the shirt, years later, even as he mourns the demise of Northland as a place of belonging in twentieth-century Detroit. "It can still feel as fresh as it did back then," Foley says, with its murals of famous Black people and Detroit's own Motown stars, with stores selling Black youth fashion from Timberlands to Tommy Hilfiger.

> When Rihanna's last album, "Unapologetic," leaked ahead of its release, many of the boutiques were knocking its tunes loudly, as if they knew which songs would be the favorites. It's not as trafficked as it used to be, but teens still frolic, wandering around the halls aimlessly, gossiping while clutching shopping bags.

In the iconic mall scenes, white teens take center stage quite literally. In the less iconic parallel script written by and for teens of color, to be seen is to be under suspicion. Jubilee's light show, Rock's toddler "on the move," Rainbow's friends' playful lip-syncing—these actions don't gain them the spotlight but instead get them hustled into a back room. What made arcades so seductive and, ultimately, subversive was that teens got to choose their own back room. Mall security, CCTV, and arcade panic took that darkness and privacy away from them in the 1990s, spilling their activities back out into the light of the atrium and food court. There, in media and in real life, twenty-first-century teens of color still found themselves excluded from the "alternate world" of the mall, thanks to new laws of shopping land: codes of conduct and parental escort policies. In 2017, just over 100 of the country's more than 1,200 malls had some constraint on young people in their official codes of conduct, up from 39 in 2007. Parental escort policies, the most popular choice, became widespread in the 2000s, setting limits on how many teenagers could move around the mall together, or setting curfews for unaccompanied teens on weekend nights. The Mall of America was the first to write such a policy, in 1996. Today's version reads:

At Mall of America, safety is a top priority.

We welcome all youth to Mall of America, however, youth under 16 must be accompanied by an adult 21 years or older from 3 p.m. to close, daily and during mall hours on Black Friday, the day after Black Friday, December 26–31 and other dates as posted in advance by Mall of America.

One might ask, *Whose* safety is a top priority? While worded as confusingly as possible, the policy comes down to this: The only time kids can come to the mall unaccompanied are Saturday and Sunday mornings, and times when they should be in school.

"We had essentially become a baby sitter," MOA director of public relations Julie Hanson told the *Christian Science Monitor* when asked about the policy in 2005. When Holyoke Mall in Ingleside, Massachusetts, instituted an escort policy the same year, stating that teens under sixteen would not be allowed in the mall without adult supervision in the evenings, fifteen-year-old Mike Lemme started an online petition that gathered one thousand signatures. "There are not that many places where teenagers can go and socialize," Lemme said at the time. "Instead of banning all teenagers, they should find a way to get the people causing the trouble out."

One of the best-known examples of such a policy was instituted at the Atlantic Terminal Mall in Brooklyn in 2010, where groups of four or more people under twenty-one were not allowed to linger without a parent at any time—more restrictive than others across the country. The justification given for the anti-teen policy sounded reasonable at first glance: A 2009 incident in which an invitation posted on social media prompted thousands of teens to arrive at the mall's Buffalo Wild Wings on the same night. After most were turned away, a stabbing and two shootings occurred on nearby streets. Atlantic Terminal is located, as its name suggests, over a large subway and commuter rail hub, and at the nexus of several bus lines. It could have been a popular after-school destination—if then-owner Forest City Ratner wanted teenagers there. Months after the violence, twenty guards were employed to approach groups of young people in groups of four or more, asking them for ID and then to split up or leave. The whole mall was designed to prevent lingering; while suburban malls sprawl, and offer indoor food courts, fountains, and sittable steps, Atlantic Terminal, built in 2004, shrank its atrium into a narrow escalator hall, with no benches and no carve-outs for socializing. Food is sold in discrete restaurants, and the public bathrooms are tucked at the back of the large Target.

After the Mall of America imposed its curfew, the policy was immediately opposed by the American Civil Liberties Union. The ACLU targeted the policy as infringing on the rights of young people, while Minneapolis advocates cautioned that, while the language of the curfew was race-neutral, it had been "drawn up in reaction to and in large part because of the large number of young people of color who congregate in the mall in the evening." Marcus Wilson, eighteen, and one of those young people of color, called it "a little racist."

In 1998, Alysa B. Freeman argued in the *Dickinson Law Review* that the two major public policy reasons for repealing the parental escort policy at the Mall of America were "(1) to repair relations with the black community, and (2) to repair relations with teen shoppers in general." Even before the escort policy was official, the MOA had already been sued twice for discrimination: once by three mothers after their daughters had gotten into a fight with mall security, and once by three minority teens in their own right. Both lawsuits argued that mall security approached more groups of Black teens than white teens and handed out copies of the conduct code more often to the former than to the latter. Freeman also suggested that the mall's policy of requiring parental escorts on weekend nights negatively stereotyped teens as a group: "The best way to ask teens to act like responsible adults may be to treat them in a more adultlike fashion." In return, mall security could enforce the laws of the state of Minnesota rather than the mall's code, using state unlawful assembly and disorderly conduct statues to target illegal behaviors rather than prejudging groups by age and race.

Private policing can extend to outdoor commercial space as well, especially when it is under the aegis of an entity like a business improvement district. Denver, Colorado's 16th Street Mall, for example, is managed by the Downtown Denver Partnership, and Downtown Denver Business Improvement District, supported by the transit and pedestrian Mall's property owners and merchants. That public-private structure has led to conflicts between the operators of the Mall and its users when they do not conform to the behaviors and demographics of ideal consumers.

Yvette Freeman, a Denver native who managed the Mall during the 1990s, told me about her professional and ethical responsibilities during her tenure. Her restorative and proactive approach seems like a much better model than the combative relationships that exist today between the Mall and teens, panhandlers, and skateboarders—conflicts played out via hostile architecture and overpolicing. "Ultimately, my salary was paid by the property owners," she told me. "I had one come to me and say, 'Yvette, we've got to get these people off this particular corner.'" The corner held a heavily used bus stop, and Black and brown young people often waited there. "The property owner was suggesting I needed to move them because people were intimidated by their presence. I had to explain they have as much of a right to be here as anybody else."

Freeman ended up using a form of restorative justice to address the issue. In collaboration with a nonprofit working to support young people, they got some of the bus-riding youth and the owner in a room together, creating a space for conversation about why they wanted to hang out on the Mall. The owner gained insight and confronted his prejudice—after that the kids were able to hang out without issue. "I did what I did because of who I am, an African American woman," she said. "I'm going to speak out for what's right and what's not right, trying to figure out ways to deal with these issues from personal experience." When property owners wanted skateboarders off the Mall, she suggested the need for a less punitive approach and worked with city council members to give them another option, which resulted in the construction of Denver's first public skate park. And when panhandlers were blocking sidewalks, she brought in social service providers to educate owners and managers about the challenges facing these individuals, and the aid the Denver Mission and nearby providers had to offer.

To include rather than exclude users of the 16th Street Mall, changes in design and behavior were required. *The Arsenal of Exclusion and Inclusion*, written by the partners at New York City–based design firm Interboro, is an encyclopedia-like collection of 156 such everyday interventions in the built environment, and comprises entries like "Armrest," "Apartment Size," "Bouncer," and "Buzzer." They are often design-as-deterrent, of teens, of skaters, of the unhoused, and of public transit users. The addition of armrests on public benches, for example, is a design to prevent homeless sleepers but also makes benches unskateable.

I counted eight entries in Interboro's *Arsenal* specifically designed to target teens: "Age-Segregated Communities," which are allowed to block residents under the age of eighteen under the Fair Housing Act; "Classical Music" and "Ultrasonic Noise" are two different aural barriers used to shoo teens away from convenience stores and public seating areas—the first by boring them to death, the second by producing a mosquito-like buzzing that only younger ears can hear. (Teen pop at the mall, with this context, begins to sound like a song of freedom rather than pablum packaged for mass consumption.) "Residents-Only Parks" and disappearing "Basketball Hoops" keep them from playing outside. "Youth Curfews" keep teens off the streets at night, while "No Loitering" signs keep them from congregating at all.

Interboro partner Daniel D'Oca first became aware of the politics of public space as a teen himself, circa 1990, in Bergen County, New Jersey, when he protested a downtown loitering ordinance: "It didn't make any sense, and it wasn't even legal. I staged a protest, but I was the only one who showed up." In 1999 the Supreme Court ruled on a case challenging a Chicago ordinance that banned congregating in groups in public; the statute was intended to combat gang violence, but the court found it so broad as to infringe on personal freedom. Justice John Paul Stevens, writing for the majority, declared that "freedom to loiter for innocent purposes is part of the 'liberty' . . . [to] engage in idle conversations or simply enjoy a cool breeze on a warm evening."

For a 2017 issue of *Harvard Design Magazine* titled "Seventeen," Interboro created a dialogue between two staff attorneys in the fictional town of Sprinkleville trying (and failing) to define "loitering" downtown by citing language from a variety of existing municipal codes. Most are circular, for example "a person is guilty of loitering when he: loiters," but others are more specific. The codes target teenagers through clothing ("wear[ing] pants, trousers, or shorts such that the known undergarments are intentional[ly] displayed/exposed to the public"), age ("groups of four or more people under 21 years old, and not traveling with a parent, are forbidden to linger"), and activity ("to linger, to stay, to saunter, to delay, to stand around and shall also include the colloquial expression 'hanging around'"), contrasting all of the above with the "proper" use of a downtown or mall: "conducting lawful business." While Interboro and the Supreme Court were both writing about lazy language in policing outdoor public space, the same laziness applies to the enforcement of mall codes. Which teens hanging around the atrium are allowed to preen and pose unmolested, and which are picked up for lingering, for sauntering, or for baggy pants?

In 2017, artist and educator Chat Travieso recruited six teenagers from the South Bronx to research the intersection, and interactions, of young people and public space. Participants interviewed experts in youth development, public space design, and the criminal justice systems, surveyed their peers, and made systematic observations of public spaces where teenagers hang out. As members of what came to be called the Yes Loitering project wrote in *Urban Omnibus*, New York City's roughly one million teenagers "face a unique spatial challenge: Old enough to be independently mobile but too young to have homes of their own, they conduct their private lives outside. There, adults set limits on youth's presence in the name of 'quality of life.'" Those limits are most often couched as a series of prohibitions cataloged in photographs by the team, including "No Loitering," "No Minors," "No Sitting on Steps," "Do Not Enter with Hoodie or Mask." But malls sell hoodies and masks. Malls are built around sittable steps. Malls wave minors in to buy, and then kick them out for loitering, congregating, and wandering. "I think we need to . . . reframe the way we think of the commons and the spaces that we all . . . share because young people and people who are experiencing homelessness are also people, human beings, who deserve spaces, and who deserve dignity," Travieso said.

When the Yes Loitering team moved from itemizing the problems to offering solutions, their ideal space came to sound very much like a mall: protected from the elements, with Wi-Fi and seating. Access to affordable food. Public bathrooms. Places to play. Open late. Among the drawings they collected during their interviews is one titled "The Center," with lights and stepped seating in two shell-shaped arrays, flanked by a basketball court and food court, "regular laying down grass," all on the river with benches along a promenade. It looks like Brooklyn Bridge Park—where Pier 2's basketball courts have been extremely popular with teens, not without conflict with park workers and police—but also like a mall. The central space, with generous, flexible stepped seating, becomes the focal point of the plan. Travieso, like Freeman, is one of the few adults in these scenarios who asked the teens what they wanted out of public space, and took the time to listen.

That what the teens came up with was a more generous version of the mall is both a commentary on how the form has captured the popular imagination and on how perfect it is as an architecture for this age cohort—from the dark attics to the skylit atriums. Commercial imperatives accidentally created an architecture that accommodates those who often have the least societal power: the young, the old, the disabled, and the poor. As the mall reinvents itself for the twenty-first century the question becomes whether, and then how, it can accommodate this cultural role with less ambivalence and more democracy. Might new codes of conduct skip the surveillance of baggy pants and focus instead on accommodating the people who need and love them, including consumers who aren't white, middle-aged, and middle class?

Chapter 6
Dawn of the Dead Mall

W hy do zombies go to the mall?

This question is asked and answered in George Romero's 1978 cult classic *Dawn of the Dead*, the second part of a planned horror trilogy. Four survivors of a zombie attack steal a TV helicopter and head north, making for Canada. As they chopper over fields and roads, they find that the virus has spread past the bounds of the city. Every open space includes dark figures that stagger toward some undefined goal. Low on fuel and sleep, the escapees reach a vast, empty parking lot. "What the hell is it?" someone asks, as if encountering the ruin of an ancient civilization. "Looks like a shopping center, one of those big indoor malls" is the reply.

Although the mall was unrecognizable from the air, once they land the helicopter on the roof and get inside, they know what to do: shop. "It's Christmastime down there, buddy," both in the real world they have left behind and the refuge in which they now play. The empty J. C. Penney provides a television, a radio, lighter fluid, chocolate. They turn on the lights, the music, the fountains. A prerecorded announcement breaks into the Muzak: "Why pay more when the sales are popping here?" Why pay more indeed? In the zombie apocalypse, everything is free.

By the mid-1970s, the mall was enough of a fixture in American life to inspire a first round of reinterpretation. The festival marketplace and Jerde's themed environments elaborated on the standard-issue model by adding

Director George A. Romero's classic zombie movie *Dawn of the Dead* (1978) was filmed in Monroeville Mall, Monroeville, Pennsylvania, 1969. (United Film Distribution Company/Photofest)

entertainment and city (or citylike) elements. Filmmakers such as Romero and writers from essayist Joan Didion to young adult author Richard Peck tried to make sense of the zoned-out (or blissed-out) feelings we have at the mall. Is this really living, or are we the undead? These artists were early to sense that all was not right in the land of consumption—1982 is considered the first "peak mall" year, the boom followed by the bust—but would not be the last. Every time malls grow unchecked, a die-off results and art is born from the entrails. *Dawn of the Dead* is cheap and cheesy and gross; *New York Times* film critic Janet Maslin lasted only fifteen minutes into the screening and filed her review from the theater lobby: "It was explained to me in the lobby, while a preview audience moaned and groaned, that . . . the bulk of 'Dawn of the Dead' had been filmed in America's largest shopping mall and is full of satirical points about consuming." The movie would set the stage for decades of similarly scavenger-driven mall art.

Malls have been dying for the past forty years. Every decade rewrites the obituary in its own terms, but the apocalyptic scale, the language and imagery of civilizational collapse, keep reappearing. These narratives suggest an inevitability. And yet, the majority of malls survive. And yet, people keep shopping. The urban and suburban landscapes in which people live don't change that rapidly. Neither does human nature.

Joan Didion's essay "On the Mall," written in 1975 and anthologized in *The White Album*, is the second significant assessment of the mall as a cultural force after Ray Bradbury's "The Girls Walk This Way; The Boys Walk That Way." While Bradbury situates himself as an observer, sitting on a bench, Didion walks with the girls. She spent time as a child at Town and Country Village outside Sacramento in the 1940s and, as a twentysomething working for *Vogue* in the 1960s, took a correspondence course on shopping center theory. "My dream life was to put together a Class-A regional shopping center with three full-line department stores as major tenants," she writes. She is disdainful of the knowledge she learned in the course but remains fascinated by the mall as an artifact, writing from the same bird's-eye vantage as Romero's helicopter crew.

Top, Ala Moana Center Honolulu, Hawaii, seen from the 1350 Ala Moana apartment building, 1970. (Bishop Museum Archives) *Bottom*, publicity photo for the Ala Moana Center, Phase II, Don Graham, 1966. (Photograph by Hawaii Visitors Bureau; Bishop Museum Archives)

They float on the landscape like pyramids to the boom years, all those Plazas and Malls and Esplanades. All those Squares and Fairs. All those Towns and Dales, all those Villages, all those Forests and Parks and Lands. Stonestown. Hillsdale. Valley Fair, Mayfair, Northgate, Southgate, Eastgate, Westgate. Gulfgate. They are toy garden cities in which no one lives but everyone consumes.

She recognizes, even embraces, the trancelike nature of mall shopping, taking herself to the open-air Ala Moana Center in Honolulu on a day in which she "wake[s] feeling low." (Opened in 1959, Ala Moana was for a time the largest mall in the United States.) In the soothing environs of its carp pools, she "moves for a while in aqueous suspension not only of light but of judgement, not only of judgement but of 'personality.' " She goes in for a *New York Times* and comes out with two straw hats, four bottles of nail polish, and a toaster. The Gruen transfer has taken hold and, like Bradbury, she is fine with that. The absence of judgment in Didion's and Bradbury's essays may come from the place they shared: California, where any public life, even with a shopping tag attached, seems better than the car-dominated alternative.

Romero's take is far harsher. Standing at the railing on the second floor of the 1.1 million square foot Monroeville, Pennsylvania, mall, watching zombies jerk their way up the escalator and into the circular fountain, blond baby-faced SWAT team member Roger (Scott H. Reininger) asks his more perceptive leader, Peter (Ken Foree), "Why did they come here?" "This was an important place in their lives," Peter responds. Over the course of the film, Romero checks in with every architectural totem of the mall—the skating rink, the feature clock, the circular fountain, the planting beds, showing the audience that the familiar landmarks remain; in one memorable sequence, a zombie topples into the fountain.

But for all the characters' sneering commentary on the automatic behavior of the zombies, it is the healthy humans who seem unable to leave the mall. Rather than seeking supplies and fuel and heading north, they stay, stealing lamps and sofas to domesticate their hideaway, going on dates in the sit-down restaurant, and posing for the security cameras with stacks of bills.

The men can analyze but not resist the allure. Francine (Gaylen Ross), the one woman in the group, grows frustrated with her compatriots' complacency and gets angry. "You are hypnotized by this place, all of you! It's so bright and neatly wrapped, you don't see that it is a prison too."

Romero inserts visual jokes, cutting between the ashen faces of the zombies and the plastic tans of the mannequins. Eventually, as morale declines, Francine makes herself up to look like one of the mannequins, all blue eyeshadow, false lashes, and blood-red lipsticked mouth. The dialogue distances the sick from the well, but the visuals underline their sameness. To survive, they must escape the soft life at the mall. In the end Francine, pregnant and desperate, breaks the hypnosis. She and the one man left alive chopper toward Canada to start civilization anew: a clear Nativity reference, given the perpetual Christmas in the mall they leave behind.

Even as fin de siècle malls shuffled tenants, shut down wings, emptied out, limped on—the language of the undead permeates all the retail reportage—they maintained cultural status through the art made by the children who grew up in their marble halls. The minute a mall shuts down, the documentation and the re-creation begins, in the work of Romero and Didion in the 1970s, John Hughes in the 1980s, mallwave composers and dystopian authors in the 2010s. For artistic creators and property developers alike, the dead mall is not the endgame, but rather the start of something new.

Owings Mills Mall opened outside Baltimore in 1986 with a trumpet fanfare and a burst of confetti, the paper drifting down its three-story central atrium. The V-shaped mall outside Baltimore boasted three department stores, marble floors, the local exclusives on a Laura Ashley, a Benetton, and a Williams-Sonoma, and was planned as the upscale centerpiece for a new suburban commercial center, with flanking office buildings and a human-made waterfront. The reception was festive, but a far cry from the flotilla that welcomed nearby Harborplace in 1980, or even the Bull Roast in the parking deck of the Mall in Columbia, the consumer centerpiece of that new town, in 1971. All three projects were developed by the Rouse Company, and all three projects were located in the same environs, but with each passing decade both the architectural and communitarian ambitions stepped down, from the logo-worthy pyramidal skylights at the Mall in Columbia to the sheltering green roofs of Harborplace to Owings Mills's faceted white concrete walls. The grandest space at Owings Mills was the food court at the top, set below another barrel-vaulted skylight, like a miniature version of Pelli and Balmori's Winter Garden in Manhattan. Owings Mills was intended to be what is colloquially called a Class A mall, after retailers' categorizations of the relative cost of merchandise from store to store. A Class A mall is located in a high-income area and offers shopping options unavailable elsewhere in the region, from marquee department store anchors on down, with average sales per square foot greater than five hundred dollars. Designed as destinations worth the drive past customers' everyday mall, Class A properties have to sell an aura of exclusivity. They also have to offer the same kinds of dining, entertainment, and pampering options as the nineteenth-century department store, alongside a well-curated roster of boutiques. This is the model by which the family-owned malls, including Dallas's NorthPark and Orange County's South Coast Plaza, have long set themselves apart from the crowd. The Jerde malls differentiated themselves by theme and oriented themselves toward families; the Pelli (and Pei and HOK) galleries differentiated themselves by class and targeted the urbane shoppers who had somehow found themselves in the land of wide roads and parking decks.

For Owings Mills to stay successful, it had to maintain that aura of exclusivity. It didn't have art or distinctive architecture. It didn't have the Baltimore harbor and the National Aquarium. It never acquired the waterfront commercial development and housing that made the Mall in Columbia a destination for both Columbia's residents and the neighboring county's. A Metro station a mile away opened in 1987, and the Mass Transit Administration initially offered free ten-minute shuttles to the mall, but transit-oriented development was slow to follow. Owings Mills wasn't a festival; it wasn't an Italian hill town; it didn't have an ice rink. Once

Williams-Sonoma went mail order, and Laura Ashley florals went out of style, why would you choose Owings Mills?

In the 2015 *New York Times* article "The Economics (and Nostalgia) of Dead Malls," Owings Mills is where we lay our scene:

> Inside the gleaming mall here on the Sunday before Christmas, just one thing was missing: shoppers.
>
> The upbeat music of "Jingle Bell Rock" bounced off the tiles, and the smell of teriyaki chicken drifted from the food court, but only a handful of stores were open at the sprawling enclosed shopping center. A few visitors walked down the long hallways and peered through locked metal gates into vacant spaces once home to retailers like H&M, Wet Seal and Kay Jewelers.
>
> "It's depressing," Jill Kalata, 46, said as she tried on a few of the last sneakers for sale at the Athlete's Foot, scheduled to close in a few weeks. "This place used to be packed. And Christmas, the lines were out the door. Now I'm surprised anything is still open."

Since 2010, writer Nelson D. Schwartz reports, more than twenty-five enclosed shopping malls had closed, and sixty more were on their way out. Fifteen percent of malls would fail in the next decade, Green Street Advisors predicted in 2014. A 2017 report from Credit Suisse augured the demise of 20 to 25 percent of U.S. malls (more than 200 of the 1,100 in existence) by 2022. During the pandemic such predictions ticked higher, to a third of all malls, with closures primarily of lower-end neighborhood and regional malls.

Owings Mills had been failing for far longer than that. In 1991, Towson Town Center, an existing mall fifteen miles away, finished a major renovation that included a Nordstrom, then an East Coast novelty. In 1992, Christina Marie Brown, a member of the cleaning staff at Owings Mills, was shot walking from her job to the Metro station via an off-grid path that shortened the distance between the mall and the trains. After her death, the path from the station to the mall was closed, but extensive local coverage of the murder led to public perception that the mall itself was dangerous. In 1996, the Saks

Fifth Avenue closed and was replaced by the more pedestrian J. C. Penney. Each event chipped away at the idea that Owings Mills was worth a trip, until no one could remember which short-lived tenants still occupied the halls.

By 2010 the mall was one quarter vacant. An entire wing on the way to the vanished Boscov's was empty, a ghostly presence. Photographs by Matthew Christopher for his project Abandoned America show dead palm trees, collapsed ceilings, boarded-up windows, and strangely pristine escalators, ready for the confetti to fall again. The mall limped on to 2016, with fewer and fewer open stores, before its new owners razed it. Today Owings Mills is not a mall at all but Mill Station, a loose collection of outdoor-facing stores including a Costco, a Lowe's, and a Burlington Coat Factory ringed by a landscaped parking lot. Its website picks up the narrative of death and rebirth, reading, "It's Time for a New Beginning."

The term for Owings Mills Mall's fate is bloody: It was "cannibalized." Two premium malls could not coexist in Baltimore County. The newer one eats the audience of its elder. Towson Town Center pushed Owings Mills to number two, and it never recovered, slipping down the mall classification system until it was the retail equivalent of the walking dead: zombified, then put out of its misery.

What happened in Owings Mills happened all over the country. The recession of the mid-1990s halted new construction, and when it resumed, developers focused on what was working—newer malls, high-end malls—and not on revivifying twenty- or thirty-year-old properties born concurrently with first- and second-ring suburbs. Retail developers, spooked by the rise of online shopping, began to experiment with ways of making real-world shopping cheaper and easier. Maybe people didn't want to spend all day at the mall, they reasoned; they just want to drive in and drive out. Power centers, grouping multiple big-box stores around a parking lot, eliminated the indoor amenities of the mall in favor of selling cheap and bulky goods. Outlet malls, which also favored a cheaper-to-build outdoor layout, offered the brand names of the mall at bargain prices, grouped for convenience. The most innovative of these real-world experiments were the "lifestyle centers," a term coined in the late 1980s by their originators, Memphis-based developer

Poag & McEwen. Famous examples include the Grove in Los Angeles, Santana Row in San Jose, and the Promenade Shops at Evergreen Walk in South Windsor, Connecticut, each designed to relate to their respective geographic setting. These centers, more than one hundred of which were built in the early 2000s, explicitly mimicked Main Streets: facing rows of retail with an emphasis on restaurants, tree-lined sidewalks, sometimes offices or apartments above, and a mix of architectural treatments, suggesting urbanity built over time. Indeed, "urbanity" was what they were selling. As Andrew Blum wrote at *Slate*, "Their developers recognize that 'shopping' is only one urban entertainment among many, like eating at restaurants, people-watching, open-air concerts, or looking at art. More incredibly, lifestyle centers do all the things that urban planners have promoted for years as ways of counteracting sprawl: Squeeze more into less space, combine a mix of activities, and employ a fine-grained street grid to create a public realm." Nonetheless, the lifestyle center, like its father, the mall, and its mother, the festival marketplace, is still a private place, owned, operated, and policed by people more interested in the comfort of paying customers than in democratic ideals.

Although the retail press also wrote of online shopping "cannibalizing" malls, that analysis hasn't borne out—at least, not prior to the disruptions of the Covid-19 pandemic, whose long-term effects on retail remain uncertain. As economist Austan Goolsbee wrote in the *New York Times* in February 2020, just before quarantine, internet shopping still represented only 11 percent of retail sales in the United States. The death of malls (and their department store anchors) rests on the rise of big-box stores such as Walmart, Costco, and Sam's Club, alongside a cultural shift toward paying for services rather than things, and compounded by rising income inequality—the 2010s analogue to that 1990s recession, which cut consumer spending and sent lower-income families in search of bargains. When malls have looked for new anchors to fill those department store holes, they first turned to Walmart; more recently, movie theaters and entertainment offerings, expanded food courts, gyms, and even co-working spaces have been used to fill those voids.

The ownership structure of malls also changed. In the first decades, family-run development companies built most of the best-known malls, and their portfolios could be counted on fingers and toes. Rouse and his 1960s competitors—Melvin and Herbert Simon, Edward DeBartolo and his architect brother Frank, Ernest Hahn on the West Coast—all specialized in malls, partnering with various department stores to make deals. By the 1990s those companies were struggling for cash and took two routes out of debt. One was consolidation—Simon bought DeBartolo; Westfield, an Australian shopping center group, bought Hahn—in hopes of finding economies of scale. Buying out the competition before it could undermine your rival property was a defense against cannibalization, but it did not save malls on the downward slide. Instead, the new megamall developers concentrated resources at the upper end, selling off and spinning off unsuccessful properties more ruthlessly now that executives had no personal relationship to their site or origins.

The other strategy, often combined with consolidation, was taking private real estate companies public. This option was pioneered by mall developer A. Alfred Taubman in 1992. Taubman began his career as an owner of strip shopping centers in the 1950s, but quickly saw the potential for the enclosed mall as a centerpiece for the expanding suburbs. He located malls near newly built highway interchanges and invested in the Mall at Short Hills in New Jersey, Fairlane Town Center outside Detroit, and other properties, eventually owning twenty malls. As he told the *New York Times* in 1977, "We were able to duplicate to a great degree what occurs in a downtown, all under one ownership and one control." In the early 1990s commercial real estate faced a credit crunch, unable to raise capital to invest in new and existing properties. Existing structures for real estate investment trusts (REITs) exposed private owners going public to capital gains taxes, but Taubman CFO Bernard Winograd and bankers at Morgan Stanley created a new way to sell shares in the company to the public, via umbrella partnerships with an ownership stake in the malls. This structure, known as an UPREIT, raised three hundred million dollars for the newly created Taubman Realty Group, allowing it greater financial flexibility to acquire new properties. Other retail developers, including Simon Property Group and Tanger Factory Outlet Centers, soon followed suit.

Before Simon acquired DeBartolo, for example, it had already trans-formed from the private Melvin Simon & Associates to the public Simon Property Group, thanks to a 1993 IPO giving the company access to more cash. Simon and Taubman would dance around each other for years, with Taubman fighting off a hostile takeover attempt in 2003, and Simon first backing out of, and then renegotiating, a merger agreement in 2020, blaming the poor pandemic performance of Taubman's holdings. Today, Simon, which owns a majority stake in more than one hundred malls, is the largest mall REIT in the United States by far. In the next tier are Macerich, which went public in 1994 and acquired a number of regional mall portfolios in the next decade; Brookfield, which acquired the Rouse Company; and Tanger Factory Outlets. With these large portfolios (Macerich owns fifty-two malls), the kind of care and feeding that the owner of one, two, even a dozen malls could provide disappears. Malls become a pure economic play. You try a few things to make them work; if they fail, you eliminate them from the port-folio. Design standards, store mix, landscaping, programming—these main-tenance concerns switch from being on-the-ground, physical acts to a matter of cultivating the share price.

Owings Mills' story reflects all the economic drama that was mall owner-ship in the 1990s and 2000s—a series of mergers, acquisitions, and IPOs that moved properties around financially but did little to service them physically. Though built as a Rouse property, by the time it was torn down and trans-formed into Mill Station, it was owned by Kimco Realty Corporation, which went public in 1991 and specializes in open-air shopping centers. Between the mall's 1986 opening and Kimco's 2016 acquisition, Rouse in 1996 purchased the Howard Hughes Corporation, which owned a number of resorts and planned communities, and was then itself acquired by larger mall owner and developer General Growth Properties in 2004. The merger resulted in GGP having ownership or management stakes in more than 250 American malls. It also sent GGP into bankruptcy in 2009, from which the company slowly emerged through restructuring. In 2012, GGP spun off thirty malls in secondary markets into a separate REIT, now confusingly known as Rouse Properties, but kept Owings Mills. GGP eventually sold the site to Kimco, which was better able to revive the location with its outdoor model.

Owings Mills was part of the last generation of malls built by specialist developers with a 1950s-era view of ever-expanding consumer demand. To open a mall was a civic gesture, to shop was a civic gesture; malls offered belonging both as places to go and through the display of shopping bags, logo wear, sneakers purchased there. The mall was manipulative, but it could also be generous—until it wasn't. Fiction writers saw this earlier than most.

Prolific young adult author Richard Peck's 1979 book *Secrets of the Shopping Mall* is an early, albeit lesser-known entry in the annals of zombie mall literature, written at the same moment as Didion and Romero's critiques. Peck places the mall at the center of teenagers' world, writing an updated and zombified version of the running-away-to-the-Met fantasy in E. L. Konigsburg's children's classic *From the Mixed-Up Files of Mrs. Basil E. Frankweiler*. In Konigsburg's book, a maybe-Michelangelo statue of an angel generates the mystery; at the mall, it's mannequins.

Peck's setup is simple: Two kids in a tough junior high run from a gang of inner-city bullies, jumping on a city bus. How far will two dollars take them? "Paradise Park," says the driver. Teresa thinks it will be a park with bridges and swans and Shaun Cassidy singing "Do You Believe in Magic?" Barnie thinks it will be a retirement home. They are both wrong.

> In front of them black pavement stretched forever—to Alaska. They were standing on the outer arrows of a parking lot. If Shaun Cassidy was anywhere around, he was buried six feet under asphalt. Teresa felt the rest of her dream crumble.
>
> In the distance past a clutter of parked cars, she could make out a vast jumble of steel, glass, and white brick. In letters of fire a neon sign read:
>
> PARADISE PARK
> "Shoot," Barnie said. "It's a shopping mall."

Every fictional shopping mall I've encountered has a name that is both linguistically symbolic and fits within the template Didion lays out. At first the mall does seem like a paradise—bigger and cleaner than the city, at least the part they've explored—but Teresa and Barnie soon find it comes with its own gang warfare. Scuba, Threads, Barbie, and Dolly, a cat named Pantyhose—the mannequins, named for their respective departments in the mall's anchor store, should not be crossed. Over nights of stealing food from the lunch counter, and days faking life as a merchandise trainee, the living kids learn their stories. The mannequins were once kids too, until they ended up at the mall. One ran away from home; another's parents used the mall as babysitter and forgot to come back; a third is supposedly at boarding school.

In today's helicopter-parenting world, this requires herculean suspension of belief, but teen media of the 1970s is filled with absent and absentminded adults, teen runaways, tough talkers. *The Hunger Games* of 1979, pitting child against child, doesn't require a real dystopia, just the inner city, the mall, and neglectful parents. The book culminates in a face-off between the parking lot gang and the department store gang. Peck's mall zombies work together to win, creating a found family for Teresa and Barnie more nurturing than the adults who left them behind. The final paragraphs show Teresa visualizing, and embracing, a future at the mall that never seemed possible in junior high.

> Teresa turned, then, and strode through knots of tussling shoppers, fighting over Amazing Reductions in Slightly Water-Damaged Goods. She had a big day ahead of her in Stemware. A whole career, in fact, unfurled before her as she started up the Up Escalator.
>
> Where do you go from merchandise trainee, she wondered. Head of the department, finally, she figured. Yes, Teresa thought, I'll be buying stemware in Czechoslovakia one day ... The future looked pretty good from where Teresa stood, rising every minute on the escalator, up to Stemware on two.

If 1982 was the first "peak mall" year, 2007 was another. That was the first year since Southdale's opening in 1956 that no enclosed shopping malls were built in the United States, down from 140 per year in the mid-1990s. A wave of closures followed for the next decade, as marginal malls, redundant malls, and outclassed malls emptied out and closed. Their abandoned hulks sparked a new wave of art exploring the themes of consumerism and death, adding suspense and science fiction to horror and teen novels.

In *Gone Girl*, the 2012 bestselling thriller by Gillian Flynn, job losses have forced Nick and Amy Dunne to move back to his Missouri hometown, but there is no escaping economic collapse. Other houses in their McMansion cul-de-sac sit empty, and the mall at the edge of town is a ruin.

"Carthage was, until a year ago, a company town and that company was the sprawling Riverway Mall, a tiny city unto itself that once employed four thousand locals—one fifth the population. It was built in 1985, a destination mall meant to attract shoppers from all over the Middle West," Nick writes in the "memoir" that forms his half of the book. His family went to opening day, "soldiers on the battlefield of consumerism," to experience the air-conditioning, the Muzak, the Orange Julius. His mother sold shoes at the Shoe-Be-Doo-Be, an apt choice, as shoe stores have been a mall staple from their earliest days; Nick wiped tables in the food court in high school. One of the last acts Nick and Amy perform as a couple before she stages her disappearance and becomes "gone girl" is a sort of foolish adult version of a teenage date, riding the carousel at the mall and eating ice cream.

On the surface the Dunnes have nothing but disdain for the squatters who have moved into the mall, creating their own semi-feral society outside the bounds of mainstream consumer culture. As Nick writes in his book-within-the-book, "It was suburbia, post-comet, post-zombie, post-humanity."

And yet, locked in the battle of wits that creates the book's mystery, both turn to the mall's denizens for help. He's looking for information. She's looking for a gun. Like the refugees in *Dawn of the Dead*, the Dunnes think they are better than the zombies but really they are the zombies. The book ends with them living a post-humanity life that is all about the appearance of prosperity—big house, glowing wife, new baby—rather than admitting their feral desires. Amy writes in her book-within-the-book: "I will write [Nick] the way I want him to be: romantic and thoughtful and very very repentant—about the credit cards and the purchases and the woodshed." They don't light out for Canada but stay in their hollow world, joining rather than fighting the horde.

The mall in Ling Ma's *Severance*, a near-future novel published in 2018, is a spiritual descendant of the mall in *Dawn of the Dead*. Neutral-colored tile, two levels, skylight in the ceiling. Potted trees, leaves made of silk. An empty fountain with pennies crusting the bottom. A group of survivors of a fungal apocalypse, including narrator Candace Chen, arrive at the parking lot of Deer Oaks Mall, "a beige complex with signs boasting a Macy's, a Sears, and an AMC movie theater with eight screens." Bob, the leader of the group, has been pushing them toward this destination. "Everything we want is here, in these stores, Bob said, gesturing to the stores as if he owned them. We have endless supplies." We know this story: The empty mall promises plenty and normalcy while fevered zombies haunt the countryside. Candace, whose pre-fever job was coordinating the production of new editions of the Bible, is pregnant. Bob, like the teens in *Secrets of the Shopping Mall*, previously found solace at this mall after his parents' divorce.

Ma puts a bit of meta-commentary into Bob's mouth:

> Let's think about the zombie narrative. It's not about a specific villain. One zombie can be easily killed, but a hundred zombies is another issue. Only amassed do they really pose a threat. This narrative, then, is not about any individual entity, per se, but about an abstract force: the force of the mob, of mob mentality. Perhaps it's better known these days as the hive mind.

Severance took on new resonance as Covid-19 spread around the world in 2020. Like Ma's Shen Fever in the novel, the coronavirus was first discovered in China. It provoked staged retreats from workplaces like Candace's Manhattan publishing office. N95 masks were in high demand. Whole regions of the United States were under quarantine. Readers seemed queasily pleased by the parallels, as long as they assured themselves the worst, as described in *Severance*, wasn't to come.

Shen Fever propels its victims into repeating everyday behaviors ad infinitum. The most popular post on Candace's photo blog, *NY Ghost*, is a video of a fevered saleslady at the Juicy Couture flagship on Fifth Avenue, folding and refolding a rainbow of clothes. As the book unfolds in the present and through flashbacks to Candace's childhood and work life, she comments on consumption patterns, from the difference between American and Chinese malls to the way the members of the survivor group choose their homes within the Facility. The department stores are communal spaces, the boutiques become bedrooms. Candace, whom we know feels connected to her own mother through skin care, chooses L'Occitane. As Jiayang Fan writes in her *New Yorker* review of *Severance*, "Maybe consumption can start to look like an inescapable disease, but, to Candace, it is also a means of participating in a place, establishing a connection to it, and, gradually, becoming part of its ecosystem." Like Peck's truant teenagers—like any teenagers searching for merchandise to reflect their own identities—the survivors are still trying to express themselves through brands.

The question lingering under these depictions is whether the mall itself is to blame for humans' zombification. Without that million-square-foot box in the middle of a parking lot, would we wreck ourselves through consumption anyway? I think of artist Barbara Kruger's highly graphic work, which combines grainy found media images with phrases that pick at stereotypical roles for women. A 1990 piece centers a red rectangle with the statement I SHOP THEREFORE I AM printed on a paper shopping bag. Postwar American culture pushed women into the role of shopper in chief, even as it judged them for overconsumption. And yet, men and women do find freedom in shopping for their true selves.

In Nana Kwame Adjei-Brenyah's 2018 short story "Friday Black," the mall makes the zombies. The virus is a sickness that grips humans shopping for bargains on Black Friday. The story stands apart from other mall zombie lit by being written from the point of view of the ultimate insider: a salesperson.

He works at a Patagonia-inspired sporting goods store at the Prominent Mall, selling SuperShell parkas and other jackets intended for extreme sports. Most don't make it out of the parking lot.

The story even starts like a race: On your mark, get set, sell. Work to the limits of your endurance. Suck it up if you get hurt. It's the Olympics of shopping. Whoever racks up the most daily sales wins the only SuperShell in size large—the gift our hero covets for Mom.

"Get to your sections!" Angela screams.

Ravenous humans howl. Our gate whines and rattles as they shake and pull, their grubby fingers like worms through the grating. I sit atop a tiny cabin roof made of hard plastic. My legs hang near the windows, and fleeces hang inside of it. I hold my reach, an eight-foot-long metal pole with a small plastic mouth at the end for grabbing hangers off the highest racks. I also use my reach to smack down Friday heads. It's my fourth Black Friday. On my first, a man from Connecticut bit a hole into my tricep. His slobber hot. I left the sales floor for ten minutes so they could patch me up. Now I have a jagged smile on my left arm. A sickle, half circle, my lucky Friday scar. I hear Richard's shoes flopping toward me. "You ready, big guy?" he asks. I open one eye and look at him. I've never not been ready, so I don't say anything and close my eyes again. "I get it; I get it. Eye of the tiger! I like it," Richard says.

A child falls and gets swept into a corner with a broom. White foam drips from the mouth of a father in a puffy vest. There are bloodstains on the floor and corpses in the food court. The Gruen transfer has taken on its final and most deadly iteration, stripping away empathy in favor of the ravening need to consume status puffers. Our hero selflessly gives away the sold-out parka after winning it, egging on the crowd with customer service language: "How can I help you today?" Adjei-Brenyah's story, like Ma's *Severance*, lives only one click away from reality. In fact, more than a hundred people in pursuit of day-after-Thanksgiving discounts are known to have been trampled, shot, and stabbed by fellow shoppers, even hit by cars—a macabre catalog recorded on websites such as Black Friday Death Count.

In his original 1979 review of *Dawn of the Dead*, Roger Ebert wrote: "The zombies are not the ones who are depraved." In *Dawn of the Dead*, in "Friday Black," it is the living who are fighting over candy, guns, coats (furs in 1978, down in 2016). They aren't 100 percent bad—they are fighting for gifts, after all, helping family members up while pushing others' family members down. Ebert: "The survivors have courage, too, and a certain nobility at times, and a sense of humor, and loneliness and dread, and are not altogether unlike ourselves. A-ha."

Photographer Seph Lawless's specialty is abandoned everything. Ranged on a nine-square grid on the first page of his website are abandoned malls, abandoned amusement parks, abandoned theme parks, abandoned houses, abandoned asylums, abandoned schools, and abandoned trolleys. (Matthew Christopher's Abandoned America project, which captured Owings Mills, is also in this mode.) The color palette is mostly greens and browns, as if every place of amusement is going back to nature. The shots are deep, sucking you into the wreck: down the length of the trolley, across the pavement to the merry-go-round, across the atrium to the escalators. Subsequent photographs pick up details and detritus—abandoned shopping carts, abandoned school desks—but there's a distancing sameness to the framing. In abandoned America, the message might be, comforts are far away. But space and scale also suggest adventure. In an action movie, it is more macho to scale a skyscraper; in abandoned-buildings photography, it is more macho to be the only man left in a one-thousand-seat theater or one-million-square-foot mall. Lawless's landscapes are bleak and dark. *Gone Girl*'s Riverway Mall would be an ideal subject.

Photographer Jesse Rieser's series *The Changing Landscape of American Retail* captured between 2015 and 2021, frames the dead mall as a pastel object, a home good from a HomeGoods inflated to architectural scale. His photos are usually taken outside the mall, with the space of the empty parking lot framing the building's beige, pink, or terra-cotta exterior like a cake in a case. Signs have been taken down or cropped out, so we see only the shapes and unfaded backgrounds where the brands used to be. Rieser's images should be more soothing, less monster movie than Lawless's, but their lack of details has its own disorienting strangeness. Again, we might be the last person here. Lawless shows us wrecks, Rieser a tidied-up desolation that seems to be in a permanent frozen state.

Directors and writers reanimated the mall, using its zombified 1980s and 2010s state as a backdrop for commentary on the consumer condition. A wave of large-format photography in the 2010s approached the dead mall differently, romanticizing and historicizing the wrecks by framing them as previous generations of photographers, painters, and engravers had framed abandoned theaters, abandoned castles, and abandoned temples. The aesthetic concept of the sublime, outlined by Edmund Burke in his 1757 treatise *A Philosophical Enquiry into the Origins of Our Ideas of the Sublime and Beautiful*, covers "whatever is fitted in any sort to excite the ideas of pain and danger" and "whatever is in any sort terrible" and connects it to pleasure. We are delighted to be afraid—this is why we go to horror movies—and depictions of architectural ruins have long been a location of such shivers.

The photographs fit into a larger visual project that also aestheticizes the skeletons of the late nineteenth century; the same symmetrical, large-volume, skylit, made-for-a-crowd spaces that inspired the mall architects fell on their own hard times. Visual depictions of ruins run the architectural history gamut from Piranesi's etchings of former Roman grandeur to postmodern architecture's collages of neoclassical parts, as seen in projects like Charles Moore's Piazza d'Italia or Jerde's Horton Plaza.

"Ruin porn" is a term that, as McLain Clutter wrote for the *Avery Review*, "seems to have emerged spontaneously from the hive mind of the blogosphere," circa 2011. It also emerges, quite explicitly from Burke's terror-pleasure principle. If "shelter porn" is looking at pretty pictures of houses you'll never afford, "ruin porn" is looking at pretty pictures of places you'll never go. In photographs like Lawless's we imagine ourselves exploring the wreck; in photographs like Rieser's we see the ghosts of past shopping trips. But we are also, less comfortably, exulting in waste. Critic Jonathan Glancey wrote in 2014, "The demolition of such huge buildings could only appear to be a case of conspicuous consumption and wastefulness on a truly titanic scale."

A key essay for twenty-first-century thinking about ruins is John Patrick Leary's "Detroitism," published in *Guernica* in January 2011, which assembles a visual bibliography of that city's select deterioration. Detroit had become a nexus of creative activity around detritus—derelict buildings, within the city limits, whose size spoke to the city's former prosperity, and whose continuing decay spoke to the city's financial status. The star of any Detroit ruin porn narrative is Michigan Central Station, a 1913 edifice, centrally located on Detroit's radiating grid, that was once the transportation gateway to the Motor City, with architecture on par with New York's Grand Central Terminal. Photographer Andrew Moore shot *Detroit Disassembled*, a photo essay whose title is a play on the assembly lines that once fueled urban growth; photographers Yves Marchand and Romain Meffre shot *The Ruins of Detroit*; and Dan Austin and Scott Doerr's architectural history *Lost Detroit: Stories Behind the Motor City's Majestic Ruins* makes it look and sound as if the best of the city is already in the past. Detroit was not alone in its appeal to photographers; other cities built around a single industry have also suffered. Detroit was special, Leary argues, because the remaining wealthy residents are happy staying in the suburbs. Because of their lack of desire to shop, or eat, or wander in the city, Detroit has never "been able to do on any significant scale what Pittsburgh has accomplished with its defunct Homestead steel mill, now a shopping mall, or what New York has done with upscale condos in old warehouses—leverage the hollow shells of a productive economy into the shell games of the credit economy." Malls were part of a larger ecosystem of architecture that once worked and had now ground to a halt.

Leary labels this recent documentation "the Lament." "The Lament signals a fascination with what seems to be all that we have of our twentieth-century history (at least besides those war memorials): the brick-and-steel spectacles of the industrial age, out of which some explanation could be found for the present desperate predicament of urban America." To him the photographs suggest a civilization hurriedly deserted, like stills from a zombie movie. He doesn't reference *Dawn of the Dead*, but the description would suit; in Romero's film the lights, sounds, and movement of the mall crank on without human visitors. British filmmaker Julien Temple referred to the few living people he encountered while scouting his documentary *Requiem for Detroit?* as "street zombies," negating their humanity and agency. Leary writes, "One often finds oneself asking of . . . all ruin photographs, first, 'What happened?' followed swiftly by, 'What's your point?'" For this photography to be successful it has to feel like the end rather than a new beginning, and the viewer needs to accept that end as an inevitability and not fight back. If you believe in a city, it is difficult to accept its demise as sublime.

In the years after 2011, a lively debate about the merits of ruin porn sprang up, centered on the out-of-town visitors treating a city like Detroit as a post-apocalyptic playground. In *Vice*, Brian Merchant wrote about *Tracing Skylines*, a 2013 "freestyle skiing video wherein a band of white thrill-seekers treat the abandoned, crumbling detritus of a once-mighty American city as an edgy terrain park." The residents of Detroit interviewed for the film are all Black. They talk about jobs while the white stars of the video talk about thrills, treating a still-occupied city as wilderness.

As a location Detroit carries numerous layers of mall-related irony. The assembly lines that stretched architecture to its limits, forcing architects to span and daylight some of the largest interior spaces in the world, created the vehicles that allowed the city to spread out. Victor Gruen had his mall epiphany on Detroit's snowy streets, realizing the downtown department stores wouldn't last the decade and planning four new out-of-town centers that would suck life from the streets. Northland, Gruen's first shopping center, opened in the Detroit suburb of Southfield in 1954. When it closed in 2015, it became the subject of the same kind of photography as the downtown office and factory buildings the suburbs had bankrupted. In the absence of commerce, Northland's three barrel-vaulted exterior entrances to the J. L. Hudson department store, lightweight structures of white metal tubing and canvas, proved to be the most enduringly photogenic elements. Empty or occupied, they reference the steel-and-glass architecture of the original European gallerias, brought down to earth in the middle of a Michigan parking lot.

Visually the malls of the 1980s and 1990s have less going on than Northland, let alone the factories, train sheds, and theaters of the late nineteenth and early twentieth centuries. Ornament is applied like a thin film—tiled columns, bolted-on neon—rather than the frosted intricacies of plaster, terra-cotta, and ironwork. Their emptiness is more empty. Their spatial qualities are more uncertain. Their contemporary design was rarely intended for timelessness, but rather to be frequently updated like a consumer product. Dead malls look like collapsing husks rather than sturdy shells, one breath (and one wrecking ball) away from destruction. What remains of life—mall plants and sculpture and blue-bottomed fountains—adds necessary visual friction, and often a spot of color, to the beige geometries.

As Clutter writes,

> If there is any promise in ruin porn, it emanates from its ability to gather an audience where there was previously none. Despite ethical transgressions, despite sometimes-kitsch aesthetics, ruin porn has turned eyes to cities in decline in volumes unseen in the latter half of the twentieth century. Regardless of whether these gazes seek authenticity, nostalgia, or some other libidinal urge, it seems the role of architecture might be to turn these spectators into citizens.

Once upon a time, malls were brimming with ideas and busy with people. The materials used to make the buildings have their own value, but they also conferred value on that corner of the interstate. Erik Pierson, the videographer behind the YouTube channel Retail Archaeology, seems as if he might be another vulture. His videos of dead and dying malls attract hundreds of thousands of viewers. But Pierson turns out to be a mall fan. He lives in Phoenix, where malls are one of few shaded, planted spaces in which to gather, and he began his YouTube career making recordings of old video games. He's a historian of the consumer experience, as happy to explore 8-bit graphics as he is the defunct stores and laughable signage of malls on their last legs. He sees his videos not as celebrating the end of an era but as preserving the artifacts of a way of life—very recent history, not archaeology of a world gone by. (And he's far from alone, at least on the internet, where the robust Reddit channel r/deadmalls and its Discord server operate as an ongoing nexus of research, memoir, and videos of then and now.) He has also documented the afterlives of malls, including a J. C. Penney (a department store chain that Covid-19 sent to its already inevitable bankruptcy) turned antiques emporium. Pierson's videos aren't pretty—the visual pleasure that gets photography of ruins labeled "porn" is absent—but there's a companionable energy to them that the still images lack. Pierson acts as a sympathetic guide, demonstrating interest in the brands and artifacts and lives lived. It makes sense that he started as an archaeologist of video games, another marginalized art form that many thought would disappear but that has come to have its own canon.

The common ground of all ruin porn is waste. A waste of materials, a waste of design, a waste of imagination. I can't admire the lines of a building if I am thinking about how its emptiness brings the city down, block by block, crime by crime, into a vicious cycle of limited economic opportunity. Any travelers in the world of dead malls must ask themselves whether they are prepared to fight to put people back into the gutted buildings, or if they merely intend to pick over the aesthetic bones.

Won't you come see about me?
I'll be alone, dancing you know it, baby

Those lyrics, from Simple Minds' 1985 number one single "Don't You (Forget About Me)," are enough to summon the closing scene in the film *The Breakfast Club* in the mind of most 1980s youths. It plays under the almost silent goodbyes of the five students—the club—who have spent their Saturday together in detention. It plays under the voice-over of their note to the principal, rejecting the categories into which high school has filed them, a Brain, an Athlete, a Basket Case, a Princess, and a Criminal. It plays under the final shot, where the Criminal (Judd Nelson) strides across the playing field and raises his fist to the sky. Over sparkling synths, Simple Minds frontman Jim Kerr sings the track's insistent title lyric, underlining the message of director John Hughes's most influential film. The song is, to pick a more recent teen idiom, a mood—a mood of adolescent angst and flailing against authority, of searching for connection and finding the right words. It is also—through its overlap of teen angst, 1980s music, and late modern buildings—the grandfather of mallwave, the latest genre to transform the dead mall.

The Breakfast Club is set at Shermer High School in suburban Chicago, played in the movie by Maine North High School in Des Plaines, Illinois, built in 1970. The exterior of Maine North appears in the movie as is, the entrance a long horizontal brow of concrete sheltering a wide set of steps. The library in which most of the action happens was constructed in the school's gymnasium—the real library was too small—and it follows the conventions of theater in the round. The tables at which the students start their day are set in the center of a deep bowl, like the floor of the stage. The mezzanine ringing the floor acts as a balcony for private chats and a proscenium for group dances. The clerestory windows lighting the room bring in daylight but block out the outside world.

The fishbowl layout of Shermer High's library, along with its stacked levels, white columns, and liberal use of blond wood and neon edging, is reminiscent of another kind of interior space central to the 1980s teen experience: the mall. Picture it: The Princess purchases the diamond studs she later shares with the Criminal, the Athlete buys his smoothie with protein powder, the Brain stocks shelves. The floor of the mall atrium, like the floor of the Shermer High library, is the mixing space through which everyone has to pass. The Princess preens in the limelight while the Basket Case tries to stick to the dark hall near the arcade, just as she chooses the table at the back in the library. The fishbowl puts the teens under adult surveillance and, at the same time, gives them room, separated from the outside world, in which to flail, to fight, to fall in love.

The centralized layout of the shopping mall was so well known by the mid-1980s, it is hard to believe that the expanded school library built for the film isn't tipping its hat to the other architecture of teen angst. Northbrook Court Shopping Center, which appears in Hughes's *Weird Science* (also released in 1985), is a two-level mall with a cream-colored interior, its atrium courts framed by tall marble-faced columns and illuminated by triangular skylights. It is grander than *The Breakfast Club*'s library but organized on the same see-and-be-seen principle. The size made for easier and more dramatic filming, while simultaneously taking advantage of the same kind of interpersonal choreography—a floor to gather, a balcony to dance on, a niche for private conversation.

I had never considered *The Breakfast Club* set as a mall in disguise until I saw Cecil Robert's 2018 YouTube video "Simple Minds—Don't You (Forget About Me) (playing in an empty shopping centre)." The song, remixed to sound tinny and hollow, as if bouncing off the hard surfaces of an empty shopping mall, is paired with an image of the abandoned Court of the Twelve

Court of the Twelve Trees, Rolling Acres Mall, Akron, Ohio, Keeva J. Kekst Architects, 1975. Demolished 2017. Still from Dan Bell, "Dead Mall: Rolling Acres," YouTube. (Dan Bell)

Trees from Akron, Ohio's Rolling Acres Mall, with a red-stepped fountain, now dry, positioned in front of the dark maw of a department store entrance, trash and debris on the ground, the whole scene still illuminated by the cool northern light filtered through the white, three-dimensional grid of the ceiling space frame. The space frame dates the mall to the mid-1970s (Rolling Acres opened in 1975). Jon Jerde used a space frame at the Mall of America; at Rolling Acres it creates a vast column-free atrium, designed for mass gathering, now emptied of all life. The combination of color, architecture, and decay made Rolling Acres a popular destination, documented by Lawless as well as other dead-mall superstars like Dan Bell. "Don't you, forget about me," sings Kerr, again. Is he speaking as the mall, for the mall patrons, or for all of us who saw ourselves in one of the types in *The Breakfast Club*? For me it is the layering of all three possibilities that gives this video an emotional punch. "i feel like the shopping center is singing to me," commented one YouTube viewer.

"Simple Minds—Don't You (Forget About Me) (playing in an empty shopping centre)" is part of a larger body of music called "mallwave" or "mallsoft," of which Cecil Robert, now in his midtwenties, was a popular practitioner. In 2017, Robert posted his first mallwave track, a remix of Toto's "Africa" edited to sound as if it were playing in an echoey, empty mall. (The 1982 song, in its original form, was also used by the Duffer Brothers in their paean to 1980s nostalgia *Stranger Things*.) As Jia Tolentino wrote for the *New Yorker* in 2018, "A remarkably high number of people have tweeted, in the past several years, about the experience of being in a mall and listening to the song. Last May, one Twitter user wrote, 'fantasizing abt listening to africa by toto in an abandoned mall.' Cecil Robert uploaded his video a few months later, and it has now been viewed more than half a million times."

To craft the distinctive mallwave sound, Tolentino wrote, tinkerers "cut the low frequencies, raise the mid-range frequencies, and add a delay, which imitates the way sound bounces through a big, empty space." Longer compositions combine new music with pop hits from the 1970s, 1980s and 1990s, using elements associated with the songs of that era—soft drum tracks, ambient sounds, and low-quality synthesizers—to create mood music associated with a place that, in its day, wasn't necessarily considered calming. Mallwave is a subset of the broader early 2010s musical genre called "vaporwave": music born of the internet, and popularized on Tumblr, that put space and smudge back into bits and pieces of 1980s and 1990s pop music. The effect is like half listening to music in an elevator or a doctor's office.

A 2016 *Esquire* story declaring mallwave music already dead identifies James Ferraro's *Far Side Virtual* (2011) as a "founding document" of the genre. All Ferraro's song titles seem intended to situate the listener in a 1990s space: *The Far Side* was one of the most popular comics of the 1980s and 1990s; there's a song called "Palm Trees, Wi-Fi and Dream Sushi"; and, as Ferraro told *Esquire*'s Scott Beauchamp,

> if you really want to understand "Far Side," first off listen to [Claude] Debussy, and secondly, go into a frozen yogurt shop. Afterwards, go into an Apple store and just fool around, hang out in there. Afterwards, go to Starbucks and get a gift card. They have a book there on the history of Starbucks—buy this book and go home. If you do all these things you'll understand what "Far Side Virtual" is—because people kind of live in it already.

An Ultimate Guitar contributor pungently described this music as "us[ing] ambience as an instrument." "The most interesting part of 'Mallsoft' music is the inclusion of the 'space' around the music that's playing," he wrote. "When you listen to 'Mallsoft,' you're not listening to a recording of the music that was played in a mall, you're listening to how that mall sounded when music was added to it."

As Tolentino and other commenters noted, the makers of mallwave weren't children of the 1970s or 1980s but, in many cases, children of the late 1990s and early 2000s, nostalgic for an experience they never had. *Dead Mall Adventures*, a 2017 digital album by Dead Air Collective, a group of musicians from (of course) New Jersey, is probably the first of the genre, its period bona fides established by its teal-pink-and-orange album cover and whispery, echoey songs like "Saint Pepsi Playing in an Empty Mall,"

"Dumped by the Fountain," and "Neon Elevator." "Dumped" offers "I Can't Make You Love Me," popularized by Bonnie Raitt in 1991, as a super-slow, super-saxophone instrumental.

Each mallwave song on YouTube is accompanied by a still photo, many of them taken by Bell. Most commenters treat the images as generic—as if all empty malls are the same, and many of the tracks use the same photo—but as I clicked through the playlists, I found that some combinations of music and image were simply more spectral, more emotional. Just listening to tinny versions of the songs of my youth, best remembered from listening to Casey Kasem's Top 40 countdown on Saturday mornings being driven to and from soccer practice, didn't really do it for me, a person old enough to have experienced the mall in its glory days. I needed the *Breakfast Club* experience, the merge of mood, architecture, and music.

YouTube user MadArtMart plays "In the Air Tonight" by Phil Collins over a picture of a shopping mall completely gone to seed: dead plants in the planter, mildew staining the walls, a sepia cast over what must once have been a shiny, white-tiled space. The photo is by Lawless, of the Metro North Shopping Center in Kansas City, Missouri, which opened in 1976. Lawless's images of the mall, taken two years after its 2014 closure, went viral in a 2016 *Daily Mail* story that became the defining pop culture moment for mall ruin porn. In the image chosen by MadArtMart, Metro North no longer looks like a mall but like a natural history museum, the antiqued finishes showing the similarity between the bones of the 1970s commercial and 1870s institutional architecture: regular, symmetrical, with display cases and deep balconies and unseen skylights. The lyrics of Collins's song, always wistful, seem to be coming at you from some far court. What's in the air tonight? Societal breakdown, malls going back to nature, the end of twentieth-century capitalism.

One of my favorite aspects of the mallwave experience on YouTube is the comments from former mall workers, who feel the feels without irony. "Man I used to work at an amusement park in a mall, and I'd close all the time," YouTube user TheKandyCinema reminisced, commenting on one of many mallwave treatments of a Journey song. "When the mall was empty and they still played music and had lights, this is EXACTLY what it was like."

An essential part of the nostalgic mall experience is simply being exposed to music you haven't chosen. Streaming services, iPods, iPhones, and headphones have pared away the hit-or-miss nature of entertainment, of waiting for your favorite song to play on the radio, sitting through advertising or the tedious banter of disc jockeys. The mall was, Tolentino wrote, "a place where, for a change, someone else controls the music . . . someplace where you've taken the chance of being lonely in public, instead of retreating and clicking around alone." Mallwave is background music for people who can listen to whatever they want in the foreground.

When the mall was first set to music, the goal was not to soothe but to stimulate. Major General George O. Squier founded the company Wired Radio in 1934, after a stint in the army as chief signal officer during World War I. A few years later he rechristened it Muzak, following the pattern of Kodak. In the 1940s, Muzak's most successful product was something called the Stimulus Progression: fifteen-minute, prearranged instrumental recordings sold as having the ability to boost worker productivity. Muzak sold different mixes for different times of day, calming for first thing in the morning, peppy for a mid-morning music break, faster again for mid-afternoon. The scientific basis for these audio snacks was dubious, and the question of whether employees should be subject to such subliminal motivation led to a lawsuit in the 1950s. Nonetheless, employers bought the product, using it to occupy riders in early elevators and on D.C. Metro buses and trains, and energize workers in hotels, restaurants, and, eventually, shopping malls.

Alvin Collis, once senior vice president of strategy and brand at Muzak, told the *New Yorker* in 2006,

> I walked into a store and understood: this is just like a movie. The company has built a set, and they've hired actors and given them costumes and taught them their lines, and every day they open their doors and say, 'Let's put on a show.' It was retail theatre. And I

realized then that Muzak's business wasn't really about selling music. It was about selling emotion—about finding the soundtrack that would make this store or that restaurant feel like something, rather than being just an intellectual proposition.

Collis called this concept "audio architecture," and Muzak used it as an opportunity to rebrand itself as something more than "elevator music." But in truth, the background music at the mall had always been mood setting, and always been an integral part of the architecture. The malls that didn't play music—NorthPark among them—exploited other kinds of white noise, like the plash of water in a fountain, to create an aural setting. The mall without music is like a movie without a soundtrack, a sitcom without a laugh track: The audience isn't used to relying on just visuals and dialogue in order to get a read on the room.

Baby boomers, born at roughly the same time as the mall, grew up with music never more than the twist of a knob away, with hi-fis in the living room, radios in their cars and, eventually, music in their pocket via the Walkman. But that individualized access was accompanied by an ever-increasing audio architecture. In 1982, it was estimated that one in three Americans heard programmed music at some point each day; estimates only increased over the following decade. By the time the Mall of America opened in 1992, the three different sound systems built into its structure were as necessary to its functioning as ducts for air-conditioning and wiring for electricity. The facilities management team, responsible for HVAC and power, also monitored the music, which revealed its presence to the public only through small, blond, circular speakers installed at the edges of the Jerde Partnership–designed space. As cultural historian Jonathan Sterne documented in a 1997 article on the MOA's audio architecture for the journal *Ethnomusicology*, quiet background music played in its hallways, digital crickets chirped for central amusement park Camp Snoopy, and individual-ized playlists for each store were set in distant corporate headquarters. The hallway music, provided by 3M, was intended to soothe but not encourage dwelling in those transitional, non-sales spaces. If mallwave has a progenitor it is this wash of half-heard tunes and ambient noise that cues you to your location while not requiring any specific emotion. The bleakest mallwave examples are those scored over images not of mall atriums or food courts or escalators, but of those generic hallways, with their interchangeable white quarry tile, hung ceilings, and striped columns. In the contrast between these cramped settings and the angsty vocals, one receives the message: *Imagine trying to find romance here.*

Foreground music in the mall, Sterne writes, "works as an architectural element of a built space devoted to consumerism. A store deploys programmed music as part of a fabricated environment aimed at getting visitors to stay longer and buy more." Standard Muzak programs, purchased by retailers, are divided up by demographics just like the *Billboard* charts: this one to invoke nostalgia among baby boomers, that one to make teens feel sophisticated. The reason most retailers purchase programs, rather than assembling their own playlists, is money. If they played the radio, or individual albums, over the public address system, they would need to pay royalties to the individual artists. The programmers take care of the fees upfront. The programs are also standardized across different branches of the store chain, so that a Victoria's Secret in Texas sounds the same as one in Minnesota.

The exceptions to these rules are stores like Hot Topic, for which music is not background but centerpiece, their outlets issuing siren songs to angsty teens everywhere. In 2014, to celebrate its twenty-fifth anniversary, Hot Topic curated its own Spotify playlist that kicked off with Nine Inch Nails and Nirvana—the grunge that its earliest teen patrons chose to consume. John Paul Brammer devoted a January 2020 edition of his newsletter *¡Hola Papi!* to his memories of Hot Topic: "As a moody high school freshman in 2005, few places offered such respite from the wretched banality of the world as the dark, deafening interior of Hot Topic." He acknowledges the irony of shopping for countercultural merchandise—for rebukes to suburbia, the American dream, and normalcy—at a mall store, but in the end, the soundtrack rules. "It did proliferate the goth, punk ethos (combined here for simplicity's sake) to parts of the country that wouldn't have been able to access it so easily, like my neck of the woods in rural Oklahoma where 'mall goth culture' was a massive hit." Today, Hot Topic has been smoothed, he observes, from the music on out. "It no longer has its iconic portal, and it no longer blasts the music that kept many a suburban parent at bay."

→

When Metrocenter opened in 1973 it was big news in Phoenix: "the state's largest new shopping 'city,'" a "312-acre 'environmentally controlled' behemoth," "98 acres of gulpable statistics" with enough refrigeration for 1,500 homes, enough shelter for thirty-five football fields, enough asphalt to reach from Phoenix to Prescott and back. Like Owings Mills, Metrocenter was a journey and a destination and a catalyst for new residential

Metrocenter Mall, Phoenix, Arizona, Robert Fairburn for Flatow, Moore, Bryan & Fairburn, 1973. (© USA TODAY NETWORK)

development on what were then the fringes of a city's metro area. (The name was aspirational.) While Owings Mills lives on as an ersatz village, 2020 locked the doors on Metrocenter—but its cultural footprint won it an afterlife.

Metrocenter had five department stores, each with a distinctive parking-lot facade and connected via an unusual Z-shaped plan. The dual-level mall, designed by Robert Fairburn, was cast as a concrete landscape, with slant-walled staircases outside and stepped, carpeted hangout spaces inside. Curved concrete curtains descended from the triple-height ceilings, focusing light from the skylights and creating topography above mallgoers' heads. An ice-skating rink was the focal point, overlooked by a restaurant with a travel theme, down to menus printed on airline tickets and booths that looked like airplane seats. When Genghis Kahn, Mozart, Joan of Arc, and Abraham Lincoln required up-to-date equipment in *Bill and Ted's Excellent Adventure*, its protagonists took the historical figures to Metrocenter for their sporting goods, keyboard, aerobics, and photography needs. A giant Sam Goody took a central spot in the mall, attracting teenagers when music still came from a physical store; in the mall's final years it would be replaced by Forever 21. Robrt L. Pela, a self-described "mall brat," reminisced about his own teen years for the *Phoenix New Times* in 2020:

> I had grown up at Metro; I could picture its funky interiors as easily as I could conjure the shag-carpeted family room of my family home. There was no community center in any of our suburban tracts, but we had Metrocenter, where we could ice skate or go to the movies, play air hockey at Red Baron and skateboard off the loading dock behind Sears. Moms weren't thinking about sexual predators when they dropped us off at Metro on a Saturday morning; we'd spend the day playing tag in front of Rosenzweig's, grab a free lunch of cheese and sausage samples at Swiss Colony, then go make out in the photo booths in the patchouli-scented, hippie-dippy Alley.

Metrocenter's other pop culture claim to fame was more specialized: When *Transworld Skateboarding* filmed a day in the life of pro skater Chad

Muska for a 1999 video titled "Feedback," he performed a front 50/50 down a double-kinked handrail outdoors on the northeast side of the mall, which subsequently became a pilgrimage site for other skaters.

On June 30, 2020, Metrocenter shut down for good. Phoenix blogs had cataloged its ailing fortunes for more than a decade, including internal and external renovations in the mid-2000s and the 2010 withdrawal of Westcor, which had been one of the mall's original developers (along with the Sears real estate division). Ownership passed from one REIT to another during the 2000s, with Simon Property Group and Macerich each taking a stake and making "improvements" for a time. The Covid-19 pandemic simply offered the final blow. Just as Metrocenter had once cannibalized the older, more centrally located Chris-Town and Park Central Malls, Arrowhead Towne Center cannibalized Metrocenter. The neighborhoods that had eventually been built around the mall had also suffered from disinvestment; they were now low-income and perceived as high crime. In 2010, the mall was 23 percent vacant, with two of its five anchors closed. The ice rink had closed in 1990; a Vans Skatepark, which opened in 2001, closed less than a decade later. An Urban Land Institute study of the property, funded by the city, suggested education and health-care tenants as replacements for retail, as well as extending Phoenix's light rail to the property. Neither of those strategies was implemented, and Metrocenter limped along. Retail Archaeology visited twice, once in December 2016, and again after the holidays, noting the continuing absence of anchor stores, many empty storefronts, and, on a Saturday afternoon, a bare handful of people.

The slow death did allow some longtime shoppers the opportunity to say goodbye. Five days before Metrocenter's closure, Danny Upshaw, Chelsea Winkel, and a dozen of their friends decided to pay tribute with "a farewell cruise," gliding through the mall on roller skates and skateboards and posing on the mall's bright, graphic atrium carpets. Winkel, who skates as "Goldy Knocks" in the Arizona Roller Derby flat-track league, said she has never met a mall she did not want to skate: "Malls just have the perfect floor."

Upshaw, a skateboarder, grew up spending more time at the Chris-Town Mall but skated the bowls at the Vans indoor park and was familiar with the handrail from Muska's 50/50 video and a subsequent backward homage by professional skateboarder David González. The group lapped the mall and took photos and videos, performing the same smooth circles and rolling descents as previous generations of skaters, now unbounded by ticketed admission. The whole mall was a skate park. The moving camera smoothed out the economic edges of the situation—no time to dwell on individual storefronts—turning the experience into a sort of instantaneous zombie flick, all empty stores and stilled escalators, or a mallwave image awaiting its perfect 1980s tune. After thirty minutes the mall's remaining security guards decided they'd had enough, and began slow-walking toward the group, which beat a quick wheeled retreat. Subsequently Winkel discovered she wasn't the first to roller-skate the mall: Metrocenter hosted a "Roller Disco Demo" in 1979, with swinging couples boogying in front of the Joske's store.

Upshaw returned on Metrocenter's final night with a *Bill &Ted* cosplay group and found one of the few remaining vendors, an airbrush shop, had decided to go out with a mordant bang. The shop was selling METROCENTER 1973–2020 T-shirts, black, with the dates under a photo of one of the mall's distinctive tile-roofed entrances. He posted the photo on Instagram, tagging Chad Muska, and Muska responded: "Long before I did the handrail, I would get dropped off as a kid to go to the skateshop and lurk around the mall, my mom had to come and pick up my skateboard from the security a few times!" What struck me most about Metrocenter's long goodbye was just how many subcultures were represented, from arcade games to roller disco, ice skating to skateboarding, teen dreamboats to custom Ts. The brutalist look of the place should have dated it, but instead it became an ongoing and ever-changing parade of consumerism and rebellion, hanging out and getting busted. Even the slow approach of the mall cops in the waning days seemed somehow poetic—even here, at the end, fun had a limit. But what fun was had, 1973–2020.

Chapter 7
The Postapocalyptic Mall

In 2019 I went to the Shops and Restaurants at Hudson Yards six times—*six times*—and yet I still kept getting lost. Hudson Yards—the twenty-eight-acre, twenty-five-billion-dollar development built on a platform over Penn Station's working railroad tracks on the West Side of Manhattan—was the biggest story in New York for months. A city within a city, it included office and residential towers, an arts center, an open plaza with Thomas Heatherwick's shawarma-shaped Vessel, and, to serve all those new visitors, workers, and residents, a mall. I went as a design critic, I went as a shopper, I went as a mother.

Was Muji on the second or third floor? Was the minty Instagram-fave Van Leeuwen ice cream shop down the hall? Forty Five Ten, the Dallas-born boutique that is the grandbaby of Neiman Marcus, was definitely up on the fifth floor, next to its ancestor, but how to get from the first to the second floor without passing Blue Bottle Coffee? And—starting to sweat now—what was the fastest route to a slice of William Greenberg rainbow cake to placate my kids, who hated the Vessel?

"It's just stairs," they said. "Can we get bubble tea?"

R. Webber Hudson, an executive vice president at the Related Companies, co-developer of Hudson Yards, didn't have this problem. He and his team curated the "vertical retail center"—he winced each time I referred to it as a "mall" as he took me on a tour—and its configuration was as clear to him as

The Shops and Restaurants at Hudson Yards, New York City, KPF, Elkus Manfredi, 2019. (Photograph by Max Touhey)

the glass in the Shops' six-story atrium. International luxury brands are on the first floor; previously only-on-the-internet brands like M. Gemi shoes and Japanese normcore faves Uniqlo and Muji are on the second; high-volume draws Zara and H&M are stacked on three and four; and so on.

There was a logic, but I just couldn't see it. Whenever I complained about this in conversation, acquaintances rolled their eyes and told me that's *mall* logic; the developers want me to get lost and spend more money. "Trust me," I told them, "I am familiar with the Gruen transfer." But that confusion wasn't my experience of "classic" indoor luxury retail: Just that March I had visited Gerald Hines's Houston Galleria, with its sweeping interior views, a conservatory-like roof, and a completely logical pattern of alternating elevators and escalators. The Gruen transfer isn't about losing yourself to confusion, but about losing yourself to pleasure. The pleasure of looking, the pleasure of touching, and increasingly the pleasure of tasting.

Almost precisely a year to the day after Hudson Yards's triumphal opening, thanks to the pandemic, the simple pleasure of touring, and critiquing, the retail manifestation of an enormous rich people's archipelago on the West Side of Manhattan suddenly felt very far away. Traveling to other cities to visit malls, stopping by multiple malls in New York City, checking out the lines at Blue Bottle, sampling the merchandise, taking my kids on an unnecessary subway trip into Manhattan and encouraging them to hold on to the pole—everything looked different when viewed at social distance. In hindsight, the Shops and Restaurants at Hudson Yards read as the last gasp of a decadent society, an architecture based on the arrogant predictions that, yes, the mall may be dead, but the best, brightest, shiniest malls continue to make bank. I did not set foot in another mall for more than a year—that tour of NorthPark with owner Nancy Nasher and architect Mark Dilworth was my last—and despite retailers' best efforts to get people back in stores in 2021, the results were spotty at best, more about pickups and drive-throughs than community or socializing. When people tweeted that they missed the mall, they missed it like they missed bars, movie theaters, concerts, parties. They missed having Somewhere To Go.

Despite the so-called retail apocalypse in the late 2010s, everyone seemed to be shopping. In the seven years it took to build Hudson Yards, a half dozen new retail hubs opened in New York City. Brookfield Place, the complex that contains Cesar Pelli's iconic Winter Garden, added a thirty-five-thousand-square-foot food court, Hudson Eats, and connected to a veritable root system of subterranean retail extending throughout the Financial District, including the Santiago Calatrava–designed Oculus (aka Westfield World Trade Center). The phenomenon was hardly confined to New York: The most valuable malls in the United States before the pandemic, based on sales per square foot and real estate value, included a number of examples that Brenda Buhr-Hancock told me were "benchmarks" for NorthPark, such as the Houston Galleria, King of Prussia in Pennsylvania, Honolulu's Ala Moana Center, and Miami's Aventura Mall.

The story was the same on the West Coast. In 2018, a three-hundred-thousand-square-foot shopping mall opened in suburban Northern California, built around a landscaped outdoor courtyard inspired by an Italian piazza; its design was overseen by Renzo Piano, the architect of Dallas's Nasher Sculpture Center. The first floor is all glass, the better to see the wares; above that, corrugated stainless steel. An Equinox gym anchors the mall at one end, a dine-in movie theater anchors the other. You can drink boba tea or a Berkeley microbrew, slurp ramen, or down a burger. From the rooftop parking garage, visitors can look down on the piazza—"it is a sweet climate," Piano said in a promotional video for the shopping mall—or out to the surrounding hills. "I don't want to be nasty to shopping malls," he added. "I just want to say, this is not a shopping mall; it is something completely different. Instead of something artificial, we need to make something very California." It's called City Center Bishop Ranch—note the absence of the word "mall."

Of course, shopping malls *are* very California. The Stanford Shopping Center, completed in 1957 in Palo Alto, was designed by Los Angeles architect Welton Becket, with a landscape by Lawrence Halprin, as at the later NorthPark. The mall, originally just a single open-air corridor with major department stores on both ends, remains similar to Gruen's Northland in its emphasis on landscaping and discrete squares for sitting and dining. The materials, textures, and trees were intended to relate the retail to the Stanford campus, although the architecture was far more modern. In 1961, Candlestick Park architect John Bolles converted an 1880s campus winery adjacent to the shopping center into an international food hall, known as the Stanford Barn, with Mexican, Chinese, and Italian restaurants, along with a donut shop and soda fountain. Like the university itself, it was meant to foster "understanding among peoples and their ways." In *Designing San Francisco*, Alison Isenberg cites the Stanford Barn as an inspiration for San Francisco's Ghirardelli Square; both are grandmothers to the food hall, without which no "city center" would be complete.

When Bloomberg released an 8-bit can-you-save-the-american-mall? game in 2018, as part of an end-of-shopping, retail-is-dead package, players' rescue options were severely limited: cutting rents, chasing rats, picking up trash, and making deals with local government to bring in the DMV and other city offices. Oh, and adding a giant slide—which Miami's Aventura Mall actually has—only to be promptly slapped with a lawsuit. If I'd written my own mall game, I would have offered more aggressive architectural interventions. Pop the top, and change the air-conditioned, enclosed food court into an open courtyard with a creek running through it. Cover the tan stucco with silvery panels to give it that au courant "industrial" look. Turn one section of the parking lot into a food truck rodeo, local vendors only. Replace the Dillard's with a Spa Castle or a Nitehawk Cinema.

The mall of the future, as seen from 2019, would be architecturally ambitious. It would include plants and water features and be judiciously sprinkled with local retailers and food options. It would be surrounded not by a donut of surface parking lot but with housing, hotels, even educational facilities.

The mall of the future, as I write this, doesn't look that different. Or that's what retail experts say. The pandemic pushed more failing properties over the edge, and it may have changed how people like to buy, but it hasn't changed human nature. In *Severance*, the mall becomes a place of comfort, an ersatz home, the brands standing in for relationships lost. The malls that will succeed will lean in to food, to family life, to design and nature. They will embrace an urbanism that may seem close to Gruen's romanticized nineteenth-century European culture but that actually derives from the way the concept of the mall has, over the past forty years, traveled around the world and picked up some new ideas. "Retail apocalypse," then a pandemic—yet the mall evolves. We can begin to imagine how.

The retail analysts weren't wrong: Malls were still dying. There isn't one culprit, but three.

Because the United States is overmalled: The country has approximately 24 square feet of retail space for every American, compared with 16.8 in Canada, 4.6 in the United Kingdom, and 2.8 in China. The number of malls and shopping centers has continued to rise, peaking at 116,000 in 2017, outpacing population growth, which has been dropping since 1993. Malls in Asia and South America, growth areas since the 1980s, have embraced urban vertical sites accessible via public transportation (like Hudson Yards); meanwhile, generation after generation of American malls continued to be built on greenfield sites near highways, and named, like City Center Bishop Ranch, for developers' hopes and the idealized agrarian past they replaced. "The United States is blessed with a tremendous amount of space, and the mall industry has taken tremendous advantage of that to the point of foolishness," said Mark Cohen, the director of retail studies at Columbia University, who was previously the CEO of multiple department store chains in the United States and Canada.

Because of the internet: "Sales per square foot had been stagnant, if not in decline, when an alternative marketplace occurred: the internet," Cohen told me. "Prior to ecommerce, you had to shop in a physical store, if not downtown, [typically] within a seven-mile radius of your home. The internet was the handcuff key that releases the consumer from that tether." E-commerce had already been growing in the double digits, year over year, pre-Covid. The latest estimates have it as 21 percent of total 2020 retail sales, up by 44 percent from 2019. "In the past, if you went to a store and browsed, if you left without it and had second thoughts, you had to come back," Cohen said. Now customers can shop in a store and then order the item at home, they can browse online and then go to a store and touch, or they can buy it online and pick it up at the curb. "They want to have it all their way and they are getting it their way." This consumer power manifests in e-commerce platforms such as Shop Now, created via a partnership between artificial intelligence company Adeptmind and mall owner Centennial. Phase 2 of the platform, launched in May 2021, allows shoppers to search the in-store inventory of participating retailers at a single mall, place items in a consolidated cart, and arrange for same-day pickup or next-day delivery from twenty of those stores—competing with Amazon on selection and turnaround time.

Because of the decline of department stores: The weakness of department stores, even before the pandemic, had robbed malls of their traditional draws. Real estate analysts Green Street Advisors estimated that about 360 mall-based department stores had closed between 2016 and 2020. Macy's planned to close 45 locations in 2021, and 125 by 2023. J. C. Penney filed for bankruptcy protection in spring 2020 and promptly closed 150 stores. Around the same time, Neiman Marcus filed for bankruptcy protection, too, and shuttered five full-price stores and seventeen Last Call outlets. Belk filed for bankruptcy protection in spring 2021.

The department store has been embattled for years. Where once it was a world unto itself (*The Ladies' Paradise*) or brought the world to Texas (Neiman Marcus), where once store owners were also cities' leading citizens (Dayton in Minneapolis, Hudson in Detroit, Wanamaker in Philadelphia), decades of consolidation have made department stores more generic, more placeless, and less central to the process of consumer discovery. The Great Recession of the late 2000s has also decimated the middle-class consumer who used to shop at stores like Macy's, J. C. Penney, and Sears (which merged with Kmart in 2005, exited bankruptcy in 2019, and has now been reduced from 3,000 stores at its peak to 86). Those consumers turned to outlets as well as to discount big-box stores like Target and Kohl's for clothes, while millennials and Gen Z found fashion inspiration online. Smart brands began to establish a direct relationship with shoppers through email, social media, and stand-alone stores, cutting out the middleman of department stores and their skilled employees.

This was the state of affairs when, on March 19, 2020, then–New York governor Andrew Cuomo closed the malls. Diagnoses of the coronavirus in New York City had begun to tick up, and teachers, parents, and elected officials were begging Mayor Bill de Blasio to close the public schools. I spent the weekend of March 13 hoping he would, trying to decide whether to keep my kids at home on Monday. It was clear that social distancing would be needed—could they get in their last blast of in-person friendship, their last trip on the subway, their last snack at the deli, before everything packed up? By Sunday night the debate was over. We would be at home together. For a year.

March 13, 2020, was also the day I saw my first quarantine mall tweet. Tanvi Misra, an immigration journalist, posted texts from her mother in India as a tweet:

> I want to go to the Mall
> There is no life without malling

That is walking in the mall
That is the best exercise
Ever

There is no life without malling. I knew exactly what she meant. But there was no quarantine life with it either. The mall, with its piped-in air and communal food courts, shiny surfaces and just-browsing adjacencies, started to look like a giant bubble of contagion. Although the mall was created to be cleaner than downtown, downtown, with its rough surfaces and uncontrolled breezes, was looking pretty good in contrast.

Hudson Yards closed on March 17, with Spanish American chef and philanthropist José Andrés's Mercado Little Spain food hall remaining open as a community kitchen for affordable daily takeout. Essex Market, a year-old food hall on the Lower East Side, stayed open for gourmet shopping and take-home meals. The Mall of America initially closed only its Nickelodeon Universe theme park but, once Nordstrom and Macy's announced all their stores were closing, the mall followed suit. On March 18, Los Angeles County officials closed all indoor malls, shopping centers, and playgrounds, following the mayors of Los Angeles and Pasadena. By April, the parking lot of the American Dream megamall in New Jersey, among others, was being used as a coronavirus testing site, thanks to all that empty outdoor blacktop.

It was not as if mall operators hadn't already seen the writing on the wall. A week before the official order to close, Elizabeth, New Jersey, mayor Chris Bollwage had called Simon Property Group—owner of the Mills at Jersey Gardens, in his city, as well as eleven other malls across the state—to ask what their plans were for closing the malls.

"What's your plan to cut my taxes?" Mike Romstad, an executive vice president at Simon, asked Bollwage, as Bollwage later reported to the *New Jersey Advance.* In Jersey City, Mayor Steven Fulop sent a prosecutor and armed police officers to the Newport Centre, another Simon mall, to make sure it was shut down as ordered. The malls needed to be closed to save us from ourselves, though photos taken of the already empty atrium showed that shoppers were smarter than Simon.

Operators' fears were not irrational, although they clashed with public health and smacked of blackmail. They were going to lose billions of dollars. A *New York Times* story on March 23 spoke of late-night phone calls between major clothing companies and department stores, asserting retail's importance to the economy alongside such hard goods as airlines, hotels, and cruise ships. "People don't understand how deeply fashion—which is often seen as nonessential—is connected to the U.S. economy," Sonia Syngal, chief executive of Gap Inc., told the *New York Times*. The mall stores were only the tip of the iceberg, their staff the first employees to find themselves potentially out of a job when there was no more mall to open. The International Council of Shopping Centers estimated that malls and shopping centers provide $400 billion in local tax revenue each year. Meanwhile, with brands suffering—no outlets to sell to, no wholesale orders—the effects ripple out nationally and internationally to the factories making the clothes, the mills manufacturing the fabric, the farmers growing the raw materials, not to mention the loss of advertising, of tenants, of boxes to ship and logistics to manage. Even the boosters were running scared: In July 2021 ICSC changed its name to the word salad Innovating Commerce Serving Communities, keeping the initials but dropping the "Shopping Centers."

"Everything that happened in the shopping center industry before Covid, Covid just accelerated a lot of those trends," said Brad M. Hutensky, a real estate investor and past member of the ICSC executive board. Malls had lost their central place in many people's lives, department stores were failing, and people turned to discount stores and the internet for basic shopping. Hutensky: "The malls that *are* successful are successful because it is an experience that is worth going to."

Cohen agreed. "Covid has accelerated the decline of retailers and retail facilities that was already in place, and already enhanced the success of some other retailers like Target, Walmart and Costco," he said. "The triple-As are fine and will outlive Covid, the Bs and Cs are in an increasingly problematic state. A few will redevelop, amp up their food and entertainment activity tenants, or renovate as a lifestyle center, but most won't succeed because they are now on the wrong side of the tracks or not economically feasible."

By January 2021, a Green Street Advisors report estimated, the values of even A-rated malls had dropped by 45 percent from 2016 levels. At that time, "the overall retail environment was much healthier," Green Street senior analyst Vince Tibone told CNBC. "The sentiment was that e-commerce was a big deal, but 'A' malls were more immune." The environment had changed by 2020.

"A mall is a fragile ecosystem," Green Street said in its report. "When conditions deteriorate markedly, a mall can enter a 'death spiral'—where the lower sales productivity leads to falling occupancy, which results in fewer visitors attracted to a diminishing group of retailers, which continues the cycle of decreasing sales and occupancy." The same dead mall narrative that dominated the early 2000s was ready to be written again, as soon as people decided it was safe to go back to the mall at all. Experts predicted a third of malls would die off within the next year. The longer malls were closed, the more businesses within them would fail. Mall owners were so worried about that death spiral, in fact, that some landlords decided to invest in their anchors, in a reversal of malls' original development structure. Simon Property Group and Brookfield Asset Management bought J. C. Penney in December 2020, allowing the company to exit Chapter 11 and keep its 690 stores open.

Neiman Marcus could and should have been more resilient. It was a luxury chain, long established in triple-A malls, known for beautiful stores and personalized service. But Neiman Marcus came late to e-commerce, thinking that its high-end shoppers would continue to come back for that human touch, now aided by new technologies such as the store's proprietary iSell, which helped sales associates keep track of years of purchases. New stores, particularly the three-story, 188,000-square-foot space at the top of the Shops at Hudson Yards, bet on in-store gadgetry to improve the experience, including a mobile point-of-sale system, touch-screen directories for product searches, customizable lighting in the dressing rooms, and more screens to summon a different size. That store also offered a gourmet restaurant, the Zodiac Room, as well as a spa and beauty salon so that women could continue to make a day of it. "The company arguably invented the concept of experiential shopping—of pampering its customers in dazzling spaces," wrote Jason Heid in a June 2020 *Texas Monthly* feature. "Reestablishing that as a priority today could help set Neiman's apart again." But in 2013, Neiman Marcus was sold to private equity firm Ares Management and the Canada Pension Plan Investment Board, a leveraged buyout that burdened the group—Neiman Marcus, Last Call, and Bergdorf Goodman— with $4.8 billion in debt. That debt meant it wasn't enough for the stores merely to continue making a profit: Not only did the group need to come up with regular interest payments, but also there was little extra cash for the ongoing improvements required to keep the stores alive as their competitors went extinct. By late April 2020, bankruptcy became inevitable. Among the first stores closed? That sixteen-month-old location at Hudson Yards, the anchor intended to draw shoppers up through the vertical maze.

Brad Hutensky's firm invests in open-air centers, whose redevelopment is far less complicated than that of malls, where department stores may own the wedge of land under their location. "It's the greatest time of my career," he said of the pandemic. "There will be a lot of properties [on the market] and we will be able to buy them. Generally a shopping center is a good location for a lot of things; it has visibility, access, roads, the buildings are cheap, and there's lots of parking." Short-term potential uses include multifamily housing and medical offices; long-term he sees parking lots as a good investment. "If they really perfect driverless cars, shopping centers could be gold mines. All that parking you are not going to need," as autonomous vehicles provide drop-off service, could be converted into other, more profitable uses.

Hutensky's businesslike joy amid the pain of the pandemic might seem predatory—and it is—until you consider the alternative. If his company buys that empty strip mall, it will become something new. While the photographs of dead palms and stilled escalators, empty parking lots and stripped signage, have an appealing bleakness, in real life that absence leads to decay, destruction, crime, and blank spots in locations now surrounded by housing, other retail, and roads. If only two thirds of America's malls reopen, we may choose to see that as tragedy—or an opportunity.

As the pandemic ground on, I became more and more convinced that the latter take was the way to go. For the mall to have a second life, radical intervention is necessary. When we think about retrofits—putting new uses in old architecture, as the creators of the festival marketplace once had—we often picture aged brick warehouses or factory halls. But at this point, the mall is historic architecture too. The sunset of its original purpose provides an opportunity to rethink, rebuild, and redesign the mall, the department store, and the parking lot. Understanding malls' complicated past provides a key to a future more community-friendly and less vehicle-focused than Amazon fulfillment centers. Schools, churches, medical offices, public libraries, and fitness complexes, even the small aquarium chain Blue Zoo, found homes in the wide-open spaces of department stores, the daylit grandeur of the atrium, the classroom-size confines of the boutique. Strip away the branding and a dead mall becomes just another building. A centrally located, highly recognizable barn of a building, with easy highway access and way too much surface parking for the current climate crisis.

That's the kind of practicality urban design professors Ellen Dunham-Jones and June Williamson have long brought to the topic of the burbs, with malls as a subset. They published their first book, *Retrofitting Suburbia*, in 2008, hard on the heels of the recession that emptied office landscapes, strip malls, shopping malls, and industrial parks—"underperforming asphalt," as they put it, that could be used to create compact, walkable, mixed-use communities. Between 2009 and 2016 the U.S. Federal Sustainable Communities Partnership gave out $240 million in planning grants and $3.5 billion in construction funds to more than one thousand communities to improve infrastructure and rewrite zoning codes. For the first time, these grant proposals were vetted by agencies including the DOT, HUD, and EPA, knitting back together transportation, housing, and environmental concerns in order to achieve a better mix of transit modes, land use, and residents' incomes.

Dunham-Jones and Williamson's second analysis, *Case Studies in Retrofitting Suburbia*, was published in January 2021. In the interim their database of retrofits grew from eighty to more than two thousand examples: half redevelopment, 2 percent regreening, and the rest some combination of retrofit and re-inhabitation. The simplest are of the least interest: that 50 percent of retrofits where architectural changes support a straightforward transition from one kind of retail to another kind of retail. That can mean examples like Owings Mills, where an outdated enclosed mall was replaced with a power center, big-box stores opening out onto a parking lot. That can mean examples like the Shops at Nanuet on Long Island, where another enclosed mall, built in 1969, was demolished and rebuilt as a lifestyle center, with outdoor store entrances, a cinema and fitness center, plus café seating and landscaping, shifting tenants toward family and entertainment options. Many high-end malls, including Durham, North Carolina's Streets at Southpoint, are built like that from scratch, combining two generations of planning but doing little to combat the car-centricity and separation of uses that had characterized the American suburb.

Given the prevalence of ruin porn, it is easy to imagine many malls going "back to nature": cracks in the tarmac, cracks in the quarry tile, the plants in the fern bar gone feral, the potted trees bursting through the glass ceiling of the atrium. But beyond postapocalyptic fantasy is the germ, literally, of economic growth. Malls are reservoirs of open space in increasingly built-up environments, both within their walls and outside in their oversize parking lots. Where else could a city, or a suburb, "find" over one hundred thousand square feet of available space for a new public library? Where else could they "find" a new park location close to existing housing, displacing no one, and with minimal demolition required? Postwar public policy created the need for the mall in the spaces between subsidized single-family homes and subsidized roadways, with single-use zoning serving as the barrier between each of these uses. Today, those barriers are crumbling, as changing patterns of work and home life mix commercial, industrial, and residential in ways never imagined by developers. The defunct mall becomes an opportunity to knit suburbs back together, via a retrofit that suits reality rather than a long-ago vision of (white) women in the suburbs and their husbands in the city. The mall is neither a joke nor a den of zombies, but a resource. America's dead malls represent millions of square feet of matériel that are not going to be reabsorbed without investment and effort.

Plans announced in 2021 for Gruen's Northland exemplify this maximalist approach. Local developer Contour Companies bought the shopping center from the city of Southfield for $11.1 million dollars, and then announced that it would take the complex back to its 1954 core, transforming the former J. L. Hudson store into a food and retail emporium and converting the ground-level shopping concourses into residential lofts. The eight-thousand-car parking lot has space for fourteen new buildings, including mid-rise, middle-income rental housing with shops and restaurants on the first floor facing surrounding roads. Total cost of what Contour is calling—I hope they are aware of the irony—Northland City Center: $403 million, with state subsidies from the Michigan Strategic Fund.

"The suburbs aren't as monolithic as some of the stereotypes seem to want to insist on," Williamson told me. That means the solutions aren't monolithic either. "It wasn't substituting one formula that got repeated across the country"—the original mall pattern—"for another formula," she added. "Malls run their course in different trajectories, so the strategy depends on local context and needs and what adjacent uses are to determine what work should happen." That local context includes major demographic changes wrought by immigration, desegregation, more diverse family structures, the aging of the baby boomers, and the loss of manufacturing jobs. In their 2021 book, Williamson and Dunham-Jones note, "Suburbanites now included young singles, one-parent families, empty-nesters, retirees, gays and lesbians, and a growing share of African Americans, Latinos, and Asian Americans. By 2016, middle class white families with a male breadwinner and a stay-at-home mom—the stereotype of 1950s suburbia—were the minority."

Young people, old people, people from countries and communities used to shopping in a very different kind of marketplace—each of these demographics will shape the rebirth of those Class B and C malls. Consider the Austin Community College (ACC) Highland campus, the Texas college's twelfth and largest. The forty-year-old, eighty-acre Highland Mall went into foreclosure in 2010, its failure blamed in part on the retrofitting of the former

Top, the Paseo at the ACC Highland Campus, Austin, Texas, Barnes Gromatzky Kosarek Architects and Perkins+Will, 2021. *Bottom*, hallway and student lounge at the ACC Highland Campus Building 2000, 2021. (Austin Community College District)

IBM Selectric manufacturing campus, six miles away, into a high-end mixed-use complex known as the Domain. Highland Mall's Dillard's, Macy's, and J. C. Penney, simply surrounded by surface parking, couldn't compete with the Domain's shaded streetscapes and dine-in theater. ACC, initially interested in just the abandoned J. C. Penney space, ultimately partnered with RedLeaf Properties to master-plan and develop all eighty acres, retrofitting the department store and setting aside adjacent spaces for future classroom and office buildings. Over the next decade the site could hold 1,200 residential units, 150,000 square feet of retail space, and 800,000 square feet of offices, instead of just 1.2 million square feet of retail.

With neighborhood support, and a successful bond initiative, RedLeaf and ACC hired McCann Adams Studio to create a design book to guide the planning moving forward. On the site plan, the bulky college buildings are surrounded by tree-lined pedestrian streets and some small green spaces. Residential buildings line the edge of the property to the west, with three additional sites for office and commercial buildings; one of the latter is practically on top of the Highland light rail station, which opened in 2010. KLRU-TV, the local public television station, moved into the former Dillard's in fall 2021, sharing office space and newly built TV studios with the college. The former J. C. Penney, now known as the ACCelerator Lab, was redesigned by Barnes Gromatzky Kosarek Architects, which cut windows into the front and skylights into the roof of what was practically a solid concrete box. Former boutiques are now classrooms with translucent walls facing an indoor, quarry-tiled street. The open selling floor contains workstations for six hundred students. A porchlike roof and a metal screen adorned with the college's symbol—people turning into stars—read as welcoming even at automotive scale.

Many suburban communities are opposed to building new housing; Caleb Pritchard, writing about ACC Highland for *Austin Monthly* in 2017, characterizes neighborhood associations as "fronts for a handful of blue-haired property owners who reflexively stand athwart proposed changes to their corner of town, yelling 'stop!'" But senior housing is frequently seen as an acceptable compromise, and former malls have begun to be repurposed as anchors to these types of developments too. Age-segregated zoning is the only exclusionary practice allowed under the 1968 Fair Housing Act, and today there are numerous "villages" that permit residents over fifty-five and limit children. Such communities are, according to historian Andrew Blechman, organized around leisure, generally economically and racially homogenous, and exempt from the high taxes many communities levy in order to pay for schools. For a county considering changing property zoning from commercial to residential, a senior housing community can seem like a guarantee of less trouble. But it is also important to make sure the location isn't an island: "Baby boomers don't want to be isolated," Dunham-Jones told the *New York Times* in 2020. "They want to be connected to the community."

The Promenade of Wayzata, built on the site of the fourteen-acre 1967 Wayzata Bay Shopping Center, has become a five-block mid-rise neighborhood, with senior housing units as well as unrestricted condominiums and rentals built over shops and alongside new offices. Its Great Lawn, facing Lake Minnetonka, as well as a children's play area were mandated by developer Presbyterian Homes' tax-increment financing; a boutique hotel is scheduled for the final phase. "By locating senior housing in walking distance of shops, libraries, gyms and recreation centers, the housing no longer needs to provide those amenities internally and may reduce costs accordingly," Dunham-Jones told the *Times*. In Wayzata, the new development attracts people to live, work, and shop, while also providing new customers for the existing downtown. The increase in traffic ended up spurring Folkestone, the senior living community, to start its own bus service to circle the town. As a bonus, the development mitigated some of the negative environmental effects of the mall, which had long been a source of polluting runoff. The new buildings on the wetland site are suspended over the swampy soil on a "land bridge" of concrete beams resting on three thousand concrete pilings. Infiltration and filtration basins for stormwater are built below the streets and parking floors, and a landscaped pond captures additional water. Despite the fact that more of the surface is covered by building, the site is far less prone to flooding, and protects the integrity of the lake.

Many malls sit atop wetlands that builders simply covered over, running culverts to capture the streams and asphalting over sandy, muddy, and swampy soil; what lay beneath would come back to haunt them, especially in a time of environmental instability. Few such malls, though, have been as thoroughly returned to open space as Meriden Green in Connecticut, another of Dunham-Jones and Williamson's case studies. Meriden Hub Mall was built in 1970, a 250,000-square-foot, single-story mall close to I-95 between New York and New Haven. The mall, anchored by New England department store chain W. T. Grant, was an urban renewal project, intended to bring shoppers back downtown after the city's silver industry went into decline. But another mall, even more convenient to the interstate, opened a year later, and Grants went bankrupt in 1976, partly as a result of the company's reluctance to adapt to suburban locations. The mall never thrived, the city was far from prosperous, and the site was never a location that should have been built up: Like many highways' paths, it fell in a riparian stream, low-lying continuous lands that earlier generations had realized were too wet for construction. The Meriden mall flooded twice, in 1992 and 1996, eventually driving out its last tenant, which was renting it as cheap office space. At that point the city decided to step in, reclaiming the mall via eminent domain, and set out to fix a flood problem that included more than two hundred downtown properties as well as a Metro-North station. The city, along with a project team that included Milone & McBroom, AECOM, the EPA, FEMA, and the Army Corps of Engineers, cleared the site and uncovered Harbor Brook winding through the middle. They built 1.5 miles of walking paths, a public amphitheater, and space for weekly farmers markets. Re-grading the park as a stormwater basin allowed the city to remove properties from the hundred-year flood plain, including the upgraded transit center, and to rezone the area around the station for mixed-use transit-oriented development, including 170 apartments over ground-floor retail. North of the site, the city plans to demolish 140 units of public housing that were also prone to frequent floods, open up more sections of the creek, and rebuild replacement housing on or near the now much more appealing area, to which current residents have the right of return.

A final strategy highlighted in the 2021 edition of *Retrofitting Suburbia* does convert retail to retail, but with a twist: transforming conventional malls, with national brands and franchises, into ethnocentric marketplaces, anchored by food and grocery vendors, and tailored to both long-standing and newly expanded immigrant communities. José de Jesús Legaspi, a Los Angeles–based consultant and developer, now has an almost twenty-year career in retrofitting dying malls for Latinx and Caribbean entrepreneurs and customers across the country. "The American dream is not to own a home," Legaspi told *Time* in 2014. "The American dream is to own your own business. To have a hold of your own destiny. That's how we build the mercado." His largest project to date, partnered with Boxer Properties, is La Gran Plaza in Fort Worth, Texas, on the site of the former Seminary South Shopping Center, built in 1962 on the drained Katy Lake. Legaspi's projects, Dunham-Jones and Williamson write, "typically incorporate a space refitted as a mercado, filled with small booths and shops for Hispanic vendors selling goods and services—a signage and print shop, a tailor, party supplies, T-shirts, real estate and travel agents—much as one would find in a town or village market in Mexico or Guatemala." Spanish-speaking radio and television stations, Spanish-language cinemas, nightclubs, and outdoor performance stages for quinceañera fashion shows, Mexican wrestling matches, and mariachi band concerts also provide a draw far beyond simply shopping. Architect David Hidalgo dressed up the mall's original white stucco with Spanish colonial details, making it read, even from the highway, as a Latinx place.

What Legaspi and others remaking the mall from the parking lot up are saying is that to survive, the American mall has to shed many of the qualities that defined it for decades: no department store anchor, less catering to an imagined middle-aged, middle-class white female shopper, more public transportation, more density. All qualities that the mall, outside America, has adopted in its relentless postwar and post-1980s spread. The element that brings all these demographic changes together is food.

In the mid-2010s, the number of food halls skyrocketed. Pre-Covid, commercial real estate firm Cushman & Wakefield counted 223 U.S. food halls, with 165 mentioned as in development; during the pandemic, they estimate, 75 percent of those were able to stay open by operating as "ghost kitchens" for takeout. Food halls were seen as a way to resuscitate real estate that had fallen on hard times—both inner-city markets in former industrial buildings and exurban courts in ailing malls—by building on the rise of "foodie culture": more people more interested in food from more places, and less interested in fine dining. "It seems almost countercultural—a way of seeking goods and services that transcends traditional corporate America with its franchises and conglomerates—and fulfills a desire to return to a time when retail felt more personal," wrote Bethany Biron for *Vox*, paraphrasing food historian Ken Albala. Furthermore, Albala told her:

> People are generally fed up with American culture writ large, which is corporate and absurdly homogenized . . . Today you can go to a Whole Foods anywhere in the country and it's exactly the same. Food halls give people a sense of place in a country that's increasingly felt uprooted and lost. The food court gives them a sense of what cities used to be, a place to interact with vendors when businesses were mom and pop.

Food halls are a variation on the Jerde transfer: Going to the mall still provides entertainment, but now the entertainment is food, often combined with shopping opportunities and retail decor specific to a foreign culture. Leave the roller coasters to the amusement parks; the mall visit could be a trip to Taipei, Bologna, or Mexico City.

David Chang, the Korean American restaurateur best known for the Momofuku restaurant group, and star of the Netflix series *Ugly Delicious*, proposed a reinvention of the food court to *GQ* in 2015. As a kid growing up in the suburbs of Washington, D.C., Chang said,

> some of my great food memories from childhood happened at Tysons Corner Center in Virginia, where I spent hours trapped in wonderfully painful indecision: Do I get the chicken sandwich at Chick-fil-a? The

fries with special sauce at Jerry's? The chow mein platter at Panda Express? Or maybe I should indulge my taste for real Italian food at Sbarro?

He even loves Cinnabon, maker of those much-mocked sugar bombs as big as your head, calling its buns "fucking delicious." Chang's argument for the return of the food court runs through the fancy food halls of Europe, stopping at Mario Batali's popular Eataly and checking in with Japan's basement eateries under department stores and subway stations. In fact, some malls were already on the case. In a nod to its Asian clientele, Ala Moana Center in Honolulu had already opened a Japanese-style food court underneath, with kiosks selling paper goods and other treats down the side, that's so authentic it's like you are in Tokyo. When Brookfield Properties remodeled the shops adjacent to Cesar Pelli's Winter Garden in 2014 and added Hudson Eats, it also fashioned Le District, a second high-end food court with a French market, Montreal bagels, and fancy grilled cheese. Chang's ideas slanted eastward. Why not offer a taste of Singapore street food? "I'm always saying that we've taken the traditional restaurant as far as it can go," he wrote. "The gastronomic future is everywhere else, starting just up the escalators from the Hot Topic, right across from the J.Crew."

As it happens, Chang got his chance to participate in the food court's reinvention in 2019, when he opened both the full-service restaurant Momofuku Kāwi and a branch of his chicken sandwich spot Fuku at Hudson Yards. Fuku, on the mall's second level, is a hole-in-the-wall only slightly bigger than a counter. Kāwi (which closed in March 2021) included a mall-facing "convenience store," where customers could pick up Korean products to go. So far, so cute, except, like the elusive ice-cream and cake shops, Chang's restaurants were not a park or a hall or a court but intermixed with the mall's other non-food offerings. There was no easy way to stop in for a snack from outside, and no communal seating if things got crowded inside.

Hudson Yards's real food success story is, like Ala Moana's Japanese ramen shops, underground. Tucked below the mall and adjacent office buildings is

Mercado Little Spain, The Shops and Restaurants at Hudson
Yards, Capella Garcia Arquitectura with Icrave, 2019.
(Photograph by James & Karla Murray)

Mercado Little Spain. Chef José Andrés has described the project as a tribute
to the indoor markets of Barcelona, with tiny "streets" with churro vendors,
carts with bountiful take-home groceries, and sit-down restaurants centered
on fish, Spanished-up "diner food," and tapas. The wild decor is dominated
by colorful tile, the domains of different counters and restaurants marked
out in different patterns and hues. "The city already has several of these
Eurocentric complexes in Manhattan, and this seemed like an Iberian clone
of Eataly and Le District," wrote *Eater* food critic Robert Sietsema. "Why
does every development of this sort have to be so European? Certainly,
Andrés could have created a Latin American food court and market with
plenty of Spanish elements; it would have been more in keeping with the
city's population." But Sietsema and *New York Times* critic Pete Wells were
both won over by the food and festive atmosphere. "With its garage-size
doors rolled all the way up almost every day this summer, Spanish Diner is
one of the few places in Hudson Yards that welcomes passers-by instead of
trying to stun them into submission," wrote Wells. By splitting the food
court from the body of the mall, the Shops and Restaurants at Hudson Yards
had literally undermined themselves.

"On a typical Friday afternoon in Fremont, California's Mission Square Shopping Center, known to regulars as 'Little Taipei,' Chinese grandmothers stake out their turf on parking lot benches while chatting with friends and comparing their grandchildren's latest feats," writes planning scholar Willow Lung-Amam. Mission Square is one of more than one hundred Asian malls in the United States, "shopping centers designed to cater to the needs, desires, and tastes of their largely Asian American, and predominantly immigrant, customers. By three o'clock, the older crowd has been replaced by after-school crews of teens from Mission San Jose High School, gathering for bubble tea and frozen yogurt. In the evenings, older teens arrive along with multigenerational family groups. Compared to their more traditional American counterparts, they tend to be more service and food oriented"—closer to the retail mix of early suburban shopping centers— with a supermarket as the anchor alongside such everyday needs as a dentist, an eye doctor, banks, nail and hair salons, and travel agencies. Food offerings are tailored to the community, with banquet-style restaurants for big occasions and smaller cafés serving pan-Asian specialties.

The changing demographics of the California suburbs that Lung-Amam describes in Silicon Valley are part of a larger growth pattern that geographer Wei Li terms the rise of the "ethnoburb." By Li's definition, "ethnoburbs are suburban ethnic clusters of residential areas and business districts in large American metropolitan areas. They are multi-ethnic communities, in which one ethnic minority group has a significant concentration but does not necessarily comprise a majority." When Li arrived in Los Angeles to study in 1991, a professor suggested she look for housing in Monterey Park, in the San Gabriel Valley. "That's a Chinese area," the professor told her, "you would feel very comfortable." Li's stereotype of the American suburbs had been white families, with stay-at-home moms and 2.5 kids. The reality was very different: Ethnoburbs had emerged as early as the 1960s but saw their greatest growth in the 1980s and 1990s, when political tension and a desire for more opportunities for their children pushed skilled workers to emigrate from China, Taiwan, and Hong Kong. By the 2010 census, 62 percent of Asian Americans lived in the suburbs of the one hundred largest U.S. cities, making such malls a necessary and ubiquitous part of twenty-first-century suburban life. Li's research focused on the ethnoburban Chinese population in the Los Angeles area, but other cities, including Bellevue, Washington, across from Seattle, and Quincy, Massachusetts, south of Boston, had seen a similar rise in Asian suburban population. Riverside County, farther east of Los Angeles, had a Latinx population of 45.5 percent by the 2010 census. Fort Bend County, west of Houston, is one of the most diverse counties in the nation, with 30 percent of its population foreign-born. In the 1970s, a Vietnamese enclave developed around the Hoa Binh (Peace) Shopping Center in Midtown; in the 1980s, a Chinese and Taiwanese ethnoburb sprang up around Sharpstown, whose 1961 centerpiece had been Houston's first air-conditioned shopping mall.

"The malls of the future will be much more diverse than the malls of the past, when every mall had a J.C. Penney or Sears," Britt Beemer of America's Research Group told the *Los Angeles Times* in 2017. "The only way to win in the long term is to become different, and one way is appeal to an ethnic group." Lung-Amam's study of Asian malls in Silicon Valley is specifically tailored to address two lacunae she sees in the study of suburbs. First, "the shopping mall has been a particularly popular object of scholarly disdain," she writes, with too much stress on its "commercialization, consumption, privacy, and security" and not enough on its community. Her research, which involved seventy interviews with the owners, managers, developers, and customers of Asian malls, clearly demonstrates the necessity of these malls, and how their activities, centered on food, connect the Asian diaspora. "They are places of vibrant social and cultural life that, for many, embody what it means to be Asian American in suburbia," she writes.

Beemer was quoted in a *Los Angeles Times* story on the Westfield Santa Anita, an enclosed mall located in Arcadia, California, a Los Angeles suburb that transformed from chicken ranches to house lots after World War II and to a majority-Asian city by 2010. The Santa Anita mall thrived by bringing in retailers and restaurants that were Asian imports or Asian-themed, from Japanese design store Muji to the Taiwanese Din Tai Fung dumpling chain. Westfield, which purchased the mall in 1998 and expanded it in 2014, also added a second floor "Food Alley" in 2016. "Alley eateries are sandwiched close together, resembling traditional food complexes known as hawker centers that are popular in countries such as Malaysia and Singapore," wrote the *Los Angeles Times*. "Uncle Tetsu Japanese Cheesecake chose the alley to locate its first continental U.S. spot." Where once malls reflected homogenized franchise American culture, largely owned and operated by white people, now they represent the business interests and consumer tastes of diverse ethnic populations—often food-first. Being able to shop for familiar ingredients is an immediate need for new immigrants; food businesses have often also been a first step on the road to entrepreneurship and ownership for new Americans.

By the early 2000s, a number of bubble tea chains owned by immigrants of Taiwanese descent began to populate the food courts and shopping strips of the San Gabriel Valley, selling a drink made from flavored sweet tea, with or without milk, poured over ice and mixed with large, black, chewy spheres of "boba"—a combination of sugar and tapioca flour. "As a Taiwanese-American kid growing up in the early 2000s in the San Gabriel Valley, the concoction was an integral part of my social life," Clarissa Wei, who went to Arcadia High School, wrote in 2017. "We, after all, were the first boba generation." The product from shop to shop was largely the same, Wei wrote, with the boba factory-made by Lollicup in Chino, California, and the tea from either there or Ten Ren. "What mattered was the space and the permanence of the shops," she said, a place for children to hang out and drink a parent-approved, relatively inexpensive beverage before coffee or alcohol were acceptable options. Places ubiquitous enough to be convenient to whatever activity—high school, SAT prep, hanging out. The Quickly chain, which opened its first Southern California franchise in 2002, at one time offered its teen patrons pop culture magazines for browsing, including the Chinese-language gossip magazine *East 38*.

As bubble tea grew more popular in the mid-2010s, attracting attention and expanding to audiences outside those enclaves, its shops underwent the same kind of transformation as coffeehouses and Chinese American restaurants before it: greater outward emphasis on the sourcing of ingredients, and drinks (or dishes) exclusive to the location. Food historian Krishnendu Ray links the rise of boba to the emergence of East Asia as a global power—a power that trickles down through young professionals with Asian roots, who want to eat and drink the foods of their youth wherever they live now. "In some ways, it is a quintessential passing of the baton from American hegemony to East Asian hegemony," Ray told writer Jenny G. Zhang in 2019. "It's symptomatic of East Asia's location—of East Asian urban culture—in the global circulation of taste." Zhang connects Asian American youths' love of boba to nostalgia for their younger selves:

> Asian-American expressions of longing for the boba shops of one's youth are not just about the physical space, or the drink, or the companionship; they're as much about the time, however fleeting, spent within the bubble of comfort and belonging. It's about missing the period of your life when you could afford to let bubble tea occupy such a large part of it.

While the food court is integral to our image of mall interiors today, and food courts often serve as the backdrop for teen mall drama in films such as *Fast Times at Ridgemont High*, the first two decades of malls did not include them. Food at the enclosed malls of the 1950s and 1960s was served at lunch counters in Woolworth's, in tea rooms within department stores, and at sit-down restaurants or casual cafeterias, whose "outdoor" café tables and chairs often strayed into the atrium. At Gruen's Southdale, fountains, plants, and the interior aviary offered the illusion of a pedestrian street. Fast food was served at stand-alone joints farther down the highway, including drive-throughs and drive-ins.

The earliest food courts—multiple vendors selling from kiosks or counters, grouped around a common seating area—appeared in malls in the early 1970s. The very first was built by the Rouse Company at the Plymouth Meeting Mall in Pennsylvania in 1971, but it quickly failed because the space was "too small" and the offerings "insufficiently varied." Rouse tried again at Paramus Park Mall in New Jersey in 1974, creating a second-floor space that helped draw shoppers upstairs. This format, with the common seating area bleeding into the second story of the atrium, was swiftly replicated by other developers. "Jim Rouse wanted to create what he saw as community picnics," Robert Rubenkonig, Rouse's communications director, said of the food courts, which were also intended to extend shoppers' time at the mall. "They're open areas—a great idea that stuck. Consumers have voted with their pocketbooks." At the same time as Rouse was experimenting with food courts in his malls, he and Ben and Jane Thompson were working on Faneuil Hall, where the indoor marketplace also included common seating, food from counters and carts, and a wide variety of local merchants. "The food courts of the '80s also had their fair share of restaurants with roots in the ethnic immigrant communities," notes *Mental Floss* in its history of the type, even though Sbarro pizza, Panda Express orange chicken and Greek gyros might only gesture at the food served in their respective home countries.

Orange Julius was a mainstay of those early food courts, with its distinctive neon *O*, loud blenders, and panoply of colorful fruits. Orange Julius kiosks often served as a sentry of sorts, welcoming people to the food court and offering a quick stop for those not quite ready for a meal. Many mall-food mainstays fall more into the category of snacks than food—cheap, quick, and often sugar-laden, they are for teenagers who need a reason to sit down and something to do with their hands. Where adults might meet for drinks, or a blind date could begin with coffee, teens slurped first Orange Julius, then smoothies, and then bubble tea. In his 2020 reconsideration of the suburbs, *The Sprawl*, critic Jason Diamond writes, "Truth is, I hardly recall ever buying anything from ages fourteen to about eighteen, besides the occasional order of fries or a used CD from the independent music store . . . That's not what mall owners wanted, but who cares? That's what made it special; that feeling my friends and I were planting a flag at the food court or on a bench by Pacific Sunwear, saying that was our place, and we were going to enjoy our time there."

Other prototypical mall foods include Mrs. Fields, founded in Palo Alto in 1977, which opened franchises selling its large and odoriferous desserts in malls and airports throughout the 1980s, and Cinnabon, given a shout-out by David Chang, which opened in Seattle's SeaTac Mall in 1985. Like Mrs. Fields's cookie counters, those at Cinnabon emit a force field of warm baking smells, advertising by scent in malls that (save for perfume departments) mostly sell by sight and sound. According to the *Wall Street Journal*, Cinnabon franchisees are told to put their ovens at the front of their stores, and to use the least effective vent hoods, to maximize the aroma zone as they bake fresh buns every thirty minutes.

Bubble tea doesn't have the scent of a cookie or a cinnamon bun, but it does have a distinctive look, which, as Zhang notes in her report on the "boba generation," may be more important in our Instagram age, when photographing a pastel drink, and geotagging your location, can be as important a social gesture as the food court hangout. Bubble tea also combines a number of previous mall-food traits: colorful like Orange Julius, sugary like a cookie, portable like a Cinnabon, snack-size like all of the above. The big difference is bubble tea's origins in Taiwan, though in the United States the drink is sold alongside pan-Asian foods including Japanese ramen, Vietnamese banh mi, and Hawaiian Spam musubi. Boba Guys, one of the most successful second-generation bubble tea chains, has mixed and matched ethnic food traditions in its boba inventions, offering fusion flavors like "dirty horchata" (Mexico) and "strawberry matcha" (Japan).

Diamond writes in *The Sprawl* that in most cases, if you'd been to a mall in South Carolina by the early 2000s, you had a pretty good idea of what a mall in Michigan would be like. The exception to that rule was destination malls like the Mall of America, a scale beyond. Over the last decade, that has become less true. Places like Mission Square and Westfield Santa Anita, not to mention La Gran Plaza, couldn't be anywhere else and are destinations unto themselves. They don't try to represent all of America but *an* America. Plaza Fiesta, a "mall/cultural gathering spot" on the edge of metro Atlanta— another Legaspi project—illustrates that we have already reached the second generation of ethnic malls and ethnoburbs. Built in 1968 as the Buford-Clairmont Mall, Plaza Fiesta started as a standard suburban supermarket plaza, became an outlet mall, was reborn as the Oriental Mall [*sic*], and then, in 2000, retrofitted into a place for the area's growing Latinx community.

Plaza Fiesta, Atlanta, Georgia, opened in 1968 as the
Buford-Clairmont Mall, remodeled by Ozell Stankus
Associates Architects, 2000. (Plaza Fiesta)

Food writer Jennifer Zyman wrote an ode to Plaza Fiesta in February 2020:
"Growing up in the South, I struggled to locate my Mexican roots," she
writes. The local A&P did not carry tortillas or canned chipotles, the butcher
did not carry marinated pork; instead, relatives arrived with suitcases full of
ingredients. Looking for a way into her mother's culture, Zyman explored
the Mexican food everywhere but at home—until the late 1990s, when
Atlanta, too, developed ethnoburbs.

> After years of longing for Mexico, Mexico came to me. Work at
> nearby chicken processing plants and construction sites for the 1996
> Olympics caused a surge in Atlanta's Mexican population. My mother
> tongue popped up everywhere, in written signs and overheard conver-
> sations. Carnicerias, mercados, and taquerias too started opening as
> a happy consequence of the growth. Soon, we only had to go as far as
> Buford Highway 20 minutes northeast to get everything we needed.
> That nearly 30-mile-long stretch of road eventually became home to
> 1,000 immigrant-owned businesses and more than 100 international
> restaurants representing Bangladesh, Cambodia, China, Colombia,

Ethiopia, Korea, Malaysia, Mexico, and Vietnam. I learned the proper way to eat pho, the joy of Hainanese chicken rice, the superiority of charcoal-fired Korean barbecue. Everything was there, and eventually, Plaza Fiesta would be too.

By 2020 Plaza Fiesta had 280 stores, thirty food businesses, and a similar variety of services as Little Taipei: dentists, hair salons, barbers, insurance agents, and a bus company with routes from Georgia over the Texas border into Mexico. A whiteboard detailed the process to become a U.S. citizen. The bland stucco entrances gained park benches crowned with state emblems and a blue-and-yellow-tiled fountain. PLAZA FIESTA, in big red letters, framed a cartoon sun. If in Asian malls bubble tea emporiums replaced smoothie shops, in this mall, Mexican shaved ice replaced frozen yogurt. Declining mall properties provided convenient real estate: inexpensive square footage, often already fitted out for food service, close to the suburbs where new immigrants and new residents could afford to settle. When the International Rescue Committee and Salt Lake County in 2013 launched the Spice Kitchen incubator, a training center for food entrepreneurs from Salt Lake City's growing refugee population, they built out the four-thousand-square-foot space in a strip mall down the road from big-box stores like Best Buy.

The form is so easy—a square lined with food carts or counters, tables in the center—that bonus food courts sprang up in the oddest places during the Covid-19 pandemic. After the Jerde-designed Glendale Galleria was closed for indoor dining in July 2020, Gevik Baghdassarian—the owner of the Armenian chain Massis Kabob, a three-decade resident of the Galleria's indoor food court—decided he could keep serving if he took the food outside. Customers waiting in their cars outside the mall's doors for drive-through delivery morphed into customers eating in the parking garage on a hastily assembled "patio," the lines of parking spots covered by small mats of artificial turf suggesting "eat here." As Alissa Walker wrote for *Curbed*,

The setup isn't all that much worse than eating from a food truck. From certain angles, the endless concrete expanse, accented with the primary-colored arrows and centerlines, could almost work as a dining concept. And with the cavernous shade and cross-breeze, the garage is, in many ways, an improvement over in-street dining on a busy road, where your meal is served with an uneasy feeling that a speeding vehicle could land on your table at any moment.

While the owners, entrepreneurs, and customers at Plaza Fiesta and Little Taipei tailored suburban forms to their communities from the bottom up, putting food first and adding culturally specific fountains, tilework, and flags to cookie-cutter shopping centers and indoor malls, there has also been a top-down push for food as a savior of malls. "Foodie culture" may embrace street food and teen sugar highs, but it can also be as snobbish as fine dining.

The splashiest entry in the don't-call-it-a-food-court category was Eataly, which opened its first U.S. store in Manhattan in 2010. The idea of an Italian supermarket came from Oscar Farinetti, who turned a decommissioned vermouth factory in Turin into the first Eataly in 2007. Like Ghirardelli Square and Faneuil Hall, the site was a former industrial building, into which Farinetti packed specialty restaurants, counters for bread, cheese, wine, and salumi, and a grocery for nonperishables and kitchen items. Farinetti saw the marketplace as a consumer-friendly outlet for products made following the principles of the region's Slow Food movement: Buy local, buy quality, buy sustainability, buy from the maker. As the franchise expanded—first to Japan, then to the United States, South America, and ultimately three dozen locations worldwide—both the architecture and the localism fell by the wayside. Eataly became a food theme park, popularized in America by co-owners Mario Batali and Lidia Bastianich. Ben and Jane Thompson sold Rouse on a vision of European amenities reborn in Boston, and eventually Farinetti and his celebrity-chef partners would make the same trip, forty years later. When Sam Sifton reviewed Eataly's Flatiron location in the *New York Times* in 2010, he called it "a circus maximus," an exhausting and exhaustive carnival ride of foods, loud and expensive but also rather delicious. In 2017, Eataly would open an actual theme park on twenty-five acres outside Bologna, with livestock, a dairy plant, and a truffle forest complete with hounds, as if filling in the backstory for the stores' extensive offerings. My mind wants to make this over for Wisconsin, also with livestock and a dairy plant, or for California, with a boba factory. The next malls of America could also take their themes from their culinary roots.

$$\rightarrow$$

In February 2021, architecture critic Eva Hagberg went back to Hudson Yards. She had first visited the complex in spring 2019, when she was on the brink of divorce, and, as she later recalled, had a surprisingly emotional reaction: "in the wide and empty hallways with absolutely nowhere to sit . . . I realized that Hudson Yards, with its luxurious emptiness and deep striving to be a better, brighter, glitzier, bigger image that could be sold and bought, was revealing me to myself." When she returned in 2021, it was in the middle of the pandemic, with a new boyfriend. There was still nowhere to sit. But there were Christmas lights on the escalator. There were lines for the women's bathroom. There was shopping for professional clothes. There was a sign at Mercado Little Spain: CHURROS ARE BACK! She finally found a seat on "a plush banquette . . . it was empty and isolating and also at the same time pregnant with possibility. Soon large groups of people will sit there again, I thought. Soon this will be different." She was talking about the banquette, I think, but also about malls.

Her reaction reminded me of a conversation I had with film and television critic Matt Zoller Seitz months before. "One of the many ironies of this age is that it has transformed ordinary photographs into a form of pornography. I've been watching old documentaries like *On the Bowery* from 1956, and the whole thing is set in bars. I keep thinking, God I miss bars," he told me. "I'm looking at newspaper clippings of my grandmother, who was a concert pianist, playing in a recital, and there are forty people in chairs in a room. I'm thinking, God I miss live music. Give me more of that sweet, sweet crowd imagery!"

I hypothesized, and he agreed, that the end of quarantine could provoke a great rush out. "I think it is built in the DNA to want to move freely in a space with other people," Seitz said. "I lived in New York for twenty-three years, and then I moved to Cincinnati, where there's more of a mall culture, and I actually really like malls. Those little benches where you can sit and take a load off, watching people going by, up and down the escalators . . . I like the food court, that's how much of mall guy I am."

What they were both saying, in different ways, was that people want to be together. That joy I had in seeing families walking hand in hand at American Dream was a version of the same joy Gruen found, at the beginning and end of his life, at Vienna's sidewalk cafés. Why we are out—a movie, a sweater, a concert, boba—does not matter as much as having the space in which to be out in the comfort of strangers. The future for the mall won't be on the template laid out by all those shopping center manuals, but it could be on the ruins of the architecture of that era. The future for the mall can't be as restricted, expensive, and policed as it became in the 1980s, but it could adapt the totemic art programs of the 1960s and the adaptive reuse strategies of the 1970s.

The ambivalence at the heart of the mall remains. Seventy years on, the mall has to learn from its mistakes and be willing to embrace the messiness and variety once thought to be the exclusive (and frightening) province of downtown. But the mall has already proved itself to be malleable. It has already stretched to include amusement parks and ethnic markets and aviaries. It can stretch to accommodate new anchors. Intervention is necessary, and that intervention should be fueled not by the historic disdain malls have engendered but by a positive spin on nostalgia. What would draw the consumers of 2022 and beyond back out? What gives the forty-year-old the same joy she once found at Hot Topic, or he once found at an attic arcade? But also: How can the next life of malls repair some of what suburban development put asunder, introducing walking, and work, and waterways back into pavement-dominated sprawl? Shopping isn't going anywhere, and it's so much nicer to do it together.

Conclusion
The Mall Abroad

I n 2013, Arlene Dávila, now a professor of anthropology and American studies at New York University, attended the International Council of Shopping Centers' John T. Riordan Global Professional Development School in Mexico City, taking courses in development, design and construction, administration, and marketing and leasing alongside young professionals from Latin America. When the organization was founded in 1956, its "international" designation was thanks to a handful of Canadian members. It wasn't until the early 1990s that ICSC held its first conferences outside North America, and its first Latin American convention was in 2009.

The group's late attention to the Latin American market didn't mean there had been no malls there: Sears and similar U.S. retailers opened stores in Mexico in the 1940s, and enclosed malls with department store anchors were built in larger Latin American cities beginning in the late 1960s. Dávila's interest in the trajectory of malls south of Texas was spurred, in part, by noticing that more than three hundred malls had been built across the region in the early 2010s, adding to hundreds built since the 1980s. Yet at the Riordan school, knowledge flowed only in one direction, north to south. Instructors pitched the classic North American business model of the mall—single owner, with leasing based around two or three large anchor stores, on a greenfield site, accessed via car—as the template for new opportunities in Latin America. The North American mall was dying, and rather than rethinking the model, why not spin it off around the world? U.S. mall developers seemed conditioned to always seek "new frontiers"—now internationally—rather than trying to solve their problems at home.

But why should the U.S. way of malling be held as central? When I mentioned to people that American Dream had an indoor ski slope, the most common response was "What? Like in Dubai?" People told me about the mall at the Changi Airport in Singapore (which also has a waterfall and all-ages play nets). A friend of mine from Los Angeles, who grew up in Orange County and worked at both South Coast Plaza and its rival, Fashion Island, visited Santiago, Chile's Costanera Center in 2015. She says she and her husband "felt like the poor U.S. cousins" at the "fancy-pants mall."

As the weeks passed, Dávila found herself more fascinated by all the permutations described by her knowledgeable classmates than by the standardized curriculum. In Latin America, malls had always been seen as part of a modernizing project, one as varied as the political groups in power across the region. While initially their inspiration had come from the United States, different countries had long since made the mall their own, with retail, entertainment, architecture, and transit options tailored to the economic and urban politics of specific countries and cities. Dávila's classmates "expressed skepticism about learning lessons from representatives of what they saw as a failing industry, relative to the current success of shopping malls back home."

The world of malls is both planetary and highly localized, vast and specific, in terms of design, amenities, funding, and location. Dávila was not alone among scholars wondering why the solution to the problem of dying malls was supposed to come from expansion to "virgin" mall territory, rather than learning from success and bringing it back to the United States.

"My lunch mates were bragging among themselves about the types of amenities and entertainment choices that are regular offerings at Latin American malls," Dávila writes in her 2016 book, *El Mall*, "re-creations of snowflakes or sandy beaches for children during holidays; bowling alleys or temporary skating rinks; amenities like gardens and fountains; innovative architectural features such as spiral-shaped hallways," while her professor offered up only the Mall of America as an example of a shopping center that embraced entertainment. While analyzing the ways *el mall* diverges from the mall, Dávila also questions its central place in the urban development process as a driver of consumerism and credit, and as a privatization of public space, with police forces empowered to judge who does and does not belong. Latin American malls' economic, cultural, and symbolic importance doesn't negate critique.

Jose, a Spanish classmate of Dávila's who had worked in Puerto Rico and Venezuela, praised a Venezuelan mall development model—based on assembling small stores and boutiques rather than chasing international brands—as an alternative in countries, including Mexico, where there are only two department store companies and two movie theaters that are even an option as an anchor. Developers who want a Forever 21 or an H&M may have to pay the brand to get the latest in fast fashion in their mall.

Chilean students described the incorporation of museums and libraries into their malls. "Chilean malls can deduct up to 50 percent of monies spent on cultural contributions, and by placing libraries within malls they increase their value as destinations, expand the number of visitors, and generate goodwill in ways that far exceed any initial investment in building these spaces," she writes.

Distinctive mall architecture is also more important than it has ever been in the United States, as Latin American visitors are more likely to compare amenities, green space, and public leisure areas than specific department stores. Malls have become the drivers of public transit extensions and residential development, rather than the other way around, making them more likely to be surrounded by density than to sit alone in a parking lot. In many countries, the ownership structure is completely different from the U.S. single-proprietor model: Interested parties raise money from a group of retailers, which then own the space in common, and make group decisions, as in a condominium building.

Parque Arauco in Santiago, opened in 1982, is run by a development company of the same name that today owns and co-owns malls in Chile, Colombia, and Peru. Over the decades it has grown into a sprawling district of its own, organized around a private, palm-lined street winding between buildings devoted to luxury brands, home and decoration, international cuisine, and, yes, a food hall. There's a cinema, an ice rink, a bowling alley, and a venue for Centro Cultural Mori, a theater organized around the principle of democratizing drama. Parque Arauco's rival, Costanera Center, was completed in 2012 and is one of the largest malls in South America, tucked under an elegant skyscraper designed by Cesar Pelli's firm.

The mall is a form that, over the past forty years, has outgrown the original. Each region has its own innovations, and each regional variation deserves the type of examination Dávila devoted to *el mall*. In 2017 Nolan Gray wrote "Triumph of the Latin American Mall," in CityLab, attributing its success to the growing middle class with money to spend—an economic condition parallel to that during the U.S. expansion after World War II—as well as a dearth of "high-quality urban environments" given the violent crime and lack of investment in public infrastructure, a condition which also parallels the postwar retreat of white shoppers from downtowns and the creation of malls as an alternative.

"American mall managers trying to survive the retail meltdown might learn a few things from their southern neighbors," Gray writes: ditching department stores for supermarkets, considering malls organized around a single industry, and, yes, incorporating offices and residential development. In other words, all the elements suburban zoning tried so hard to keep separate have at last been put back together. Their reassembly doesn't make the need for the mall as a structure disappear, any more than the increasing urbanization of the American suburbs makes it so. Rather, in the alternative paths of development, location, and organization, it is possible to see a new future for this North American innovation.

In fact, layered functions, urban density, and embedded public services were part of the malls of one country from the beginning, and far earlier than the 1980s: the United Kingdom. The New Towns Act of 1946 was the British government's response to the deprivations of World War II, setting aside government funds under the control of development corporations to rebuild and replace bombed and substandard housing. The first wave of that development was largely suburban, literal new towns on greenfield sites,

Town Centre Phase I, Cumbernauld New Town,
Cumbernauld, Scotland, Geoffrey Copcutt,
Cumbernauld Development Corporation, 1967.
(Photograph by Bill Toomey; RIBA 1968)

while other locations swallowed up traditional villages. Central to their
concept, and central in their planning, were replacements for traditional
high street shopping districts. The critical response to the New Towns, with
their oversized concrete architecture and paternalistic view of what the
people want, has waxed and waned over the years. But when they were
young, they were proving grounds for postwar architecture, built by publicly
funded developers at a scale, style, and density far different from the United
States' privately built little boxes and Levittowns.

Cumbernauld, in the Clyde Valley outside Glasgow, was the fifteenth in
the sequence of towns built from scratch. The second wave of New Towns
was meant to be denser by design, and this Scottish site was the smallest to
date: four thousand acres, atop a windy ridge. Cumbernauld Town Centre,
which opened in 1967, was planned as a megastructure—a then au courant
architectural form, popular in Britain and Japan, which envisioned multi-
farious urban functions assembled under one infinitely extendable roof, and
variously modeled as a tree, a three-dimensional grid, and a lumbering
robot. Architect Geoffrey Copcutt described his plans in futuristic terms

(and one of the center's twin row of penthouses later served as a lair for more than one movie villain), with "clip-on" elements stacking the commercial, religious, and residential needs of the town atop a base of parking. Plans extended it to a half mile, door to door, with theaters, sports facilities, department stores, apartments, and offices. The jury of an international community architecture award that year wrote, in praise, "The jury believes the Cumbernauld Town Centre is the prototype of the form that must evolve, sooner or later, for the central business districts in our cities in the United States."

The megastructure was supposed to be infinitely adaptable to suit the needs of the community, a high-design and high-tech version of being able to swap stores in and out while maintaining architectural control. Cumbernauld Town Centre remains one of few built examples of the "plug-in city" form and was spoken of in its time as a "giant vending machine through which the motorized user drives." Like so many 1960s experiments with flexible form, it never quite worked as intended. Centrality rather than sprawl dominated the design, to the detriment of the surrounding environment. In the twenty-first century, Cumbernauld has deteriorated into a ragged, flat, decentralized suburban environment known for cheap goods: "The remains of the old town center loom up like industrial ruins from a shapeless ocean of gigantic supermarkets, logistics areas, parking lots, leftover green spaces, and gas stations," writes Regina Bittner in *The World of Malls*.

The concrete grid Copcutt laid out made it difficult to fit in mass entertainment facilities such as a cinema or a skating rink, while outdoor walkways—designed to offer expansive views—were windy and cold. The raw concrete, now an aesthetic, looked unfinished, especially in contrast to enclosed, climate-controlled shopping elsewhere. Retailers doubted they would be able to attract customers to the upper floors, given the climb. When critic John Grindrod finally visited, he found "the much-vaunted 'Megastructure' existed largely in the minds of a handful of architectural critics and academics, with the central area never reaching a size that merited a name." That said, while most of the shopping had devolved into ground-level big boxes, up in the structure "the entire centre feels like a flea market . . . it has developed *character*. The lack of chain stores, the irregularly shaped paths between the shops, the brown and orange wall tiles, the internal ramps—they all give the place a quirky, independent feel." He might almost be describing Ray Bradbury's vision of the mall's magic-filled attic.

Birmingham's Bull Ring, a "Brutalist, introverted concrete form—occupying 32,515 square metres with 140 shops and 500 car parking spaces," was built at the same time, replacing the English city's historic market square in 1964. The Bull Ring itself was demolished in 2000, replaced with a shiny new mall in two parts connected by an underground passage. Nicholas Jewell, a British architect who practices in China, has argued that a new generation of mall projects in the U.K. would do well to learn from Asian examples, which connect to transit; layer small shops, department stores, food halls, offices, and residences in a vertical sandwich; and provide a needed, climate-controlled respite from the city streets of Singapore and Hong Kong. While Jewell considers the new Bull Ring an improvement on its 1960s predecessor, it still lacks the "more rounded conception of urbanity in its Asian counterparts" by maintaining its single-minded focus on retail and excluding the public by offering seats only to customers. In China, where developers were building hundreds of malls per year in the late teens, those structures "occasionally . . . stand as individual buildings in their own right, but most commonly their atrium binds together a complex mixed-use city section that combines public transport infrastructure, shopping, work and housing within a bounded city block."

Diana Martinez, who studies the particulars of the post-dictatorship mallification of the Philippines, connects this Asian complexity back to the birth of the mall in Edina. Gruen, who turned his back on his own invention by the late 1960s, would have recognized his original vision for Southdale in Manila. "When Victor Gruen first designed Southdale, he imagined a medical center, schools, and residences, not just a parade of stores," she writes. "In the United States the mall never achieved this form. Thus, a disjunction

SM Mall of Asia, Bay City, Pasay, Philippines, Arquitectonica, 2006. (Photograph by Joel Lozare; Arquitectonica)

exists between the now failing American mall and the still thriving and evolving Philippine supermall." The Philippines are not alone in that grander definition of what a mall can do. Iran opened the world's largest mall in 2017, Thailand has two malls with close to six million square feet of leasable space, and Saudi Arabia had plans to triple its mall space by 2025. These un-American malls are so large they cannot be decoupled from the city, the economy, or society. They do not swim in parking lots but are connected on multiple levels to the urban environment and, even more deeply, to culture.

The story of malls in the Philippines also begins in the 1940s. Sy Zhicheng, a Chinese immigrant, sold American shoes to GIs stationed on the islands during World War II and used the profits to open a shoe store in Manila in 1948. In 1958, Sy launched his first air-conditioned Shoe Mart superstore. By 1980 he owned six department stores, which served as destinations, thanks to their climate control. In 1985 he opened his first mall, SM City North EDSA, with one million square feet of leasable space and, of course, air-conditioning. While other investors feared a socialist uprising as the result of the deposing of dictatorial president Ferdinand Marcos, Sy saw those newly empowered masses as customers. While the Filipino mall industry launched in earnest thirty years after the U.S. version, it soon surpassed its progenitor.

"The Philippines is home to some of the world's largest shopping malls—it boasts five with gross leasable areas in excess of four million square feet. Each of these shopping malls is significantly larger than the US's gargantuan Mall of America, which has a comparatively modest leasable area of 2.7 million square feet," Martinez writes. While American malls have reduced their physical and psychological footprint, Philippine malls remain at the center of society: Somewhere To Go to shop, to eat, to ride a carousel, to ice-skate, to file government paperwork, to pay a utility bill, to see the doctor, or to drop a child at daycare. Sy's SM company, which owned forty-two malls in 2020, serves three million customers a day, focused not on luxury objects and international brands—the Philippines is one of the poorest countries in Asia—but on high volume, low-cost activities and goods. SM Mall of Asia, the largest in the country when it opened in 2006, now fourth, is currently undergoing an expansion that will bring it to over six million square feet in gross floor area by 2024. A relationship that began informally, with bus stops and jeepneys lining up outside the mall to capture loaded-down shoppers, has evolved into a system where new light rail stops follow the lead of new mall projects, malls absorb city functions into their vast architectural bodies, and malls are one of the few places with generators to keep the lights and air-conditioning on in a state with limited public investment. Martinez again: "The mall, however, is now so deeply intertwined with the Philippine society and economy that the former would be dysfunctional without it, while the latter might fail in its absence—a sure sign that the mall has become infrastructural."

One in ten Filipinos works overseas, and in 1994 Sy estimated that 30 percent of funds spent at his malls came from abroad. Martinez writes that "spending the money of someone both loved and absent is a form of communion for millions of separated Filipino families." Those monies are spent at home, but also abroad, in countries such as Saudi Arabia, Qatar, and Dubai, where Filipino overseas workers make up a sizable portion of the population (as high as 21 percent, in the case of Dubai). There, workers can eat the same food as their families back at home via Filipino fast-food chain Jollibee, which has multiple franchises in Middle Eastern malls. Both the cuisines and architecture on offer, at least in Dubai, reflect the increasing diversity of the United Arab Emirates population. Even Filipino slang has absorbed the mall's status: "Only in the Philippines is 'malling' used as a verb," note other mall scholars. "Malls are not used solely for entertainment, as they also serve as avenues of escapism for most Filipinos, whose daily hardships have made them feel despondent. Malls provide a mirage of comfort, security and affluence."

Despite the innovation and lavishness of homegrown malls from Beijing to Bogotá, top shopping for many elites is still to be found in the United States, where prices for brand-name goods are often lower, and the trip is a way to demonstrate status. In 2010 the *Financial Times* reported that at Sawgrass Mills, a Simon-operated outlet mall in Sunrise, Florida, more than 40 percent of shoppers were from Latin America. Miami's Dolphin Mall is a long-standing destination for shopping tourists from Brazil and Colombia, while NorthPark advertises in Mexico, offers bilingual concierge services, and is also a popular destination for Asian tourists, thanks to nonstop flights from the Dallas–Fort Worth airport to China, Japan, and South Korea. Nine percent of South Coast Plaza's pre-pandemic 22 million annual visitors were from abroad, many of them from China. Sitting in Orange County, which has the country's third-largest Asian American population, SCP is just one of many local destinations that accept Chinese credit cards, hire Mandarin-speaking sales associates, and stock traditional red gift-giving envelopes. When my own Brazilian and Israeli relatives visit New York City, they add on a day in Elizabeth, New Jersey, where the outlets at the

Amorepacific Headquarters, Seoul, South Korea, David Chipperfield Architects, 2010–2017. (Photograph by Noshe)

Mills at Jersey Gardens provide a year's worth of inexpensive cotton clothes for the grandchildren. The mall runs a shuttle directly to Newark Liberty International Airport, and there's a New Jersey Transit bus from Manhattan. These malls have hooked themselves up to public transportation, despite precedent, to cater to audiences used to shopping being closely linked to the subway. It's telling, but not unexpected, that some of these efforts have been made to attract international visitors rather than a more racially and economically diverse local audience. When Dávila spoke to Latinx mall developer José Legaspi, he marveled at the developers' willingness to leave rather than pivot: "Legaspi has shown that making a shopping mall relevant demands a transformation of the concept of the mall to make it more culturally and community relevant."

Meanwhile, on the other side of the globe, my last international pre-pandemic trip was to Seoul. I was there to interview Teo Yang, an emerging design star who has chosen to live, work, and sell skincare products in the city's historic Bukchon neighborhood. The area was charming, with its narrow streets and wood-and-plaster houses, a preserved and pedestrianized village among the skyscrapers. I couldn't help noticing, however, that everywhere else in Seoul seemed to be built on top of a mall. Train stations, universities, office buildings, hotels: Everywhere I went I found rows of shops, delicious smells from cubby-size counters, artificial lighting, and indoor plants. Yang designed a boutique European coffee shop, with wooden curves inspired by the work of Alvar Aalto, and the flagship location wasn't in the luxury precincts of Gangnam but on the lower floor of the brand-new Amorepacific Headquarters building by David Chipperfield. A striking piece of contemporary architecture, the beauty company's offices also house a hanging garden, a skincare store, a contemporary art museum, an art book library, a subway station, and, of course, a mall. The question was not Where's the mall? but Where isn't the mall?—so thoroughly had the idea of convenient, varied, sociable shopping infiltrated all levels of this technologically advanced city. I had seen something with this mix and this energy before in just a few places in New York City: Rockefeller Center, built in the 1930s, and Brookfield Place, built in the 1980s and updated in the last decade.

The more recently built Oculus at the World Trade Center and Shops at Hudson Yards feel empty and exhausting by contrast, their spaces too vast to make hopscotching between transit, coffee, office, and shopping a route of convenience rather than enervation.

After a pandemic layered on top of a retail apocalypse, it is hard to imagine everyone's mall isn't going to require a retrofit. If you believe, as I do, that it is human nature to want the feeling of communal space the mall affords, the most fertile sources for inspiration may not be the department store anchors, overlarge parking lots, and underdiversified food courts of the past life of the (North) American mall, but the transit-centered, community-embedded, active uses of present-day successes—wherever in the world they might be. The next time you see a picture of a dead mall looking like a lonely sculpture, look again. Imagine the return of the grove it was named after, or the growth of housing into the parking lot from the surrounding neighborhoods. Imagine the department store reborn as a spa or a rec center, community college classrooms cheek by jowl with Forever 21 and a branch library. Imagine the mall being as physically embedded in place as it already is in culture. The mall was made to be responsive. It can still be Somewhere To Go.

Acknowledgments

Thank you to Anne Trubek, the first person with whom I discussed the idea of a mall book, for her generous advice and encouragement. Thank you to Ben Hyman, Nancy Miller, Katya Mezhibovskaya, Morgan Jones, Barbara Darko, Maureen Klier, Tanya Heinrich, Kay Banning, and the rest of the team at Bloomsbury for being so great to work with the first time that I wanted to do it again. Thank you to Joe Veltre for helping me pivot. Thank you to Kelsey Keith, Amy Plitt, Sara Polsky, and Asad Syrkett, all lately of Curbed, for assigning and editing the pieces that inspired this book.

Writing a book during a pandemic can be a lonely task. Mine was made a little less lonely by Zoom meetings of Architecture Writers Anonymous (you know who you are), as well as by the sprawling online design community, with whom I continued to bitch about the built environment through texts, tweets, emails, DMs, and Instagram messages. Members include Greg Allen, Jessica Anshutz, Sarah Archer, Liz Arnold, Rebecca Baird-Remba, Elizabeth Blasius, Ian Bogost, Alex Bozikovic, Charles Birnbaum, Diana Budds, Garnette Cadogan, Kriston Capps, Sara Jensen Carr, Bree Davies, Jason Diamond, Phil Donohue, Chappell Ellison, Neil Flanagan, Gina Ford, Brian Goldstein, Eva Hagberg, Sara Hendren, Jen Hewitt, Jennifer Howard, Amanda Kolson Hurley, Brock Keeling, Austin Kleon, Mark Lamster, Sarah Larson, Bruce Levenson, Josh Lipnik, Deane Madsen, @mallchitecture, Carolina Miranda, Aaron Naparstek, @nickhasthoughts, Jennifer Komar Olivarez, Antonio Pacheco, Anthony Paletta, Jeff Pleshek, Anne Quito, Anjulie Rao, Fred Scharmen, Timothy Schuler, Benjamin Shaykin, Jill Singer, Patrick Sisson, Rachel Syme, Avery Trufelman, Alissa Walker, Liz Waytkus, Alex Weinberg, Nord Wennerstrom, Alexa Winton, and many more whose handles escape me.

IRL friends including Kyra Caspary, Angelyn Chandler, Rebecca Goldsmith, Kristen Nutile, Rose Kob, Meredith Johnson, Francine Rosado-Cruz, Varsha Rosenblatt, and especially Jennifer Weyburn (many weekend walks) kept my spirits up.

Thank you to Brenda Buhr-Hancock, Kristen Gibbens, Mark Dilworth, Andi York, and especially Nancy Nasher and David Haemisegger for being generous with their time, knowledge, and archives of NorthPark Center, the only mall field trip I was able to take before quarantine. Thank you to Tom Martinson for background on the Minneapolis trip I was not able to make. Thank you to Danny Upshaw and Chelsea Winkel for skating Metropark and sharing their experience, and to Alison King for being my Phoenix scout. Thank you to June Williamson (and Ellen Dunham-Jones in absentia) for being generous with her retrofit knowledge. Thank you to Sarah Streit for generously sharing her mall movie supercut.

This book would have no pictures without the skills of archivists, architects, media coordinators and photographers like David Zaballero at Arquitectonica, Dan Bell, DeSoto Brown at the Bishop Museum, Capella Garcia Arquitectura, Tricia Gilson at the Columbus Indiana Architectural Archives, Michael Galinsky, Anne Mar at Glendale Library, Arts & Culture, Matthew Parrent at Gruen Associates, Emily Lowthian and Greg Rodgers at JERDE, Matt Reeves at the Kansas City Public Library, Lindsey Loeper of Special Collections at the Albin O. Kuhn Library at UMBC, Ivana Kostic at LHP Architects, Ross Mantle, Michael Nock and Celia Toche at Pelli Clarke Pelli, Steve Rosenthal, Louise Sandhaus, Sara Crown at the Santa Monica History Museum, Max Touhey, and Claire Weisz at WXY. While I was only able to benefit for the first two months of 2020, my time in the Shoichi Noma Reading Room at the New York Public Library provided the foundation for everything that came after.

Thank you to Gere Kavanaugh, a Zelig of design, who created both colorful toys (last book) and colorful shopping experiences (this book), and who always understood the assignment.

Last but never least, thank you to my family—Mark, Paul, and Romy—for weathering a pandemic with grace and humor intact, for being fellow introverts, and for giving me the time and space to write a whole book from home.

Notes

INTRODUCTION: WHY WE GO TO THE MALL

9   he made sure to stop at the local mall: Michael Galinsky, *The Decline of Mall Civilization* (n.p.: Rumur, 2019).

11   Lifestyle centers are designed: Andrew Blum, "The Mall Goes Undercover," *Slate*, April 6, 2005, https://slate.com/culture/2005/04/the-latest-incarnation-of -the-shopping-mall.html, accessed September 27 2021.

11   "asking private landowners": Jeff Furman, vice president of development for Northwood Ravin, quoted in Thomas McDonald, "Durham Mayor Claps Back at Testy Letter from Northgate Mall Developer," *IndyWeek*, May 7, 2021, https:// indyweek.com/news/durham/durham-mayor-northgate-mall-northwood -developer/, accessed September 28, 2021.

12   "The theme park presents": Michael Sorkin, ed., *Variations on a Theme Park: The New American City and the End of Public Space* (New York: Hill and Wang, 1992), xv.

12   Justice Thurgood Marshall described: Amalgamated Food Employees Union Local 590 v. Logan Valley Plaza, 391 U.S. 308 (1968).

CHAPTER 1: EVERY DAY WILL BE A PERFECT SHOPPING DAY

This account of the origins of the American shopping mall is indebted to Victor Gruen, *Shopping Town: Designing the City in Suburban America*, ed. and trans. Anette Baldauf (Minneapolis: University of Minnesota Press, 2017); M. Jeffrey Hardwick, *Mall Maker: Victor Gruen, Architect of an American Dream* (Philadelphia: University of Pennsylvania Press, 2003); and Richard W. Longstreth, *The American Department Store Transformed, 1920–1960* (New Haven, CT: Yale University Press, 2010).

15   "I decided to wander": Victor Gruen, *Shopping Town: Designing the City in Suburban America*, ed. and trans. Anette Baldauf (Minneapolis: University of Minnesota Press, 2017), 110–111.

16   was the brainchild: Lindsay Turley, "'I Have Seen the Future': Norman Bel Geddes and the General Motors Futurama," Museum of the City of New York: New York Stories, blog, November 26, 2013, https://wp.me/p1kGOJ-1Yr, accessed September 28, 2021; Lawrence W. Speck, "Futurama," in *Norman Bel Geddes Designs America*, ed. Donald Albrecht (New York: Abrams, 2012), 288–315.

17   "a pitcher plant captures flies": Lewis Mumford, "The Sky Line: New Faces on the Avenue," *New Yorker*, September 9, 1939, 62.

18   Krummeck, a skilled artist: Myrna Oliver, "Elsie Krummeck Crawford; Artistic Industrial Designer," *Los Angeles Times*, June 3, 1999; Victor Gruen, "Store Designing for the 'Feminine Touch': Famed Store Designer Tells Interior Secrets," *West Coast Feminine Wear*, April 29, 1947, quoted in M. Jeffrey Hardwick, *Mall Maker: Victor Gruen, Architect of an American Dream* (Philadelphia: University of Pennsylvania Press, 2003), 39.

18   "shops were the advance messengers": Robert A. M. Stern, David Fishman, and Thomas Mellins, *New York 1960: Architecture and Urbanism Between the Second World War and the Bicentennial* (New York: Monacelli Press, 1995), 574.

19   For the Hollywood Grayson's: Hardwick, *Mall Maker*, 62.

19   Gruen had surveyed the postwar shopping scene: Victor Gruen, "What's Wrong with Store Design?" *Women's Wear Daily*, October 18, 1949.

20   *House Beautiful* published: Quoted in Richard W. Longstreth, *City Center to Regional Mall: Architecture, the Automobile, and Retailing in Los Angeles, 1920–1950* (Cambridge, MA: MIT Press, 1998), 149–150.

21   Nichols set a design standard: Sara Stevens, "J.C. Nichols and the Country Club District: Suburban Aesthetics and Property Values," The Pendergast Years: Kansas City in the Jazz Age & Great Depression (2018), https://pendergastkc .org/article/jc-nichols-and-country-club-district-suburban-aesthetics-and -property-values, accessed September 28, 2021; Judy L. Thomas, "'Curse of Covenant' Persists—Restrictive Rules, While Unenforceable, Have Lingering Legacy," *Kansas City Star*, July 27, 2016.

22   a comparison not lost: Hardwick, *Mall Maker*, 96–97.

24   *Architectural Forum* asked: Victor Gruenbaum and Elsie Krummeck, "New Buildings for 194X: Shopping Center," *Architectural Forum*, May 1943, 101–103; Gruen, *Shopping Town*, 97.

25 editor George Nelson: George Nelson to Victor Gruenbaum, March 3, 1948, letter in American Heritage Center Victor Gruen Collection (AHCVGC), quoted in Hardwick, *Mall Maker*, 82–83.

26 Gruen wrote a ten-page letter: Gruen, *Shopping Town*, 114ff.

27 Northland, Eastland, Westland, and Southland: Victor Gruen and Larry Smith, *Shopping Towns USA: The Planning of Shopping Centers* (New York: Reinhold Publishing, 1960), 36; Victor Gruen, "Victor Gruen's Speech at Press Preview, Northland," March 15, 1954, AHCVGC, quoted in Hardwick, *Mall Maker*, 128. Gruen and Smith first used this phrase in the study "Shopping Centers: The New Building Type," *Progressive Architecture*, June 1952, 69.

29 even Jane Jacobs: Jane Jacobs, "Northland: A New Yardstick for Shopping Center Planning," *Architectural Forum*, June 1954, 103; Grady Clay, "What Makes a Good Square Good?" *Fortune*, April 1958, 236, reprinted in *The Exploding Metropolis*, ed. William H. Whyte (New York: Doubleday, 1958), 154.

30 "the character and atmosphere": Gruen, *Shopping Town*, 129.

30 Gruen transfer: Elena Gooray, "There's a Name for That: Gruen Transfer," *Pacific Standard* (December–January 2018), https://psmag.com/magazine/gruen-transfer, accessed September 28, 2021.

30 French novelist Émile Zola: Émile Zola, *Au bonheur des dames* (1883); *The Ladies' Paradise* (London: Vizetelly, 1886), consulted via Project Gutenberg, https://www.gutenberg.org/files/54687/54687-h/54687-h.htm, accessed September 28, 2021.

32 "fostered women's mobility": Chuihua Judy Chung, "Ms. Consumer," in *Harvard Design School Guide to Shopping*, ed. Chung, Jeffrey Inaba, Rem Koolhaas, and Sze Tsung Leong (Cologne: Taschen, 2001), 506–507.

32 the earliest American department stores: Robert Hendrickson, *The Grand Emporiums: The Illustrated History of America's Great Department Stores* (New York: Stein and Day, 1979), 34ff; Lewis Mumford, *The Culture of Cities* (New York: Harcourt Brace Jovanovich, [1938] 1970), 259.

33 thought it would revolutionize consumption: William Leach, *Land of Desire: Merchants, Power, and the Rise of a New American Culture* (New York: Vintage, 1994), 74.

34 "The elevator is ideal": Quoted in Srdjan Jovanovic Weiss and Sze Tsung Leong, "Escalator," in Chung et al., *Guide to Shopping*, 337.

34 positioning of the escalators: "A Break-Through for Two-Level Shopping Centers," *Architectural Forum*, December 1956, 115.

35 "blight-proof neighborhood": Gruen and Smith, *Shopping Towns USA*, 108; Victor Gruen, "Urban Renewal," *Appraisal Journal* (American Institute of Real Estate Appraisers), January 1956, n.p., quoted in Hardwick, *Mall Maker*, 154.

36 "Inventions sometimes": Gruen, *Shopping Town*, 131.

37 "regardless of unpleasant outdoor weather": Carrier advertisement (1930), quoted in Chung et al., *Guide to Shopping*, 108; Victor Gruen, Morris Ketchum, Morris Lapidus, Daniel Schwartzman, and Kenneth Welch, "What Makes a 1940 Store Obsolete?" *Architectural Forum*, July 1950, 62.

38 "Pleasure-Domes with Parking": "Pleasure-Domes with Parking," *Time*, October 15, 1956, 96; "Design for a Better Outdoors Indoors," *Architectural Record*, June 1962, 174; "Southdale Is 11th of Its Kind in Nation," *Minneapolis Sunday Tribune*, October 7, 1956, 5, quoted in Hardwick, *Mall Maker*, 148.

38 the Garden Court: Gruen, *Shopping Town*, 133.

39 "Reviewers rarely noticed": Hardwick, *Mall Maker*, 153; Frank Murray, "Wright Asks City to Seek 'Truth, Not Just Facts,'" *Minneapolis Star*, November 28, 1956, https://www.startribune.com/nov-28-1956-frank-lloyd-wright-at-southdale/126070188/, accessed September 28, 2021; "Minneapolis Crucified by Architect," *Rapid City (SD) Journal*, November 29, 1956, quoted in Hardwick, *Mall Maker*, 151.

39 downtown takeover of Edina: "Work Begins on 10 Million Dollar Southdale Shopping Center," *Minneapolis Star*, October 29, 1954, 52, quoted in Hardwick, *Mall Maker*, 154; Hardwick, *Mall Maker*, 157.

40 one contemporary community-planning guidebook: *The Community Builders Handbook*, prepared by the Community Builders' Council of the Urban Land Institute (Washington, D.C.: ULI, 1947, and annually thereafter).

42 One such owner: "Missouri: The Shelley House," National Park Service, https://www.nps.gov/places/missouri-the-shelley-house-l.htm, accessed September 28, 2021; Shelley v. Kraemer, 334 U.S. 1; 68 S.Ct. 836, 92 L.Ed. 1161 (1948), vote 6–0.

42–43 "This blow to racial segregation": Thurgood Marshall, *News from NAACP* (May 6, 1948), quoted in Amina Hassan, *Loren Miller: Civil Rights Attorney and Journalist* (Norman: University of Oklahoma Press, 2015), 176.

43 "African American suburban dreams": Andrew Wiese, "'The House I Live In': Race, Class and African American Suburban Dreams," in *The New Suburban History*, ed. Kevin M. Kruse and Thomas J. Sugrue (Chicago: University of Chicago Press, 2006), 99.

43   "did not insure mortgages": Jake Blumgart, "Redlining Didn't Happen Quite the Way We Thought It Did," *Governing*, September 21, 2021, https://www.governing.com/context/redlining-didnt-happen-quite-the-way-we-thought-it-did, accessed September 28, 2021; Andrew Herscher, "Black and Blight," in *Race and Modern Architecture*, ed. Irene Cheng, Charles Davis, and Mabel Wilson (Pittsburgh: University of Pittsburgh Press, 2020), 294; Ira Katznelson, *When Affirmative Action Was White: An Untold Story of Racial Inequality in Twentieth-Century America* (New York: W. W. Norton, 2005), 140.

CHAPTER 2: THE GARDEN

46   "In the dream stage": "NorthPark Fact Sheet," August 1965, NorthPark Center, Dallas; Peter Blake, *God's Own Junkyard* (New York: Holt, Rinehart and Winston, 1964), 7.

47   The Simon brothers: Thomas Derdak and Tina Grant, "Simon Property Group, Inc.," in *International Directory of Company Histories*, vol. 27 (Detroit: St. James Press, 1999), 399; Martha Weinman Lear, "A Master Builder Sites a Shopping Mall," *New York Times Magazine*, August 12, 1973, 224ff.

48   "more than a conventional shopping center": "Two Schools of Thought Clash Head-On in Battle over Planned Shopping Center," *Dallas Morning News*, July 10, 1961, NorthPark Center.

50   young architect E. G. Hamilton: "2300 Riverside Apartments, Tulsa," *Architectural Record* 125 (June 1959): 208–209; Mark Lamster, "Remembering E. G. Hamilton, the Architect Who Made Dallas," *Dallas Morning News*, May 12, 2017, https://www.dallasnews.com/arts-entertainment/architecture/2017/05/12/remembering-e-g-hamilton-the-architect-who-made-dallas/, accessed September 28, 2021.

50   "'going to be a millionaire'": E. G. Hamilton, "Shopping Texas Style: E. G. Hamilton, Omniplan, and NorthPark Center," April 30, 2010, Nasher Sculpture Center, Dallas. Thank you to Dr. Kathryn E. Holliday, director, Dillon Center for Texas Architecture, for sharing this transcript.

50   Raymond Nasher: "The Collector," *Duke Alumni Magazine*, May–June 2003, https://alumni.duke.edu/magazine/articles/collector; Janet Kutner, "Nasher Leaves Dallas a Better Place," *Dallas Morning News*, March 18, 2007, https://web

.archive.org/web/20070320023210/http://www.dallasnews.com/sharedcontent /dws/dn/latestnews/stories/031707dnmetnasherappreciate2.1ff4e0f8.html, accessed September 28, 2021; Alan Peppard, "The Heart of NorthPark," *Dallas Morning News*, September 29, 2015.

51   her mother deserves equal credit: "Patsy Nasher, 59, Dies; Was Sculpture Patron," *New York Times*, July 9, 1988, https://www.nytimes.com/1988/07 /09/obituaries/patsy-nasher-59-dies-was-sculpture-patron.html, accessed September 28, 2021; Nancy Nasher, interview with author, February 25, 2020.

54   "educating most of the architects": Stanley Marcus, quoted in James Adams, "A Curiosity in Architecture: The Legacy of Stanley Marcus," *Columns: AIA Dallas* 34, no. 4 (Fall 2017), https://www.aiadallas.org/v/columns-detail/A-Curio sity-in-Architecture-The-Legacy-of-Stanley-Marcus/s4/, accessed September 28, 2021.

55   "installing play areas": Virginia Postrel, "NorthPark's Secret," *D Magazine*, April 2006, https://www.dmagazine.com/publications/d-magazine/2006/april /spaces-northparks-secret/, accessed September 28, 2021.

56   "the bug": "From the Archives: The NorthPark Logo," NorthPark Center website, https://northparkcenter.com/posts/from-the-archives-the-northpark-logo, accessed September 28, 2021.

57   "A sculpture to see through a car window": Advertisement, *Dallas Morning News*, April 2, 1973, NorthPark Center.

58   "The ultra-modernist": *The Community Builders Handbook*, prepared by the Community Builders' Council of the Urban Land Institute (Washington, D.C.: ULI, 1947), viii.

59   basics of planning: *Community Builders Handbook* (1947), 127–128; Richard W. Longstreth, *The American Department Store Transformed, 1920–1960* (New Haven, CT: Yale University Press, 2010), 173.

60   a white, suburban mother: Longstreth, *American Department Store*, 163.

60   "active features": *Community Builders Handbook* (1968), 370–371.

62   "customer-appealing centers": *Community Builders Handbook* (1968), 313.

62   Pall Mall: "'Mall': It's Not Just for Shopping," *Merriam-Webster*, https://www .merriam-webster.com/words-at-play/the-history-of-the-word-mall, accessed September 28, 2021; Longstreth, *City Center*, xiv.

64   "Like the department store interior": Longstreth, *American Department Store*, 249.

64   mall be a single path: E. G. Hamilton, panel at the Texas Society of Architects Annual Conference, 2007, transcript, NorthPark Center, Dallas; Hamilton, "Shopping Texas Style"; "NorthPark Regional Shopping Center," *Architectural Record*, April 1966, 150–159.

64   smoothly strolls the center's wide halls: *True Stories*, directed by David Byrne (Burbank, CA: Warner Brothers, 1986). Amazon Prime.

67   Forbes Company: Daniel Duggan, "Developing High-End Malls an Award-Winning Strategy for Forbes," *Crain's Detroit Business*, April 15, 2012, https://www .crainsdetroit.com/article/20120415/SUB01/304159982/developing-high-end -malls-an-award-winning-strategy-for-forbes, accessed September 28, 2021.

67   South Coast Plaza: Stephie Grob Plante, "The Case for the American Mall," *Racked*, August 2, 2016, https://www.racked.com/2016/8/2/12290506/american -malls-south-coast-plaza, accessed September 28, 2021; Dana Goodyear, foreword to *South Coast Plaza: 50 Years of Quality* (New York: Assouline, 2017), 8–9.

69   the expansion: "NorthPark Center," Omniplan website, https://www.omniplan .com/work/case-studies/northpark-center.html, accessed November 9, 2021; Postrel, "NorthPark's Secret."

69   "all the greats": Nancy Nasher and Mark Dilworth, interview with author, February 24, 2020.

71   a previous weakness: Holly Haber, "NorthPark Shoots for Top with $225M Revamp," *WWD*, May 3, 2006.

71   interest in maintenance: Steven J. Jackson, "Rethinking Repair," in *Media Technologies: Essays on Communication, Materiality, and Society*, ed. Tarleton Gillespie, Pablo J. Boczkowski, and Kristen A. Foot (Cambridge, MA: MIT Press, 2013): 221–239; Andrew Russell and Lee Vinsel, "Hail the Maintainers," *Aeon*, April 7, 2016, https://aeon.co/essays/innovation-is-overvalued-main tenance-often-matters-more, accessed September 28, 2021.

71   types of decay: Shannon Mattern, "Maintenance and Care," *Places Journal*, November 2018, https://placesjournal.org/article/maintenance-and-care/, accessed September 28, 2021; Vicki Howard, *From Main Street to Mall: The Rise and Fall of the American Department Store* (Philadelphia: University of Pennsylvania Press, 2015), 174.

72   "good citizenship and good consumer-ship": Lizabeth Cohen, *A Consumers' Republic: The Politics of Mass Consumption in Postwar America* (New York: Vintage Books, 2004, c2003), 112; Ruth Schwartz Cowan, *More Work for*

Mother: The Ironies of Household Technology from the Open Hearth to the Microwave (New York: Basic Books, 1983), 89, 100.

73 "I wouldn't know how": Jack Follett, quoted in Cohen, *Consumers' Republic*, 278.

73 "The longest letter": Brenda Buhr-Hancock, interview with author, February 25, 2020.

74 "They took too much space": Nancy Nasher, interview with author, February 24, 2020.

CHAPTER 3: THE MALL AND THE PUBLIC

76 "this scene of ruin and litter": Bernard J. Frieden and Lynne B. Sagalyn, *Downtown, Inc.: How America Rebuilds Cities* (Cambridge, MA: MIT Press, 1989), 4.

77 "Use it, enjoy it": Mayor Kevin White, quoted in Joshua Olsen, *Better Places, Better Lives: A Biography of James Rouse* (Washington, D.C.: Urban Land Institute, 2014), 259.

78 first enclosed urban shopping mall: Alex Wall, *Victor Gruen: From Urban Shop to New City* (Barcelona: Actar, 2005), 145–148; Will Astor, "Original Tower Was Jewel of National Wonder," *Rochester Business Journal*, November 18, 2016, https://rbj.net/2016/11/18/original-tower-was-jewel-of-national-wonder/, accessed November 20, 2020.

79 more down to earth: Simon Breines and William J. Dean, *The Pedestrian Revolution: Streets Without Cars* (New York: Vintage Books, 1974), 9.

79 "so little understanding of popular taste": Frieden and Sagalyn, *Downtown, Inc.*, 16–17.

80 "Some may reject the whole thing": Olsen, *Better Places*, 240.

81 a "housekeeping" crisis: Alison Isenberg, *Downtown America: A History of the Place and the People Who Made It* (Chicago: University of Chicago Press, 2004), 167.

82 "how our cities grow": James W. Rouse, "How to Build a Whole New City from Scratch," lecture given at the National Association of Mutual Savings Banks, Philadelphia, May 16, 1966.

83 nine small "villages": Jimmy Stamp, "James W. Rouse's Legacy of Better Living Through Design," *Smithsonian Magazine*, April 23, 2014, https://www.smithsonianmag.com/history/james-w-rouses-legacy-better-living-through-design-180951187/, accessed November 20, 2020.

83 "It was so romantic": Olsen, *Better Places*, 241.

84 to design a modernist subdivision: Amanda Kolson Hurley, "The Rise of the Radical Suburbs," *Architect Magazine*, April 9, 2019, https://www.architectmagazine.com/design/the-rise-of-the-radical-suburbs_o, accessed November 20, 2020.

84 in a clapboard row house: Jane Thompson and Alexandra Lange, *Design Research: The Store That Brought Modern Living to American Homes* (San Francisco: Chronicle Books, 2010), 34ff.

85 "we must live with it": Geoffrey Hellman, "Talk of the Town: New Store," *New Yorker*, December 28, 1963.

85 an equally diverse career: Bryan Marquand, "Jane Thompson, 89, Award-Winning Designer, Urban Planner," *Boston Globe*, August 28, 2016, https://www.bostonglobe.com/metro/obituaries/2016/08/28/jane-thompson-award-winning-designer-urban-planner/AG1qpKIZ5kPRhM5gIGbmsN/story.html, accessed November 20, 2020.

86 "the vast middle-class slum": Benjamin Thompson, "Visual Squalor, Social Disorder or A New Vision of the 'City of Man,'" 1968 Wayne State University Centennial Lecture, Detroit, revised and reprinted in *Architectural Record*, April 1969, 161–164.

87 "They don't want the hassle": Edward J. DeBartolo, quoted in Martha Weinman Lear, "Master Builder Sites Shopping Mall," *New York Times Magazine*, August 12, 1973, 82–83.

87 More came the first year: Frieden and Sagalyn, *Downtown, Inc.*, 6.

88 robust urban places: Roberta Brandes Gratz, "Downtown Devitalized," *Progressive Architecture*, July 1981, 82.

88 "a conspicuously empty stage": Jane Davison, "Bringing Life to Market," *New York Times Magazine*, October 10, 1976, 74–78.

89 Rouse made the cover: "Cities Are Fun! Master Planner James Rouse," *Time*, August 24, 1981.

89 One hundred new downtown retail centers: Frieden and Sagalyn, *Downtown, Inc.*, 171.

90 fewer than twenty-four of those original malls: Jessica Schmidt, "Revisiting Pedestrian Malls," prepared for the Technical Conference and Exhibit, Institute of Transportation Engineers, Savannah, GA, 2010, https://nacto.org/wp-content/uploads/2015/04/revisiting_pedestrian_malls_scmidt.pdf, accessed November 20, 2020.

90 covered the plans: "Downtown Needs a Lesson from the Suburbs," *Business Week*, October 22, 1955, 64–66; Jim Vachule, "Plan for 'City of Tomorrow' Outlined to Civic Leaders," *Fort Worth Star-Telegram*, March 11, 1956, 1, 10, 12, http://gruenassociates.com/wp-content/uploads/2016/02/Fort-Worth_Star -Telegraph.pdf, accessed November 20, 2020.

91 what he would do for Manhattan: Andy Logan and Brendan Gill, "Talk of the Town: New City," *New Yorker*, March 17, 1956, https://www.newyorker.com /magazine/1956/03/17/new-city, accessed November 20, 2020.

91 suggested a similar ring: Louis I. Kahn, "Traffic Study Project, Philadelphia, Pennsylvania (1952)," collection of the Museum of Modern Art, https://www .moma.org/collection/works/488, accessed November 20, 2020.

91 "Cities saw Gruen's concept": M. Jeffrey Hardwick, *Mall Maker: Victor Gruen, Architect of an American Dream* (Philadelphia: University of Pennsylvania Press, 2003), 197.

92 "a more perfect downtown": Lizabeth Cohen, "From Town Center to Shopping Center: The Reconfiguration of Community Marketplaces in Postwar America," *American Historical Review* 101, no. 4 (1996): 1059.

92 first became a shopping destination: Rosten Woo, "Invisible Street: A History of Fulton Mall," in *Street Value: Shopping, Planning, and Politics at Fulton Mall*, ed. Meredith Tenhoor and Rosten Woo (New York: Inventory Books, 2010), 33ff.

93 hired to rationalize the street: "Fulton Street Pedestrian Mall and Transitway," Lee Harris Pomeroy Architects website, https://www.lhparch.com/fulton-street -pedestrian-mall-transitway, accessed November 20, 2020.

93 The first BID: Jennifer Yang, "The Birthplace of BIAs Celebrates 40 Years," *Toronto Star*, April 18, 2010, https://www.thestar.com/news/gta/2010/04/18/the _birthplace_of_bias_celebrates_40_years.html, accessed November 20, 2020.

95 "What was once an emergency measure": Max Rivlin-Nadler, "Business Improvement Districts Ruin Neighborhoods," *New Republic*, February 19, 2016, https://newrepublic.com/article/130188/business-improvement-districts-ruin -neighborhoods, accessed November 20, 2020.

96 epicenter of hip-hop style: Biz Markie and Big Daddy Kane, "Albee Square Mall," March 1, 1988, quoted in Tenhoor and Woo, *Street Value*, 83.

96 "when new sneakers came out": Regina Myer, president, Downtown Brooklyn Partnership, interview with author, September 9, 2019.

97   the project's biggest enemy: Ben Thompson and Jane Thompson to the Rouse Company, "Guiding the Future of Faneuil Hall Marketplace," December 5, 1978, quoted in Nicholas Dagen Bloom, *Merchant of Illusion: James Rouse, America's Salesman of the Businessman's Utopia* (Columbus: Ohio State University Press, 2004), 163.

97   "The brick exposed": Calvin Trillin, "Thoughts Brought on by Prolonged Exposure to Exposed Brick," *New Yorker*, May 9, 1977, 101ff, https://www.new yorker.com/magazine/1977/05/16/thoughts-brought-on-by-prolonged -exposure-to-exposed-brick, accessed November 20, 2020; Andrew Kopkind, "Kitsch for the Rich," *Real Paper*, February 19, 1977, republished in JoAnn Wypijewski, ed., *The Thirty Years' Wars: Dispatches and Diversions of a Radical Journalist, 1965–1994* (London: Verso, 1995), 293–294.

99   toured Faneuil Hall: Olsen, *Better Places*, 283.

100 "When he started Harborplace": Ethan McLeod, "What Happened to Baltimore's Harborplace?" CityLab, January 16, 2020, https://www.bloomberg.com/news /articles/2020-01-16/what-happened-to-baltimore-s-festival-marketplace, accessed November 20, 2020.

101 seller of local relishes and sauces: Olsen, *Better Places*, 289; Marian Burros, "An Excursion to Baltimore's Inner Harbor," *New York Times*, August 14, 1983, https://www.nytimes.com/1983/08/14/travel/an-excursion-to-baltimore-s -inner-harbor.html, accessed November 20, 2020.

102 "Faneuil Hall's Promised Retail Revolution?": Janelle Nanos, "Faneuil Hall's Promised Retail Revolution? We're Still Waiting," *Boston Globe*, January 12, 2019, https://www.bostonglobe.com/metro/2019/01/12/faneuil-hall-promised -retail-revolution-still-waiting/pgkDvRrovqZzxRFI3zzAwJ/story.html, accessed November 20, 2020.

102 "It's hard to overstate": McLeod, "What Happened to Baltimore's Harborplace?"

103 "every town's got two malls!": Chris Rock, *Saturday Night Live*, November 2, 1996, SNL Transcripts Tonight, https://snltranscripts.jt.org/96/96emono .phtml, accessed November 20, 2020.

105 *"It was successful from the start"*: Dan McQuade, "It's the End of the Gallery as We Know It (and That's a Shame)," *Philadelphia Magazine*, March 22, 2015, https://www.phillymag.com/news/2015/03/22/gallery-mall-philadelphia -closing-future-history/, accessed November 20, 2020.

105 David Morton, "Suburban Shopping Downtown?" *Progressive Architecture* (December 1978), 64.

106 "Here, in the gap between the well-to-do areas": Elijah Anderson, *The Cosmopolitan Canopy: Race and Civility in Everyday Life* (New York: W. W. Norton, 2011), 73.

106 "the Fashion District appears likely": Inga Saffron, "Philadelphia's Renovated Downtown Mall Still Focuses on the Inside, Instead of on Market Street," *Philadelphia Inquirer*, September 21, 2019, https://www.inquirer.com/real-estate /inga-saffron/philadelphia-fashion-district-gallery-mall-architecture-preit -market-street-20190921.html, accessed November 20, 2020.

107 a disaster movie looking for a hero: Victor Gruen Associates, *Fresno: A City Reborn* (1968), https://www.pbs.org/video/byyou-newspublic-affairs-fresno -city-reborn-1968-documentary/, accessed November 20, 2020.

107 stylized wave pattern: Harvey M. Rubenstein, *Central City Malls* (New York: Wiley, 1978), 105–109.

109 "I am sitting contentedly": Bernard Taper, "A City Remade for People," *Reader's Digest*, October 1966, 146, quoted in Wall, *Victor Gruen*, 157.

109 "precisely the people who chose": Wall, *Victor Gruen*, 154.

110 entire pedestrian mall phenomenon: Cole Judge, "The Experiment of American Pedestrian Malls: Trends Analysis, Necessary Indicators for Success and Recommendations for Fresno's Fulton Mall," International Downtown Association, November 2015, https://doi.org/10.13140/RG.2.1.3502.7280.

112 concepts for the 240-acre public realm: Downtown Brooklyn Partnership, Bjarke Ingels Group, WXY Architecture + Urban Design, "Downtown Brooklyn Public Realm Action Plan," 2019, https://www.downtownbrooklyn.com/about/big-ideas /public-realm-vision-plan, and press release, December 18, 2019, https://www .downtownbrooklyn.com/news/2019/downtown-brooklyn-partnership-unveils -sweeping-public-realm-vision-to-pedestrianize-downtown-brooklyn, accessed November 20, 2020.

CHAPTER 4: MAKE SHOPPING BESIDE THE POINT

114 "In Mexico, in any small-town plaza": Ray Bradbury, "The Girls Walk This Way, the Boys Walk That Way," originally published in *West: The Los Angeles Times Magazine* (April 5, 1970), republished in Bradbury, *Yestermorrow: Obvious*

Answers to Impossible Futures (Santa Barbara, CA: Joshua Odell Editions/Capra Press, 1991), 33.

116 at an amusement park on the ocean cliffs: Ann Bergren, "Jon Jerde and the Architecture of Pleasure," *Assemblage* 37 (December 1998): 10, https://www.jstor.org/stable/3171353.

117 "That's your Galleria": Ray Bradbury, "The Pomegranate Architect," *Paris Review*, January 29, 2015, https://www.theparisreview.org/blog/2015/01/29/the-pomegranate-architect/, accessed September 29, 2021.

119 in a revealing 2002 profile: Ed Leibowitz, "The Solitary Existence of L.A.'s Mall Mastermind," *Los Angeles Magazine*, February 1, 2002, https://www.lamag.com/longform/crowd-pleaser/, accessed September 29, 2021.

119 Jerde later reminisced: Jon Jerde, Southern California Institute of Architecture, lecture, October 28, 1998, SCI-Arc Media Archive, https://www.youtube.com/watch?v=WGyVPEqb4RE, accessed September 29, 2021.

119 "To be lost": Ray Bradbury, "The Aesthetics of Lostness," *Designers West*, November 1988, republished in Bradbury, *Yestermorrow*, 45ff; Margaret Crawford, "The Architect and the Mall," in *You Are Here: The Jerde Partnership International*, ed. Frances Anderton (London: Phaidon, 1999), 45.

121 black turtlenecks of stagehands: Frances Anderton, "Urban Transformations," in Anderton, *You Are Here*, 9.

121 The spine of the mall: Anderton, *You Are Here*, 34–43; Bernard J. Frieden and Lynne B. Sagalyn, *Downtown, Inc.: How America Rebuilds Cities* (Cambridge, MA: MIT Press, 1989), 147.

122 "Horton Plaza follows the rules": John Simones, interview with author, April 29, 2020.

123 vanished in the featureless private floating world: Charles W. Moore, "You Have to Pay for the Public Life" (1965), reprinted in *You Have to Pay for the Public Life: Selected Essays of Charles W. Moore*, ed. Kevin Keim (Cambridge, MA: MIT Press, 2001), 124.

125 "introduced colonnades and side streets and sidewalk cafes": Leibowitz, "Solitary Existence"; Anderton, *You Are Here*, 122–135.

126 "the aesthetic of the 2010s": Scott Gairdner, quoted in Steven Blum, "'90s Neon Wonderland or 'Ominous Parallel Universe'? How CityWalk Became a Polarizing L.A. Landmark," *Los Angeles Magazine*, November 26, 2019, https://www.lamag.com/culturefiles/universal-citywalk/, accessed September 29, 2021.

126 "a metaphorical LA": Jerde, Southern California Institute of Architecture lecture, 1998.

126 "ominous parallel universe": Mike Davis, quoted in Nancy Spiller, "There's No There Here, Either," *Mother Jones*, January–February 1993, https://www .motherjones.com/politics/1993/01/motherjones-jf93-theres-no-there-here -either/, accessed September 29, 2021.

126 Jerde introduced new chaos: Daniel Herman, "Jerde Transfer," in *Harvard Design School Guide to Shopping*, ed. Chuiha Judy Chung, Jeffrey Inaba, Rem Koolhaas, and Sze Tsung Leong (Cologne: Taschen, 2001), 403.

127 Gehry's evil twin: Quoted in Crawford, "Architect and the Mall," 53, from a lecture by Rem Koolhaas, "The Metropolis and Big Buildings," delivered at the conference "Learning from the Mall of America: The Design of Consumer Culture, Public Life, and the Metropolis at the End of the Century," University of Minneapolis, November 22, 1997.

127 Gehry and Rouse's first proposal: Paul Goldberger, *Building Art: The Life and Work of Frank Gehry* (New York: Knopf, 2015), 187–189.

128 "Both utilize a profusion": Crawford, "Architect and the Mall," 53.

129 "Frank, you don't like Santa Monica Place": Goldberger, *Building Art*, 208.

129 provided a corrective to this attitude: Jeffrey Meikle, "The Malling of the Mall: Cultural Resonances of the East Building," *Southwest Review* 66, no. 3 (Summer 1981): 233–244.

130 "poshest of suburban shopping malls": "P/A on Pei: Roundtable on a Trapezoid," *Progressive Architecture*, October 1978, 52, 55.

132 "like a mayfly on steroids": Leibowitz, "Solitary Existence."

132 "a glass building and a container of landscape": Louise Wyman, "Crystal Palace," in Chung et al., *Guide to Shopping*, 230; Susan Buck-Morss, *The Dialectics of Seeing: Walter Benjamin and the Arcades Project* (Cambridge, MA: MIT Press, 1991), 83, 85.

134 "It is because of the Galleria": Gerald Moorhead et al., "The Galleria," in *SAH Archipedia*, ed. Gabrielle Esperdy and Karen Kingsley (Charlottesville: University of Virginia Press, 2012), http://sah-archipedia.org/buildings/TX -01-HN88, accessed September 10, 2020.

134 "Corporations are today's equivalent of the Medici": Gerald Hines, quoted in Paul Goldberger, "Gerald D. Hines, Developer and Architects' 'Medici,' Is Dead at 95," *New York Times*, August 27, 2020, https://www.nytimes.com/2020/08/27 /obituaries/gerald-d-hines-developer-dead.html; Richard West, "My Home, the

Galleria," *Texas Monthly*, July 1980, https://www.texasmonthly.com/articles/my -home-the-galleria/, accessed September 29, 2021.

135 "after watching the ice skaters in the Galleria": West, "My Home."

136 attempts to retrofit the outdoors for pedestrians: Judith K. DeJong, *New SubUrbanisms* (New York: Routledge, 2014), 157–159.

136 "a parade, a football game and a shopping center": Anderton, *You Are Here*, 100.

137 which visitors could tour by submarine: Tracy Mumford, "The Original Plan for the Mall of America Was Bananas," MPR News, March 21, 2017, https://www.mpr news.org/story/2017/03/21/history-mall-of-america-origins, accessed September 29, 2021.

137 WEM provided both an escape: Margaret Crawford, "The World in a Shopping Mall," in *Variations on a Theme Park: The New American City and the End of Public Space*, ed. Michael Sorkin (New York: Hill and Wang, 1992), 3–4; Nader Ghermezian, quoted in Neal Karlen, "The Mall That Ate Minnesota," *New York Times*, August 30, 1992, https://www.nytimes.com/1992/08/30/style/the-mall -that-ate-minnesota.html, accessed September 29, 2021.

139 MOA has actually absorbed and roofed: Deborah Karasov and Judith A. Martin, "The Mall of Them All," *Design Quarterly* 159 (Spring 1993): 23, 25, https://www .jstor.org/stable/4091328, accessed November 9, 2021.

140 "Gruen languishes in the rogue's gallery": Karlen, "Mall That Ate Minnesota"; Maureen Bausch, quoted in "MOA Moments: Truly Groundbreaking," Mall of America blog, February 27, 2017, https://blog.mallofamerica.com/truly -groundbreaking/, accessed September 29, 2021.

141 "a post-shopping mall": Amanda Hess, "Welcome to the Era of the Post-Shopping Mall," *New York Times*, December 27, 2019, https://www.nytimes.com/2019/12 /27/arts/american-dream-mall-opening.html, accessed September 29, 2021.

142 Black Lives Matter protesters stood beneath a pair of silvery multistory Christmas trees: Brandt Williams, Curtis Gilbert, and MPR News staff, "#BlackLivesMatter Protest Fills Mall of America Rotunda; 25 Arrested," MPR News, December 20, 2014, https://www.mprnews.org/story/2014/12/20/moa -blacklivesmatter-protest; Libby Nelson, "The Mall of America Wants to Stop a Black Lives Matter Protest with a Restraining Order," *Vox*, December 22, 2015, https://www.vox.com/2015/12/22/10651676/mall-of-america-black-lives-matter, accessed September 29, 2021.

142 Marsh sued to overturn her conviction for criminal trespass: Marsh v. Alabama, 326 U.S. 501 (1946), https://www.law.cornell.edu/supremecourt/text/326/501, accessed November 9, 2021.

143 The supermarket hired nonunion workers to stock shelves: Food Employees v. Logan Valley Plaza, Inc., 391 U.S. 308 (1968), https://www.law.cornell.edu/supremecourt/text/391/308, accessed November 9, 2021.

145 agreeing to de-map eight acres of public streets: Lloyd Corp. v. Tanner, 407 U.S. 551 (1972), https://www.law.cornell.edu/supremecourt/text/407/551, accessed November 9, 2021.

146 "does not offer the full range of public experience": Moore, "You Have to Pay," 128.

146 "extended an express invitation": Jennifer Niles Coffin, "The United Mall of America: Free Speech, State Constitutions, and the Growing Fortress of Private Property," 33 U. Mich. J. L. Reform 615 (2000), https://repository.law.umich.edu/mjlr/vol33/iss4/5, accessed November 9, 2021.

147 considered the rights of antifur protesters: State of Minnesota v. Wicklund, no. C7-97-1381 (1999), https://caselaw.findlaw.com/mn-supreme-court/1224143.html, accessed November 9, 2021.

147 "the minimal cost of providing a space for real public discourse": New Jersey Coalition Against the War in the Middle East v. JMB Realty Corp. 138 N.J. 326, 650 A.2d 757, 1994 N.J. 52 A.L.R.5th 777, https://law.justia.com/cases/new-jersey/supreme-court/1994/a-124-93-opn.html, accessed November 9, 2021.

149 "Columbus looked all too much like any Midwestern town": John Morris Dixon, "Piazza, American Style," *Progressive Architecture*, June 1976, 64–69; *Columbus Indiana: A Look at Architecture* (Columbus, IN: Columbus Area Chamber of Commerce, 1974), 5.

150 "This is not a mall": Michael J. Crosbie, ed., *Cesar Pelli: Selected and Current Works* (Mulgrave, Victoria: Images Publishing, 1993), 13.

151 Xenia Miller: Connie Ziegler, "Xenia Simons Miller," *Commercial Article* 11 (2018).

151 one element that was replicated was a free indoor play structure: Aaron Smithson, "Remembering Cesar Pelli's Lost Mark on the Midwest," *Architect's Newspaper*, August 28, 2019, https://www.archpaper.com/2019/08/remembering-cesar-pelli-lost-midwest/, accessed September 29, 2021.

151 Pelli revised and glamorized the idea: Crosbie, *Cesar Pelli*, 54–63.

152 "a kind of living room for the locals": Amy Frearson, "NL Architect Unveils Forum Groningen as a 'Cultural Department Store,'" *Dezeen*, January 19, 2020,

https://www.dezeen.com/2020/01/19/forum-groningen-nl-architects-cultural -centre/, accessed September 29, 2021. Oliver Balch, "The New-Look Shopping Mall That Doesn't Sell Stuff," *Guardian*, March 11, 2020, https://www.theguardian .com/world/2020/mar/11/dutch-mall-groningen-netherlands-forum-urban-hub.

CHAPTER 5: WHOSE MALL IS IT ANYWAY?

153 popular parenting manual: Anthony E. Wolf, *Get Out of My Life, but First Could You Drive Me and Cheryl to the Mall? A Parent's Guide to the New Teenager* (New York: Farrar, Straus and Giroux, 1995).

153 only one place to spend it: Dennis H. Tootelian and Ralph M. Gaedecke, "The Teen Market: An Exploratory Analysis of Income, Spending and Shopping Patterns," *Journal of Consumer Marketing* 9, no. 4 (April 1, 1992): 35; William Severini Kowinski, *The Malling of America: An Inside Look at the Great Consumer Paradise* (New York: William Morrow, 1985): 349–350.

154 "mall rats (males) and bunnies (females)": Susan Nigra Snyder, "Codes of Conduct: Mall Rats and Bunnies and the Shopping Agenda," *Harvard Design Magazine* 44 (Fall–Winter 2017): 30–31.

155 get one free hour of babysitting: Donald L. Curtiss, *Operation Shopping Centers: A Guidebook to Effective Management and Promotion* (Washington, D.C.: Urban Land Institute, 1961), 21–23.

157 describes teenagers perched along the second-floor railings: Jennifer Smith Maguire, *Hanging Out and the Mall: The Production of a Teenage Social Space* (Saarbrücken, Germany: VDM, 2008), 46.

158 shares the self-delusion and queen-bee fashion sense: *Clueless*, directed by Amy Heckerling (Hollywood, CA: Paramount Pictures, 1995). Amazon Prime.

158 "the mall functions as a microcosm of society": Sean O'Neal et al., "Scenes from the Malls: 15 Films with Pivotal Moments Set in Shopping Malls," *A.V. Club*, August 20, 2012, https://film.avclub.com/scenes-from-the-malls-15-films-with-pivotal-moments -se-1798233258, accessed September 29, 2021; Smith Maguire, *Hanging Out*, 59.

159 scene of literal primate behavior: *Mean Girls*, directed by Mark Waters (Hollywood, CA: Paramount Pictures, 2004). Amazon Prime.

159 more digital places like the mall: Alexandra Lange, "Where Teens Are Hanging Out in Quarantine," CityLab, November 24, 2020, https://www.bloomberg.com /news/articles/2020-11-24/teens-lead-the-way-in-adapting-to-online-public -space, accessed September 29, 2021.

160 Tiffany, the red-haired singer: Steven R. Churm, "Tiffany Will Hang Out All Summer in Shopping Malls and Try to Meet New Friends," *Los Angeles Times*, July 2, 1987, https://www.latimes.com/archives/la-xpm-1987-07-02-hl-1724 -story.html, accessed September 29, 2021.

160 "You see all these little kiosks": Mariah Eakin, "Tiffany on 'I Think We're Alone Now,' Being the Queen of the Mall, and Dubstep," *A.V. Club*, August 21, 2012, https://music.avclub.com/tiffany-on-i-think-we-re-alone-now-being-the -queen-o-1798233135, accessed September 29, 2021.

161 "the loudest store in the mall": Hot Topic Obsessed, http://history.hottopic.com /1991-we-become-known-as-the-loudest-store-in-the-mall/; Alice Newell-Hanson, "How Hot Topic Became America's Outsider Teen Haven," *i-D*, November 21, 2017, https://i-d.vice.com/en_us/article/vb3abm/how-hot-topic -became-americas-outsider-teen-haven, accessed September 29, 2021.

161 "limitations of the printed word": David Carr, "The Vampire of the Mall," *New York Times*, November 16, 2008, https://www.nytimes.com/2008/11/17/movies /17twil.html, accessed September 29, 2021.

162 "the original mall walker": Cara Pallone, " 'Original' Mall Walker Still Going Strong After 30 Years," *Salem (OR) Statesman Journal*, January 9, 2013, https://www.usatoday.com/story/news/nation/2013/01/09/mall-walking -health-routine/1566166/; Marcia Saft, "Going to the Mall for Better Health," *New York Times*, July 21, 1985, https://www.nytimes.com/1985/07/21/nyregion /going-to-the-mall-for-better-health.html, accessed September 29, 2021.

163 resource guide on mall walking: B. Belza, P. Allen, D. R. Brown, L. Farren, S. Janicek, et al., *Mall Walking: A Program Resource Guide* (Seattle: University of Washington Health Promotion Research Center, 2015), 2–3, http://www.cdc.gov /physicalactivity/downloads/mallwalking-guide.pdf.

164 praised malls as spaces that accommodate: Amina Yasin, @bambinoir, "We also have this . . . ," September 6, 2020, https://twitter.com/bambinoir/status /1302675625149259776?s=21; Gabrielle Peters, @mssinenomine, "Apropos of nothing really [smirk] . . . ," February 23, 2020, https://twitter.com/mssine nomine/status/1231729045118697472.

165 "watch the action": Elijah Anderson, *The Cosmopolitan Canopy: Race and Civility in Everyday Life* (New York: W. W. Norton, 2011), 78, 81.

165 buying only coffee and french fries: Stacy Torres, "Old McDonald's," *New York Times*, January 21, 2014, https://www.nytimes.com/2014/01/22/opinion/old -mcdonalds.html, accessed September 29, 2021.

165 "This is a family": Aditi Shrikant, "But Where Will the Mall Walkers Go?" *Racked*, March 6, 2018, https://www.racked.com/2018/3/6/16946482/mall-walkers-death-of-retail, accessed September 29, 2021.

166 "made such great friendships": Florence Henderson, "Mall Walkers Seek Earlier Hours During Cold Weather," letter to the editor, *Pittsburgh Tribune-Review*, November 7, 2020, https://triblive.com/opinion/letter-to-the-editor-mall-walkers-seek-earlier-hours-during-cold-weather/, accessed September 29, 2021.

167 created the runaway arcade hit *Pong* in 1972: Laura June, "For Amusement Only: The Life and Death of the American Arcade," *Verge*, January 16, 2013, https://www.theverge.com/2013/1/16/3740422/the-life-and-death-of-the-american-arcade-for-amusement-only; N. R. Kleinfeld, "Video Games Industry Comes Down to Earth," *New York Times*, October 17, 1983, https://www.nytimes.com/1983/10/17/business/video-games-industry-comes-down-to-earth.html; Lynn Langway, "Invasion of the Video Creatures," *Newsweek*, November 16, 1981, 90, http://gamearchive.askey.org/General/Articles/ClassicNews/1981/Newsweek11-16-81.htm, accessed September 29, 2021.

168 from safe spaces *for* teens: Kyle Riismandel, "Arcade Addicts and Mallrats: Producing and Policing Suburban Public Space in 1980s America," *Environment, Space, Place* 5, no. 2 (Fall 2013): 65–89, https://doi.org/10.7761/ESP.5.2.65; Dan Kane and Cheryl Imelda Smith, "Mall Rats Bring Thefts, Fights, and Drugs," *Syracuse Post-Standard*, March 20, 1988, link via Syracuse Nostalgia, "Penn-Can Mall," https://www.syracusenostalgia.com/penn-can-mall, accessed November 9, 2021; Bob Levey, "Teens View Center as 'Their' Community," *Washington Post*, January 1, 1981.

169 terrors of game-addicted teens: Spencer Buell, "Please Enjoy This Wildly 1980s News Clip About the Scourge of Video Games in Boston," *Boston Magazine*, October 30, 2020, https://www.bostonmagazine.com/news/2020/10/30/arcade-games-boston-1982/, accessed September 29, 2021.

169 arcade-specific legislation: Riismandel, "Arcade Addicts," 73.

169 Shoplifting, loitering, drinking, and vandalism: *Shopping Center World*, November 1978, 39, quoted in Riismandel, "Arcade Addicts," 74.

170 The total number of security guards: Riismandel, "Arcade Addicts," 77.

170 hall of moral panic: June, "For Amusement Only."

171 George Weinstein, "The Pinball Business Isn't Child's Play," *Better Homes and Gardens* (October 1957), 6.

171 "*Pac-Man* elbow": Dmitri Williams, "The Video Game Lightning Rod," *Information, Communication and Society* 6, no. 4 (December 2003): 541, https://doi.org/10.1080/1369118032000163240; Rochelle Slovin, "Hot Circuits," in *The Medium of the Video Game*, ed. Mark J. P. Wolf (Austin: University of Texas Press, 2001), http://www.movingimagesource.us/articles/hot-circuits-20090115, accessed November 9, 2021; Maaike Lauwaert, *The Place of Play: Toys and Digital Cultures* (Amsterdam: Amsterdam University Press, 2009), 41–42; "The Nintendo Kid," *Newsweek*, March 6, 1989.

172 "adults play too": Williams, "Video Game Lightning Rod," 536; Buell, "Please Enjoy."

173 "Malls target teenagers with age-specific clothing stores": Smith Maguire, *Hanging Out*, 44.

173 one of vanishingly few Chinese American characters: Sara Century, "Whatever Happened to X-Men's Jubilee?" Syfy Wire, December 21, 2018, https://www.syfy.com/syfywire/whatever-happened-to-x-mens-jubilee; XMenXPert, "Uncanny X-Men #244 (May 1989)," https://xmenxpert.wordpress.com/2017/04/10/uncanny-x-men-244-1989-may/, accessed September 29, 2021.

174 teenage Chris goes to a department store: "Shopping While Black," *Everybody Hates Chris*, CBS, November 30, 2011, https://www.youtube.com/watch?v=rfgBXEo5T-w&list=PL8xnBZ4_y8wR4qcfTqzWsoiFnTf9lwxgl; "You Got It All," *Mixed-ish*, ABC, May 5, 2020. Hulu.

174 real-world version of the oppositional relationship: Aaron Foley, "Requiem for Northland Center," *Belt Magazine*, January 27, 2015, https://beltmag.com/requiem-northland-center/, accessed September 29, 2021.

176 "safety is a top priority": "Parental Escort Policy," Mall of America website, https://www.mallofamerica.com/pep; Robyn Meredith, "Big Mall's Curfew Raises Questions of Rights and Bias," *New York Times*, September 4, 1996, https://www.nytimes.com/1996/09/04/us/big-mall-s-curfew-raises-questions-of-rights-and-bias.html, accessed September 29, 2021.

176 "essentially become a baby sitter": Sara B. Miller, "At Shopping Malls, Teens' Hanging Out Is Wearing Thin," *Christian Science Monitor*, August 11, 2005, https://www.csmonitor.com/2005/0811/p01s01-ussc.html, accessed September 29, 2021.

177 thousands of teens to arrive at the mall's Buffalo Wild Wings: Al Baker and Karen Zraick, "Brooklyn Malls Try to Limit Youth Loitering," *New York Times*,

September 17, 2010, https://www.nytimes.com/2010/09/18/nyregion/18mall .html, accessed September 29, 2021.

177 infringing on the rights of young people: Alysa B. Freeman, "Go to the Mall with My Parents?? A Constitutional Analysis of the Mall of America's Juvenile Curfew," *Dickinson Law Review* 102, no. 2 (1998): 481–539, 530, reprinted in *Children and the Law*, vol. 3, *Child vs. State*, 277–334.

178 a Denver native who managed the mall: Yvette Freeman, interview with author, September 15, 2020.

179 design-as-deterrent: Tobias Armborst, Daniel D'Oca, Georgeen Theodore, and Riley Gold, eds., *The Arsenal of Exclusion and Inclusion* (New York: Actar, 2017).

180 protested a downtown loitering ordinance: Daniel D'Oca, interview with author, November 28, 2017; Chicago v. Morales, 527 U.S. 41 (1999).

180 trying (and failing) to define "loitering": Tobias Armborst, Daniel D'Oca, and Georgeen Theodore of Interboro Partners, "Linger, Stay, Saunter, Delay," *Harvard Design Magazine* 44 (Fall–Winter 2017): 183–187.

180 recruited six teenagers from the South Bronx: Yes Loitering Project, https://www .theyesloiteringproject.com; Yes Loitering Project, "Yes Sitting, Yes Skating, Yes Music," *Urban Omnibus*, March 8, 2018, https://urbanomnibus.net/2018/03/yes -sitting-yes-skating-yes-music/; Adele Peters, "The Yes Loitering Project Asks Kids of Color to Rethink Public Space," *Fast Company*, April 18, 2018, https://www.fastcompany.com/40558755/the-yes-loitering-project-asks-kids -of-color-to-rethink-public-space, accessed September 29, 2021.

181 Pier 2's basketball courts have been extremely popular: Emma Whitford, "Neighbors Blame Basketball Courts and Teenagers for 'Trauma' at Brooklyn Bridge Park," *Gothamist*, May 18, 2016, https://gothamist.com/news/neighbors -blame-basketball-courts-teenagers-for-trauma-at-brooklyn-bridge-park, accessed September 29, 2021.

CHAPTER 6: DAWN OF THE DEAD MALL

183 Four survivors of a zombie attack: *Dawn of the Dead*, directed by George A. Romero (Italy/USA: Laurel Group, 1978). DVD.

185 lasted only fifteen minutes: Janet Maslin, "Film: 'Dawn of the Dead,'" *New York Times*, April 20, 1979, C14, https://www.nytimes.com/1979/04/20/archives/film -dawn-of-the-deadmorning-after.html, accessed September 30, 2021.

185 Ray Bradbury's "The Girls Walk This Way; The Boys Walk That Way: Ray Bradbury, "The Girls Walk This Way, the Boys Walk That Way," originally published in *West: The Los Angeles Times Magazine* (April 5, 1970), republished in Bradbury, *Yestermorrow: Obvious Answers to Impossible Futures* (Santa Barbara, CA: Joshua Odell Editions/Capra Press, 1991).

185 Didion walks with the girls: Joan Didion, "On the Mall" (1975), in Didion, *The White Album* (New York: Simon and Schuster, 1979), 180–186.

188 opened outside Baltimore in 1986 with a trumpet fanfare: Scapino Media, "Owings Mills Mall—the Rise and Fall," YouTube, December 27, 2019, https://www.youtube.com/watch?v=hbx0vibVhj4&feature=youtu.be, accessed September 30, 2021; "The Mall in Columbia," Columbia Maryland Archives, https://www.columbiaassociation.org/facilities/columbia-archives/history/the-mall-in-columbia/, accessed October 6, 2020.

190 "just one thing was missing: shoppers": Nelson D. Schwartz, "The Economics (and Nostalgia) of Dead Malls," *New York Times*, January 3, 2015, https://www.nytimes.com/2015/01/04/business/the-economics-and-nostalgia-of-dead-malls.html, accessed September 30, 2021.

190 had been failing for far longer: Meredith Schlow, "In Towson, Toward a Bigger, Better Mall," *Baltimore Evening Sun*, April 1, 1991, https://www.nydailynews.com/bs-xpm-1991-04-01-1991091197-story.html; Ed Brandt, "Owings Mills to Close Pathway to the Mall," *Baltimore Sun*, November 24, 1992, https://www.baltimoresun.com/news/bs-xpm-1992-11-24-1992329028-story.html; Matthew Christopher, "Owings Mills Mall," Abandoned America, https://www.abandonedamerica.us/owings-mills-mall, accessed November 9, 2021.

191 not a mall at all but Mill Station: Alison Knezevich, "Redevelopment of Former Owings Mills Mall Site Starts with Announcement of a New Costco," *Baltimore Sun*, November 21, 2017, https://www.baltimoresun.com/maryland/baltimore-county/bs-md-co-owings-mills-mall-20171120-story.html; Mill Station website, https://millstation.shopkimco.com, accessed September 30, 2021.

191 The most innovative of these real-world experiments: Andrew Blum, "The Mall Goes Undercover," *Slate*, April 6, 2005, https://slate.com/culture/2005/04/the-latest-incarnation-of-the-shopping-mall.html, accessed November 9, 2021.

192 represented only 11 percent of retail sales: Austan Goolsbee, "Never Mind the Internet. Here's What's Killing Malls," *New York Times*, February 13, 2020,

https://www.nytimes.com/2020/02/13/business/not-internet-really-killing -malls.html, accessed September 30, 2021.

193 began his career as an owner of strip shopping centers: Robert D. McFadden, "A. Alfred Taubman, 91, Dies; Developer, Sotheby's Owner and Focus of Scandal," *New York Times*, April 18, 2015, https://www.nytimes.com/2015/04 /19/business/a-alfred-taubman-shopping-mall-tycoon-involved-in-price -fixing-scandal-dies-at-91.html; Laurence Arnold, "Bernard Winograd, Who Helped Devise Taubman REIT IPO, Dies at 63," Bloomberg, March 6, 2014, https://www.bloomberg.com/news/articles/2014-03-06/bernard-winograd -who-helped-devise-taubman-reit-ipo-dies-at-63, accessed September 30, 2021.

194 blaming the poor pandemic performance: Brent Nyitray, "Simon Property Renegotiates Its Merger with Taubman," Motley Fool, November 18, 2020, https://www.fool.com/investing/2020/11/18/simon-property-renegotiates -merger-with-taubman/, accessed September 30, 2021.

194 It also sent GGP into bankruptcy: Michael J. De La Merced, "General Growth Properties Files for Bankruptcy," *New York Times DealBook*, April 16, 2009, https://dealbook.nytimes.com/2009/04/16/general-growth-properties-files -for-bankruptcy/; Ilaina Jonas, "General Growth Cleared to Exit Bankruptcy," Reuters, October 21, 2010, https://www.reuters.com/article/us-generalgrowth /general-growth-cleared-to-exit-bankruptcy-idUSTRE69K41320101022, accessed September 30, 2021.

195 "black pavement stretched forever—to Alaska": Richard Peck, *Secrets of the Shopping Mall* (New York: Delacorte Press, 1979), 40, 184.

197 "a destination mall meant to attract shoppers from all over the Middle West": Gillian Flynn, *Gone Girl* (New York: Crown, 2012), 71–72, 113, 406.

198 "a beige complex with signs boasting a Macy's": Ling Ma, *Severance* (New York: Farrar, Straus and Giroux, 2018), 160, 29.

199 "an inescapable disease": Jiayang Fan, "Ling Ma's 'Severance' Captures the Bleak, Fatalistic Mood of 2018," *New Yorker*, December 10, 2018, https://www .newyorker.com/books/under-review/ling-ma-severance-captures-the-bleak -fatalistic-mood-of-2018, accessed September 30, 2021.

199 printed on a paper shopping bag: Barbara Kruger, *I Shop Therefore I Am* (1990), photolithograph on paper shopping bag, collection of the Museum of Modern Art, https://www.moma.org/collection/works/64897.

200   "Get to your sections!": Nana Kwame Adjei-Brenyah, "Friday Black," in *Friday Black* (Boston: Mariner Books, 2018): 104–114.

201   "are not the ones who are depraved": Roger Ebert, "Dawn of the Dead," *Chicago Sun-Times*, May 4, 1979; republished on RogerEbert.com, https://www.rogerebert.com/reviews/dawn-of-the-dead-1979, accessed September 30, 2021.

201   abandoned malls, abandoned amusement parks, abandoned theme parks: Seph Lawless website, https://sephlawless.com; Jesse Rieser website, https://jesserieser.com.

202   Edmund Burke, *A Philosophical Enquiry into the Origin of Our Ideas of the Sublime and Beautiful* (London: printed for R. and J. Dodsley, 1757), 13–14.

202   "emerged spontaneously from the hive mind": McLain Clutter, "Notes on Ruin Porn," *Avery Review* 18 (October 2016), http://averyreview.com/issues/18/notes-on-ruin-porn; Jonathan Glancey, "The Death of the US Shopping Mall," BBC Culture, October 21, 2014, https://www.bbc.com/culture/article/20140411-is-the-shopping-mall-dead, accessed September 30, 2021.

203   that city's select deterioration: John Patrick Leary, "Detroitism," *Guernica*, January 15, 2011, https://www.guernicamag.com/leary_1_15_11/, accessed September 30, 2021.

204   "street zombies": Julien Temple, "Detroit: The Last Days," *Guardian*, March 10, 2010, https://www.theguardian.com/film/2010/mar/10/detroit-motor-city-urban-decline, accessed January 10, 2022.

204   "a band of white thrill-seekers": Brian Merchant, "The Ultimate Detroit Ruin Porn," *Vice*, December 10, 2013, https://www.vice.com/en_us/article/xyw8g7/the-ultimate-detroit-ruin-porn-skiing-through-the-apocalypse, accessed September 30, 2021.

205   behind the YouTube channel Retail Archaeology: Retail Archaeology, YouTube channel, https://www.youtube.com/channel/UCR2LNeZSqINp0WTd_eWCIGg; Dead Malls, Reddit, https://www.reddit.com/r/deadmalls/, accessed September 30, 2021.

207   spent their Saturday together in detention: Simple Minds, "Don't You (Forget About Me)," by Keith Forsey and Steve W. Schiff, track 1 on *The Breakfast Club* (Original Motion Picture Soundtrack), A&M Records, 1985; *The Breakfast Club*, directed by John Hughes (Universal City, CA: Universal Pictures, 1985). Amazon Prime.

208   remixed to sound tinny and hollow: Cecil Robert, "Simple Minds—Don't You (Forget About Me) (playing in an empty shopping centre)," YouTube,

March 1, 2018, https://www.youtube.com/watch?v=um6M7cDnfQs, accessed September 30, 2021.

208 *Weird Science*, directed by John Hughes (Universal City, CA: Universal Pictures, 1985). Amazon Prime.

209 "A remarkably high number of people": Jia Tolentino, "The Overwhelming Emotion of Hearing Toto's 'Africa' Remixed to Sound like It's Playing in an Empty Mall," *New Yorker*, March 15, 2018, https://www.newyorker.com/culture/rabbit-holes/the-overwhelming-emotion-of-hearing-totos-africa-remixed-to-sound-like-its-playing-in-an-empty-mall, accessed September 30, 2021.

210 situate the listener in a 1990s space: Scott Beauchamp, "What Happened to Vaporwave?" *Esquire*, August 18, 2016, https://www.esquire.com/entertainment/music/a47793/what-happened-to-vaporwave/; Milesdavidoconnor21, "Micro Genre Within a Micro Genre That Uses Ambience as an Instrument: Learn About Mallsoft," *Ultimate Guitar*, October 12, 2018, https://www.ultimate-guitar.com/articles/features/micro_genre_within_a_micro_genre_that_uses_ambience_as_an_instrument_learn_about_mallsoft-80334, accessed September 30, 2021.

211 dead plants in the planter: MadArtMart, "In the Air Tonight (Playing in an Empty Shopping Centre," YouTube, March 24, 2018, https://www.youtube.com/watch?list=PL4pGkk3QBW29yqnarnVkA1qHB7cyAwX9Q&v=CQln04ALz2A; "Inside America's Creepiest Malls," *Daily Mail*, November 15, 2016, https://www.dailymail.co.uk/news/article-3936978/Apocalyptic-photos-Seph-Lawless-capture-abandoned-Metro-North-Mall-Kansas-City.html, accessed September 30, 2021.

212 "this is just like a movie": David Owen, "The Soundtrack of Your Life," *New Yorker*, April 3, 2006, https://www.newyorker.com/magazine/2006/04/10/the-soundtrack-of-your-life, accessed September 30, 2021.

214 Foreground music in the mall: Jonathan Sterne, "Sounds like the Mall of America: Programmed Music and the Architectonics of Commercial Space," *Ethnomusicology* 41, no. 1 (Winter 1997): 25, https://www.jstor.org/stable/852577, accessed November 9, 2021.

214 "moody high school freshman": John Paul Brammer, "A Requiem for Hot Topic," *¡Hola Papi!*, January 11, 2020, https://holapapi.substack.com/p/a-requiem-for-hot-topic, accessed September 30, 2021.

215 "'environmentally controlled' behemoth": Manya Winsted, "Metrocenter," *Phoenix Magazine*, November 1973, 42–44.

216 "I could picture its funky interiors": Robrt L. Pela, "Mall Brat: A Late '70s Class Trip of Sorts to Metrocenter," *Phoenix New Times*, July 16, 2020, https://www .phoenixnewtimes.com/arts/mall-brat-a-late-70s-class-trip-of-sorts-to -metrocenter-11481204; *Transworld Skateboarding*, "Chad Muska Feedback [1999]—TransWorld SKATEboarding," YouTube, September 20, 2012, https://www.youtube.com/watch?v=8og8sGKvEhs, accessed September 30, 2021.

216 shut down for good: Max Jarman, "Westcor Abandoning Metrocenter Mall," *Arizona Republic*, March 3, 2010, http://archive.azcentral.com/arizonare public/business/articles/2010/03/03/20100303biz-metrocenter0303.html; Retail Archaeology, "Metrocenter Mall's Bogus Journey," YouTube, June 9, 2019, https://www.youtube.com/watch?v=YjIuSTD_XRg, accessed November 9, 2021.

217 "Malls just have the perfect floor": Chelsea Winkel and Danny Upshaw, inter- view with author, July 1, 2020.

CHAPTER 7: THE POSTAPOCALYPTIC MALL

220 told me that's *mall* logic: Alexandra Lange, "New York City Is a Mall," *Curbed*, June 26, 2019, https://ny.curbed.com/2019/6/26/18693372/new-york-mall-hud son-yards-empire-outlets, accessed September 30, 2021.

221 everyone seemed to be shopping: Abha Bhattarai, "'Retail Apocalypse' Now: Analysts Say 75,000 More U.S. Stores Could Be Doomed," *Washington Post*, April 10, 2019, https://www.washingtonpost.com/business/2019/04/10/retail -apocalypse-now-analysts-say-more-us-stores-could-be-doomed/, accessed September 30, 2021.

221 built around a landscaped outdoor courtyard: Alexandra Lange, "Malls and the Future of American Retail," *Curbed*, February 15, 2018, https://archive.curbed .com/2018/2/15/17014230/malls-califonia-america-renzo-piano-victor-gruen, accessed September 30, 2021.

222 grandmothers to the food hall: Alison Isenberg, *Designing San Francisco: Art, Land, and Urban Renewal in the City by the Bay* (Princeton, NJ: Princeton Architectural Press, 2017), 74.

222 players' rescue options were severely limited: *American Mall*, game, Bloomberg, February 8, 2018, https://www.bloomberg.com/features/american-mall-game/, accessed September 30, 2021.

223 United States is overmalled: Michael Brown and Matt Lubelczyk, "The Future of Shopping Centers," Kearney, February 6, 2018, https://www.kearney.com /consumer-retail/article/?/a/the-future-of-shopping-centers-article, accessed November 9, 2021; Mark Cohen, interview with author, January 28, 2021.

224 E-commerce had already been growing in the double digits: "US Ecommerce Grows 44.0% in 2020," Digital Commerce 360, https://www.digitalcommerce360 .com/article/us-ecommerce-sales/; Ben Johnson, "The New Elements in Centennial's Shopping Center–Level e-Commerce Platform," *Shopping Centers Today*, January 27, 2021, https://www.icsc.com/news-and-views/icsc-exchange /the-new-elements-in-centennials-shopping-center-level-e-commerce -platform, accessed November 9, 2021.

224 weakness of department stores: Bethany Biron, "Neiman Marcus Is Closing Another Department Store, Bringing Its Total Closings to 22 Locations," *Business Insider*, August 24, 2020, https://www.businessinsider.com/nemain -marcus-and-last-call-closing-stores-list-addresses-2020-7, accessed September 30, 2021.

225 embattled for years: Jason Del Rey, "The Death of the Department Store and the American Middle Class," *Recode*, November 30, 2020, https://www.vox.com /recode/21717536/department-store-middle-class-amazon-online-shopping -covid-19, accessed September 30, 2021.

225 "I want to go to the Mall": Tanvi Misra, @tanvim, March 14, 2020, "My mom is having some feelings," https://twitter.com/Tanvim/status/1238833773346783232.

226 what their plans were for closing the malls: S. P. Sullivan, "Where's Our Tax Cut? As N.J. Mayor Tried to Shut City, Mall Owner Pushed Steep Tax Break," *New Jersey Advance*, March 21, 2020, https://www.nj.com/news/2020/03/wheres -our-tax-cut-as-nj-mayor-tried-to-shut-city-mall-owner-pushed-steep-tax -break.html, accessed November 9, 2021.

227 Operators' fears were not irrational: Vanessa Friedman and Sapna Maheshwari, "'Our Industry Will Fail': Retail Leaders Ask for Emergency Aid," *New York Times*, March 23, 2020, https://www.nytimes.com/2020/03/23/style/coronavirus -retail-bailout.html, accessed September 30, 2021.

227 "Covid just accelerated a lot of these trends": Brad M. Hutensky, interview with author, January 25, 2021.

228 "the overall retail environment was much healthier": Lauren Thomas, "America's Top-Tier Malls Were Resilient, but Values Are Now Crumbling," CNBC,

January 26, 2021, https://www.cnbc.com/2021/01/26/top-tier-mall-values-have -dropped-45percent-from-2016-levels-green-street.html?__source=sharebar %7Cemail&par=sharebar, accessed September 30, 2021.

229 "pampering its customers in dazzling spaces": Jason Heid, "Should Neiman Marcus Exist?" *Texas Monthly*, June 2020, https://www.texasmonthly.com/news /should-neiman-marcus-exist/, accessed September 30, 2021.

230 compact, walkable, mixed-use communities: Ellen Dunham-Jones and June Williamson, *Retrofitting Suburbia: Urban Design Solutions for Redesigning Suburbs* (Hoboken: John Wiley and Sons, 2008, 2013), 4.

231 retrofits grew from eighty to more than two thousand examples: June Williamson and Ellen Dunham-Jones, *Case Studies in Retrofitting Suburbia: Urban Design Strategies for Urgent Challenges* (Hoboken: John Wiley and Sons, 2021).

232 "Suburbanites now included": Williamson and Dunham-Jones, *Case Studies*, 45. For a detailed discussion of ACC Highland, see 138ff.

234 "fronts for a handful of blue-haired property owners": Caleb Pritchard, "The Plan to Turn Highland Mall into a Neighborhood," *Austin Monthly*, July 19, 2017, https://www.austinmonthly.com/the-plan-to-turn-highland-mall-into-a -neighborhood/, accessed November 9, 2021; Andrew Blechman, "Age-Segregated Community," in *The Arsenal of Exclusion and Inclusion*, ed. Tobias Amborst, Daniel D'Oca, Georgeen Theodore, and Riley Gold (New York: Actar, 2017), 32–24; John F. Wasik, "Once Meccas of Retail Therapy, Now Homes to Elder Americans," *New York Times*, October 24, 2020.

235 five-block mid-rise neighborhood: Williamson and Dunham-Jones, *Case Studies*, 152ff.

236 as thoroughly returned to open space: Williamson and Dunham-Jones, *Case Studies*, 229ff.

237 retrofitting dying malls for Latinx and Caribbean entrepreneurs: Sam Frizell, "Mercado of America," *Time*, April 17, 2014, https://time.com/66282/hispa nic-malls-capture-trillion-dollar-market/, accessed September 30, 2021; Williamson and Dunham-Jones, *Case Studies*, 127ff.

238 more people more interested in food from more places: Bethany Biron, "Food Halls Are Everywhere Now. It's Because We Crave 'Authenticity,'" *Vox*, October 30, 2018, https://www.vox.com/the-goods/2018/10/30/18039790/food -halls-local-vendors-court-modern, accessed September 30, 2021.

238 "wonderfully painful indecision": David Chang, "Are You Ready for the Foodie Court?" *GQ*, February 5, 2015, https://www.gq.com/story/david-chang-food -court, accessed September 30, 2021.

240 tribute to the indoor markets of Barcelona: Robert Sietsema, "What to Order at José Andrés's Impressive New Hudson Yards Spanish Market Right Now," *Eater*, May 10, 2019, https://ny.eater.com/2019/5/10/18536763/mercado-little -spain-what-to-order-first-look-review-jose-andres-hudson-yards; Pete Wells, "The 20 Most Delicious Things at Mercado Little Spain," *New York Times*, July 23, 2019, https://www.nytimes.com/interactive/2019/07/23/dining/mercado -little-spain-review-pete-wells.html, accessed September 30, 2021.

241 "On a typical Friday afternoon in Fremont": Willow Lung-Amam, "The Vibrant Life of Asian Malls in Silicon Valley," in *Making Suburbia: New Histories of Everyday America*, ed. John Archer, Paul J. P. Sandhul, and Katherine Solomonson (Minneapolis: University of Minnesota Press, 2015), 208, http://www.jstor.com/stable/10.5749/j.ctt17t77s8.16, accessed November 9, 2021.

241 the rise of the "ethnoburb": Wei Li, "Anatomy of a New Ethnic Settlement: The Chinese Ethnoburb in Los Angeles," *Urban Studies* 35, no. 3 (March 1998): 479, https://www.jstor.org/stable/43083884; Christopher Cheung, " 'Ethnoburbs': The New Face of Immigrant Cities," *The Tyee*, August 5, 2016, https://thetyee .ca/News/2016/08/05/Ethnoburbs/, accessed September 30, 2021; Son Mai, "From Chinatown to Little Saigon," in *Lone Star Suburbs: Life on the Texas Metropolitan Frontier*, ed. Paul J. P. Sandul and M. Scott Sosebee (Norman: University of Oklahoma Press, 2019), 218–220.

242 "The malls of the future will be much more diverse": Shan Li, "As Other Malls Die Off, This One in Arcadia Focuses on Asian Shoppers," *Los Angeles Times*, April 2, 2017, https://www.latimes.com/business/la-fi-santa-anita-westfield -mall-20170331-story.html, accessed September 30, 2021.

243 large, black, chewy spheres of "boba": Clarissa Wei, "How Boba Became an Integral Part of Asian-American Culture in Los Angeles," *LA Weekly*, January 16, 2017; Jenny G. Zhang, "The Rise (and Stall) of the Boba Generation," *Eater*, November 5, 2019, https://www.eater.com/2019/11/5/20942192/bubble-tea-boba -asian-american-diaspora, accessed September 30, 2021.

244 Rouse tried again at Paramus Park Mall: "Rouse Left Mark on All Malls, Not Just His Own," *Shopping Centers Today*, May 2004, http://web.archive.org/web/2012

1017075432/http://www.icsc.org/srch/sct/sct0504/page42.php; Leigh Raper, "A History of the Food Court," *Mental Floss*, February 8, 2016, https://www .mentalfloss.com/article/71414/history-food-court, accessed September 30, 2021.

245   "I hardly recall ever buying anything": Jason Diamond, *The Sprawl: Reconsidering the Weird American Suburbs* (Minneapolis: Coffee House Press, 2020), 176–177.

246   ovens at the front of their stores: Sarah Nassauer, "Using Scent as a Marketing Tool, Stores Hope It—and Shoppers—Will Linger," *Wall Street Journal*, May 20, 2014, https://www.wsj.com/articles/using-scent-as-a-marketing-tool-stores -hope-it-and-shoppers-will-linger-1400627455, accessed September 30, 2021.

247   wrote an ode to Plaza Fiesta: Jennifer Zyman, "I Went Looking for My Mexican Identity and Found It at Atlanta's Plaza Fiesta," *Bon Appétit*, February 13, 2020, https://www.bonappetit.com/story/plaza-fiesta, accessed September 30, 2021.

248   eating in the parking garage: Alissa Walker, "Is This the Saddest Pandemic Dining Experience in America?" *Curbed*, July 28, 2020, https://archive.curbed .com/2020/7/28/21340646/coronavirus-outdoor-dining-glendale-galleria, accessed September 30, 2021.

249   don't-call-it-a-food-court category: Whitney Filloon, "How Eataly Became an Italian Food Superpower," *Eater*, October 30, 2017, https://www.eater.com/2016 /8/12/12442512/eataly-history-store-locations; Sam Sifton, "Eataly Offers Italy by the Ounce," *New York Times*, October 19, 2010, https://www.nytimes.com /2010/10/20/dining/reviews/20Eataly.html?_r=0, accessed September 30, 2021.

250   surprisingly emotional reaction: Eva Hagberg, "Love and Death in Hudson Yards," *Architect*, February 8, 2021, https://www.architectmagazine.com/design /culture/love-and-death-in-hudson-yards_o, accessed September 30, 2021; Matt Zoller Seitz, interview with author, August 29, 2020.

CONCLUSION: THE MALL ABROAD

253   malls had always been seen as part of a modernizing project: Arlene Dávila, *El Mall: The Spatial and Class Politics of Shopping Malls in Latin America* (Berkeley: University of California Press, 2016), 64.

253   "expressed skepticism about learning lessons": Dávila, *El Mall*, 53–54.

255   growing middle class with money to spend: Nolan Gray, "The Triumph of the Latin American Mall," Bloomberg CityLab, November 25, 2017, https://www

.bloomberg.com/news/articles/2017-11-25/the-triumph-of-the-latin-american
-mall, accessed September 30, 2021.

256 The critical response to the New Towns: Steve Rose, "Sterile or Stirring? Britain's
Love-Hate Relationship with New Towns," *Guardian*, May 19, 2019, https://www
.theguardian.com/cities/2019/may/15/sterile-or-stirring-britains-love-hate
-relationship-with-new-towns, accessed September 30, 2021.

256 planned as a megastructure: John Grindrod, *Concretopia: A Journey Around
the Rebuilding of Postwar Britain* (Brecon: Old Street Publishing, 2014),
297–299; quoted in Regina Bittner, "Futures Past: The Shopping Mall as
Megastructure," in *The World of Malls: Architectures of Consumption*, ed.
Andres Lepik and Vera Simone Bader (Berlin: Hatje Cantz, 2016), 69, 73.

258 "Brutalist, introverted concrete form": Nicholas Jewell, "Bringing It Back Home:
The Urbanization of the British Shopping Mall as the West Goes East," *ARENA
Journal of Architectural Research* 1, no. 1, https://ajar.arena-architecture.eu
/articles/10.5334/ajar.4/; Nicholas Jewell, "The Great Mall of China," Future
Cities Project, November 25, 2015, http://futurecities.org.uk/2015/11/25/the
-great-mall-of-china/, accessed September 30, 2021.

258 post-dictatorship mallification of the Philippines: Diana Martinez, "An
Archipelago of Interiors: The Philippine Supermall as Infrastructure of
Diaspora," *Avery Review* 49 (October 2020), https://averyreview.com/issues/49
/archipelago-of-interiors, accessed September 30, 2021.

261 "Only in the Philippines is 'malling' used as a verb": Jore-Annie Rico and
Kim Robert C. de Leon, "Mall Culture and Consumerism in the Philippines,"
State of Power Report 6 (Transnational Institute, 2017), 7, https://www.tni
.org/files/publication-downloads/stateofpower2017-mall-culture.pdf,
accessed September 30, 2021.

261 40 percent of shoppers were from Latin America: Andres Schipani, "Miami
Throbs to Beat of Latin American Shoppers," *Financial Times*, November 4,
2010; Stephie Grob Plante, "The Case for the American Mall," *Racked*, August 2,
2016, https://www.racked.com/2016/8/2/12290506/american-malls-south-coast
-plaza, accessed September 30, 2021.

262 "willingness to leave rather than pivot": Dávila, *El Mall*, 28.

Index

Note: Page numbers in *italics* refer to images.

A Note on the Author

ALEXANDRA LANGE is a design critic and the author of four previous books, including *The Design of Childhood*. Her writing has also appeared in publications such as the *New Yorker*, the *Atlantic*, *New York* magazine, and the *New York Times*, and she has been a featured writer at Design Observer, an opinion columnist at *Dezeen*, and the architecture critic for Curbed. She holds a PhD in twentieth-century architecture history from the Institute of Fine Arts at New York University. She lives in Brooklyn.

Third Street

TREE
TREE
TREE
TREE
TREE
TREE
TREE
TREE

FLOWERSFLOWERSFLOWERSFLOWERSFLOWERSFLOWERSFLOWERSFLOWERS

W.C.
W.C.

phones
lockers

SNACKSICECRE
MJUICESODAPO

sitsnacktalkcoffeewatc

watch children

MAKE BELIEVE EXPLORE

tunnel

stairs
slide

climb climb
hide
climb climb
crawl
hide

PLAY
PLAY
slide

table table
games stories
slide

GAMESOUTDOOR

DN

PLAY RUN PLAY

PLAY

FIRST FLOOR

N